THE PARENT'S LAUNCH CODE

LOVING AND LETTING GO OF OUR ADULT CHILDREN

Jack Stoltzfus, Ph.D.
America's Launch Coach®
Foreword by Marshall Goldsmith

The Parent's Launch Code

Copyright © 2024 by Jack Stoltzfus, Ph.D. All rights reserved.

No part of this book may be used or reproduced in any manner whatsoever without written permission, except in the case of brief quotations embodied in critical articles and reviews. For more information, e-mail all inquiries to info@mindstirmedia.com.

MINDSTIR MEDIA

Published by MindStir Media, LLC
45 Lafayette Rd | Suite 181| North Hampton, NH 03862 | USA
1.800.767.0531 | www.mindstirmedia.com

Printed in the United States of America.
ISBN-13: 978-1-963844-64-1

TABLE OF CONTENTS

Acknowledgments vii
The Parent's Launch Code Foreword ix
Preface xi

Introduction: The Launch Code xv
    The Truth about Parents and Young Adults xvi
    The Launched "Young" Adult xvii
    Stinking Thinking xix
    Launching—Emotional Failures and Successes xxii
    The Launch Code Revealed xxv
    Do You Have the "Right Stuff" to Launch Your Young Adult? ... xxviii
    Keepers xxx

Chapter One: Let Go with Love 1
    What's Love Got to Do With It? 2
    Unconditional Love for the Young Adult 4
    What Unconditional Love Is Not 6
    Love to Let Go: My Story 8
    Love to Let Go: Your Story 15
    Barriers to Expressing Unconditional Love 21
    Expressing Unconditional Love: Our Charge 24
    Keepers 27

Chapter Two: Understand and Relate 29
   From Lawrence Welk to Rap 30
   Who Are These Emerging Adults of Today, and
      What Is Their Experience? 33
   A Work in Progress: The Young Adult 41
   A Work in Progress: Parents 44
   Three Skills to Strengthen the Relationship 45
   Listen with the Third Ear 46
   Do Your Report Card 60
   Keepers 62

Chapter Three: Apologize 65
   Opportunities to Apologize 66
   The Gift of Apology 70
   What Constitutes a Genuine Apology? 73
   Why Do We Resist Apologizing? 77
   Why Apologize if I Don't Believe I Did Anything Wrong? 79
   The Impact of an Apology 80
   Is There a Time when Parents Shouldn't Apologize? 83
   The Qualities We Need to Apologize 84
   Keepers 88

Chapter Four: Forgive 89
   Understanding Forgiveness 91
   The Benefits of Forgiveness 93
   Barriers to Forgiveness 95
   Three People We May Need to Forgive 96
   Start with Self Forgiveness 96
   To Send or Shred? 110

    Forgiveness of a Third Party..112
    Keepers 115

Chapter Five: Show Backbone 117
    What Is Parental Backbone? 119
    Principles for Demonstrating Backbone..121
    Personal Qualities Essential to Show Backbone..........................124
    Why Parents Fail to Show Backbone 128
    Show My Young Adult I Have Backbone 133
    Teach Grit 137
    The Major Types of Failure to Launch (FTL)..............................140
    Backbone Requires Self-Care 154
    Keepers 157

Chapter Six: Love and Backbone in Action 159
    Partnering on the Future and Influence Strategies 160
    Getting on the Same Page: Their Page 160
    Getting on the Same Page: Our Page...163
    Expectations for Living at Home 166
    Discussing the Five-Year Plan and Parent's Response 171
    Making Living Together Work..173
    Managing Tensions and Conflict..174
    Why Won't They Leave?..177
    The Young Adult's Openness to Change 182
    Ways to Influence Your Young Adult 185
    Teaching a Child to Ride a Bicycle 196
    Keepers 199

Chapter Seven: Let Go 201
    Letting Go: The Final Stage of the Launch Process 203
    Characteristics of a Parent Who Lets Go 208
    Why Letting Go Can Be Difficult 212
    The Practice of Letting Go of Our Young Adult Children 215
    Do You Have the "Right Stuff" to Let Go? 222
    Time to Say Goodbye 223
    My Final Report Card 227
    Keepers 229

Epilogue 231
Appendix A 233
Appendix B 245
Notes 247
Bibliography 255
Resources 263

ACKNOWLEDGMENTS

Many people deserve credit, and thanks for my work over the last ten years as I gathered the information for *The Parent's Launch Code*. These people have influenced my life personally and professionally and deserve mention. I should start with my parents, Jane and Earl Stoltzfus, without whom I would not be here. Specifically, I have used my relationship with my father to understand the parent/adult child separation process and as a source of motivation for my dissertation. I owe thanks to my kids, too. They have brought me such joy and taught me so much. They are the source of many life-giving experiences, some of which I share in this book. Now, I am exploring what it means to be a dad of married young adults; the learning continues. Last, one of my most essential supporters has been my wife. She has endured my absence while I write and has provided editorial advice and feedback. I will be eternally grateful for her patience, presence, and love, which extend far beyond this book.

My early training in family therapy and studies with Carl Whitaker influenced my work as a clinician and my understanding of family relationships. My years at 3M, especially the last eleven years managing a leadership development and coaching initiative, have informed my work with families. I have incorporated this experience into my writing. We can learn much from business leadership as it translates to family life (and vice versa). It was at 3M that I first met Marshall Goldsmith, who has become a mentor and friend over the years. He is a person who practices what he preaches. In one of his workshops, he described how he applied the concept of feedforward, which you will learn about in chapter two, to become a better father.

Beyond these influencers, I also want to thank several people with fingerprints all over this book. First and foremost is Monique Keffer, who was my primary editor and writing coach. I was fortunate to find someone with exceptional editing skills who had children at the launching stage. I asked her to wear two hats as editor and mom, and she wore them well. Second, many others have been helpful in the editing process, including my good friends Nancy Herbst, Dr. Penny Giesbrecht, Blair and Betty Anderson, Jim and Judy Grubs, and Dr. Jonathon Hoistad. I also want to recognize my sister, Janet Brownback, for her thorough reading of my manuscript, which only a former teacher can do. Finally, two people who have been with me in my writing and website creation deserve recognition. Jennifer Wreisner, my graphic design resource, has done a masterful job in creating six short books on the practices updated with more depth in this book. Ryan McGinty, my webmaster, has been working closely with me to expand the reach of my work by helping me post my blogs, videos, and writings on my website, parentslettinggo.com, and YouTube.

Finally, I extend my heartfelt thanks to the parents of young adults I've had the privilege to work with over the last decade. Their wisdom, their struggles, and their successes have been my greatest teachers. I believe in the power of community and approach my work with families as a continuous learning process. Their feedback and experiences have been invaluable, and I am deeply grateful for their contribution to this book.

THE PARENT'S LAUNCH CODE FOREWORD

BY DR. MARSHALL GOLDSMITH

As a leadership and coaching expert, I've had the privilege of guiding many through the various stages of personal and professional development. Yet there's a pivotal phase that's often overlooked: the transition young adults make from the family home into the wider world. Dr. Jack Stoltzfus's *The Parent's Launch Code* is a pivotal work that provides an invaluable road map for this journey. Having raised two adult children myself, I understand the delicate balance required in this critical phase. The process of releasing our kids into the world equipped for success and resilience is a task that, while daunting, is deeply rewarding. Dr. Stoltzfus's work is a vital companion for this task, offering sage advice that I wish had been available during my own parenting years.

In my career and life, I've seen firsthand the challenges of letting go and the importance of doing it right. This book is a testament to the delicate art of parenting young adults—a stage where conventional parenting books often fall silent. Dr. Stoltzfus offers not just his profound insights but also his heart as he shares real-life experiences from his practice and personal life. It's this blend of professional expertise and personal vulnerability that makes *The Parent's Launch Code* resonate with such authenticity and authority. Having experienced the complex emotions of watching my children venture out, I can attest to the need for a guide that embraces both the joy and trepidation of this period. Dr. Stoltzfus steps into this role with grace and wisdom, offering a light to navigate by.

THE PARENT'S LAUNCH CODE

What strikes me most about this book is its unflinching honesty. Dr. Stoltzfus doesn't shy away from the complexities of the parent-young adult relationship. Instead, he faces them head-on, acknowledging the emotional turmoil while steering clear of empty guarantees. This honest approach sets a solid foundation for the six practices he outlines, each a stepping stone towards successful independence for our children and peace of mind for us as parents. The realism in these pages speaks to those of us who have lain awake at night wondering if we've done enough, if our children are truly prepared for the challenges ahead, and how our relationship with them will evolve. It assures us that while perfection in parenting is unattainable, continuous improvement is always within reach.

I am particularly moved by the way Dr. Stoltzfus addresses the duality of parenting: the profound love we have for our children and the inherent sadness in acknowledging they will one day leave the nest. This book provides a compassionate and practical approach to managing this bittersweet reality, ensuring that the bonds we cherish remain strong, even as we encourage our children to forge their own paths. As parents, we aspire not just to raise competent individuals but also to lay the groundwork for lasting, meaningful relationships that endure the test of time and distance.

The Parent's Launch Code is an essential read for any parent at the cusp of this transformative stage. As our young adults prepare to launch into a world that we've helped them navigate from a distance, Dr. Stoltzfus's book is a powerful reminder that our roles as parents evolve but never truly end. We are forever coaches, cheerleaders, and safe harbors in the ever-changing tides of our children's lives. The launch may be theirs, but the journey is a shared one, with each successful step forward a testament to the love and effort we've poured into their upbringing. As my own children have embarked on their independent paths, the lessons echoed in this book have reinforced the importance of trust, the wisdom of restraint, and the value of unwavering support. Dr. Stoltzfus's words are not just guidance; they are a celebration of one of life's most significant milestones.

—Dr. Marshall Goldsmith is the *Thinkers50* #1 Executive Coach and New York Times bestselling author of *The Earned Life*, *Triggers*, and *What Got You Here Won't Get You There*.

PREFACE

This book is about you and me as parents. Parents of young adults are a woefully underserved segment of the parent population. For example, do a web search of "parents of young adults," and you'll see that the search results will bring up a scant one percent of the "parents of children" URLs on the internet. One of my parent clients said, "We need help, and it's hard to find." Another parent contacted me and said, "I'm desperate." This book is a response to these pleas for help.

The book describes a code or set of practices that can help avert failure to launch and enable our kids to find paths toward happiness, success, and independence while staying positively connected to us. Some readers have described the book as very packed with information and help. Some books make the main points in the first few chapters and then fill in afterward. In this book, every chapter relates to a practice that needs to be implemented or strengthened to enable a successful launch. I know you will find useful advice in each chapter on how to be a better parent at this stage of life.

This book also reflects my experience as a young adult and as a parent of three young adults. My kids attained responsible independence while maintaining close connections to my wife and me. I view the successful launching of my kids with gratitude and a degree of undeserved blessing. I see many loving parents who have done so many things right and yet have kids who act out, become drug addicts, and fail at school, relationships, or vocational pursuits. Sobbing parents in my private practice office give credence to the gut-wrenching emotional pain these parents feel. One of my colleagues said about this time of life with teenagers and young adults: "When they are young, they step on your toes; when they are older, they step on your heart."

My experience meeting with families over the past ten years has humbled me to know there is no guarantee of how our kids will turn out. Can we ultimately prevent a failed launch or estrangement? The short answer is no. But don't put this book down, because there is no excuse for not trying! With unyielding love and willingness to let go, we can influence the trajectory of their lives in meaningful and positive ways. Parenting at any stage is hard work, especially when we can no longer control or direct our kids and they make poor decisions or act irresponsibly. There is no simple answer to setting up the launch pad effectively. If you are willing to do the work, this book will help you do your best to let go with love.

This influence process doesn't start when our children turn eighteen or twenty-one. Nested inside of the intention to have children is knowing that this little being we welcome with such love will someday need to leave. The love we experience for our children comes from deep in our biology. As strong as our love for a partner may be, it is a manufactured love, something we engender. The love for a child only exists once the child arrives. When we bring a child into the world, we realize that there is something more important in life than our well-being. At the same time, as they grow, there is an inherent sadness in knowing our kids will leave us someday. When they go in the right way, we can cheer them on and joyfully celebrate their success.

Many parents navigate this development stage with minimal drama and often celebration by both parties. However, the process can be difficult and draining for some parents and young adults. Sometimes, parents will argue they are ready to let go, but the young adult seems emotionally stuck, like a toddler wrapped around a mother's leg. However, it's fair to say that parents sometimes hang on and support dependent behavior in unhealthy ways that inhibit the young adult's progress toward emotional and behavioral independence. We need to learn how to launch our kids in *the right way*. Success is not just about getting them out of the house or on their own but helping them thrive by becoming self-sufficient and autonomous while retaining an affiliative bond with their parents. As parents, we can embrace a code of practices that enable our young adults to launch in the best

PREFACE

way that preserves our relationships with them. Isn't that what we all want? Six practices that constitute the launch code are described in the chapters of this book with examples, testimonies of parents, and actions you can take to strengthen one or more of these.

At the end of the day, we all have to face the bittersweet experience of saying goodbye to our kids. No matter the circumstances under which kids leave, be they well-launched or not, all parents will feel some loss or sadness. The family we created will never be the same again when members leave. Although sorrow is inevitable, done right, the successful launch of the young adult is a cause for celebration. In this book, you will find an understanding and compassionate voice and practical actions you can take to prepare the launch pad for a successful launch.

Note: Throughout the book, I share experiences I have had both personally and in my clinical work. In all instances of the latter, I have changed the names to protect the anonymity of the families and young adults I have worked with. They have been my teachers in this journey to find the code for a successful young adult launch experience.

INTRODUCTION

THE LAUNCH CODE

> *For many parents, the sleepless nights when their infant needed comfort pale in comparison to nights worrying about a troubled young adult.*
>
> *A single-parent mother was concerned about her young adult son, who was afraid to leave the house, didn't sleep at night, and exhibited signs of depression and anxiety. Although he was close to finishing college, he had dropped out and had been home for several years. He refused to look for work because he feared the rejection of not being hired. This mom was distraught and worried he might be suicidal if she threatened to force him to leave.*

This mother and millions of mothers and fathers face a common dilemma with young adults who fail to progress toward responsible independence. The difficulty is balancing a message of love and concern with one that challenges young adults to move forward in their lives. Too much of the soft nurturing side and the adult child may never leave or grow up. Still, a harsh push to be more independent could result in increased depression and anxiety and jeopardize the relationship the parent desires to have with their child. The book doesn't contain the silver bullet or easy solution for managing this dilemma but offers the code or roadmap to do your best to launch your young adult. Many of the parents I see in my practice express guilt about their stalled young adult or feel responsible for their current immobilization. When do we no longer feel responsible for our young adult's success and happiness? The short answer is never.

A mother asked for my help deciding whether to help her son, who had become embroiled in a custody battle over a three-year-old son and needed money to hire a lawyer. He sought custody of his son because his girlfriend was a drug addict. You might imagine this son to be twenty-some years of age. At the time, this son was fifty-nine years old, and his mother was ninety-five years old, living in an extended care facility. Before you stop reading this book because you don't like to hear stories like this, let's admit that we will always love our adult children. We want the best for them, even if we must step up to help them. I've not met parents who don't love their young adult children even though their kid's behavior may challenge them. We're wired to love our kids and are heartsick when they run into trouble at any age. Many of us struggle to continue to love our kids and let them go; support their independence but allow them to stumble and fail. Do we jump in to rescue them or let them figure out how to swim? Can we love them and support their independence without rescuing them? Finding this balance or *sweet spot* is necessary to launch our young adults successfully.

THE TRUTH ABOUT PARENTS AND YOUNG ADULTS

Foundational in my work with parents and young adults is that they share three beliefs. First, both seek to love and be loved by the other, even if the relationship is contentious. It's in our DNA. Second, both share a common desire to see the young adult become happy, successful, self-sufficient, and independent. Third, both share a desire to make the process of letting go and launching amicably. These beliefs underpin my work to help parents and young adults find common ground and partner in the letting go process. A reminder is that this book provides a guide for you—parents. You can only change yourself, so I encourage you to embrace this concept and your love and desire to support a positive future for your adult child as you read on. Truly seeing our kids, touching them, hugging them, and expressing heartfelt love and appreciation become as essential as supporting autonomy in a successful launch. This book describes a set of practices representing the code for parents to let

INTRODUCTION

go. The core message of the code, which could have been the title of this book, is **loving our kids into adulthood.**

TERMS USED IN THIS BOOK

Young adult: I will interchange this term with an adult child, young person, emerging adult, or sometimes-kid. They will always be our kids. Incidentally, some of these young adults use the word "kid" to describe a friend they may be meeting.

Responsibly independent: I will use this term to describe a self-sufficient young adult who functions independently of his parents.

Differentiation/individuation: I use these terms synonymously with healthy emotional separation or connected autonomy to describe the healthy state of being separate from parents but still connected positively. A young adult may be responsibly independent but not emotionally independent. Read on.

THE LAUNCHED "YOUNG" ADULT

I put the word "young" in quotation marks because, like the example above, a fifty-nine-year-old may not have launched. However, the main stage for becoming launched is that of the young adult. The Federal Interagency Forum on Child and Family Statistics describes young adults as individuals ages 18–24. Jeffrey Arnett coined the phrase "emerging adulthood" to characterize periods between 18 and 25.[1] Arnett has co-authored a book with Elizabeth Fishel entitled *Getting to Thirty: A Parent's Guide to the 20-Something Years.* This is a very helpful guide to the parenting role during the young adult stage of development. Pew Research Center uses 18–29 to describe the period of young adulthood.[2] They describe their research as documenting the highest percentage ever of young adults (52%) living with one or both parents today. Don't assume that all of these young adults living at home are failures to launch, but I think it's safe to say that a significant number are.

My work primarily focuses on parents, consistent with the Pew definition of 18–29. We are learning more about young adults' brain development, which, some argue, continues into the mid-twenties, so extending the focus to twenty-nine for my work with parents makes sense. Parents I see with stalled young adults in their early twenties express concern, but alarm bells ring when they haven't made any progress into their late twenties. COVID has undoubtedly contributed to many young adults stuck on the launch pad.

My definition of a fully launched young adult includes the following:

1. *Identity*—a stable sense of self.
2. *Independence*—financially, physically, and emotionally
3. *Intimacy*—the development of significant sustainable relationships outside of the family.
4. A positive connection to the parent.

Healthfully launched and separated young adults demonstrate maturity in their relationships with their parents. They care about their parents and express concern and empathy. They are assertive without being defensive. They are open, trusting, and receptive to parental support. They acknowledge and are willing to apologize for their mistakes and forgive their parents. The specific attributes above are my contributions to describing a launched young adult. I have dealt with many financially independent adults who continue to be hurt, angry, and frustrated with their parents because of how they were treated or how they left home. Therapists' offices are filled with adults describing unresolved issues with their parents. These adults have physically separated from their parents, but the process didn't go well. If the relationship between young adults and parents is estranged, it's fair to assume that the transition or launch likely didn't go well, and both parties will suffer. It's important to understand that there may be circumstances where reconciliation or the retention of an amiable relationship between parents and adult children may not be possible. Such circumstances may include an abusive parent or a young adult who may be angry and threatening to the parents.

INTRODUCTION

LIVING OUTSIDE THE HOME IS NOT THE LITMUS TEST FOR A SUCCESSFUL LAUNCH

Let me clarify my belief that a young adult does not need to leave the parent's home to be fully launched. There is a trend in the United States toward multigenerational households. This trend occurs for various reasons, including economics, but does not necessarily signal young adults in these homes aren't self-sufficient. Suppose a young adult lives in an amicable relationship with parents, maybe even grandparents, works and is a contributing family member, sharing costs and home maintenance tasks. In this case, I'd be hard-pressed to label them as stuck on the launchpad. The young adult's capacity to establish healthy emotional separation from parents, whether living with parents or not, is directly related to the parents' launch practices. If young adults do not attain self-sufficiency and responsible independence, who's at fault? Okay, the answer is both. Since this is a book for and about parents of young adults, we'll focus on the parent's role. We'll start with some myths that cause much self-inflicted pain for parents.

STINKING THINKING

Many parents request my help in launching their young adults. Secretly or subconsciously, they hope that I will intervene to emancipate their young adult and free them from this responsibility. Most parents with whom I work want the answer or the secret to launching their young adult, which usually means getting them out of the house. When I ask young adults at home where they want to live five years from now, none have said, "I just want to live here with my mommy and daddy." There is a palpable sigh of relief when parents hear this. However, for various reasons, including their own young adult experience, parents are impatient with a five-year horizon and want change now. Parental myths lie beneath the emotional drivers of impatience and frustration. I refer to these myths as "stinking thinking" by parents, leading to disabling actions and the root of much self-inflicted suffering and unhappiness.

One myth is that **the parent can control or direct the young adult.** A parent attending one of my workshops addressed this myth by saying, "The problem with young adults is that they are adults." If the young adult lives at home, you have some leverage, but they may leave without changing their behavior. Lack of control does not mean you can't influence them; this book is about influencing our young adults. If you have ever attended an Al-Anon meeting or know their philosophy, you will understand that letting go of control does not mean you don't care. Letting go of the need to control the young adult may be one of your most loving actions.

Another myth is that **parents are responsible for their young adult's behavior.** Whereas the first myth deals with letting go of the belief that you can control their behavior, this myth deals with the parent's behavior. Parents are the guiltiest segment of our population. One parent told me that being a parent is "one big guilt trip." In my survey of over one hundred parents of young adults conducted in 2021, 78 percent indicated that they "believe they are responsible for their young adult's success." In this survey, 38 percent expressed guilt about raising their young adult.[3] Unless we have been perfect parents, we made mistakes, have some regrets, and wish we could have a do-over. We can acknowledge our mistakes and actions, but if we believe we are the cause of current inappropriate behaviors or signs of the stalled young adult, we are back to accepting myth number one. Young adults are responsible for their behavior and can't blame their parents for their lack of progress toward adulthood. Ultimately, it's their responsibility to move on with their lives regardless of their parents' past or current behavior. Parents and young adults cannot use the past to excuse behavior in the present.

A third myth is that **failure to launch is all about the young adult,** and we have no responsibility for our decisions or actions related to this process. You would not have picked up this book if you had believed this. It's important to understand that we are in a facilitative role, not a directive one. We play a significant real-time role in helping our young adults grow up and take responsibility for their lives. Although we can't control our young adults, we can control our decisions and actions, affecting the launch process. We prepare the launch pad. We can take steps that enable young adults to move ahead or disable them toward this end.

A fourth myth is that **success as a parent is contingent upon their child's success.** It grows out of the second myth that a parent is responsible for a young adult's behavior. Beginning with my generation, boomers, and continuing with Gen Xers, we have become more invested in children's success and happiness. The experience of Olympic athletes offers one good example of this more involved contemporary parenting style. We hear about medal winners at the Olympics expressing gratitude and praise for a parent who drove them to practice day and night so they could achieve greatness. Unfortunately, for some of these driven athletes, the overwhelming competitive pressures by others, including their parents, can lead to anxiety and depression.

When a parent invests so heavily in a young adult's achievements—whether a future Olympic athlete, a straight-A student, or an overachiever—the young adult feels the burden to excel for themselves *and* their parents. When and how should parents back off? When should young adults assume responsibility for their actions? Our society says eighteen or twenty-one, but that doesn't stop parents from still intervening and believing others' approval of their parenting hinges upon their young adults' accomplishments. We have become too vested in what our children do, not who they are. Achievement trumps character. We must let go of this myth to allow our young adults to pursue *their* vision of success and happiness.

Finally, **there is the myth that change has to occur exclusively with the young adult.** Believing this lie leads parents only to complain and point out things that need to change with the young adult. *We are not responsible for their decisions and actions, but we are responsible for ours.* Change in the young adult is unlikely to occur with threats, bribes, rewards, pleading, and so on. So, what can ultimately influence the young adult to move toward responsible independence? It comes down to an ability to influence through our changes. We must change first, and this book outlines how.

LAUNCHING—EMOTIONAL FAILURES AND SUCCESSES

Living at home and taking advantage of the parent's goodwill while playing video games, not working, and not helping around the house is only one example of a failure to launch. Failure to launch (FTL) is not just about becoming independent and self-reliant. My definition includes a failure to become emotionally independent from a parent. Below is a graph that shows the different types of failure to launch emotionally from parents: Quadrants I, II, and III illustrate the failure to connect to parents and demonstrate autonomy. Quadrant IV illustrates the combination of independence and a positive connection to parents. As you read the different types of failures to launch, where would you place your young adult? Put an X to signify this, and keep this in mind as you read on to learn how your parenting can move the X toward a higher score on both axes.

FAILURE TO LAUNCH AND LAUNCH

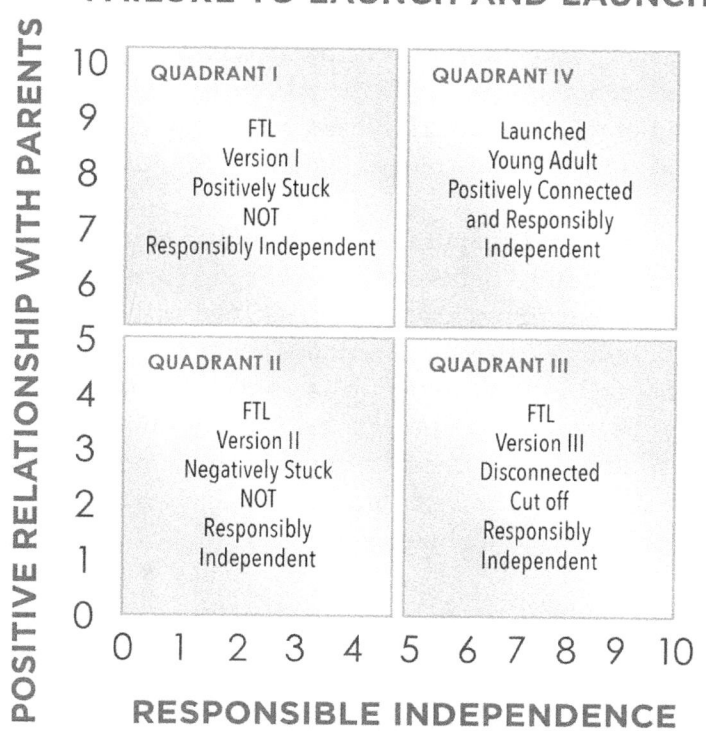

POSITIVE RELATIONSHIP WITH PARENTS		
10	**QUADRANT I**	**QUADRANT IV**
9	FTL	Launched
8	Version I	Young Adult
7	Positively Stuck	Positively Connected
6	NOT Responsibly Independent	and Responsibly Independent
5	**QUADRANT II**	**QUADRANT III**
4	FTL	FTL
3	Version II	Version III
2	Negatively Stuck	Disconnected
1	NOT Responsibly Independent	Cut off Responsibly Independent
0	0 1 2 3 4 5 6 7 8 9 10	

RESPONSIBLE INDEPENDENCE

FAILURE TO LAUNCH—DEPENDENT TYPE—POSITIVELY STUCK (SEE QUADRANT 1 ABOVE)

The first version of FTL is the young adult living the "good life." The young adult lives at home without a job, pays no rent, and is physically and financially dependent on their parents. Imagine the Matthew McConaughey character in the movie *Failure to Launch*. It is important to note that this young adult has no physical or mental health challenges. The parent may or may not have a concern or desire for this person to move out. One study found that sixty-one percent of parents have positive feelings toward their young adult living at home.[4] This type of FTL would also include a young adult who lives outside the home but is highly dependent on the parent. These young adults rely upon their parent's financial and other help and often have trouble making independent decisions. In both cases, the parent's resistance to let go may contribute to the failure to launch.

FAILURE TO LAUNCH—DEPENDENT TYPE—NEGATIVELY STUCK (SEE QUADRANT 2 ABOVE)

The second version of FTL is when the young adult lives at home or elsewhere, works, and is self-sufficient but contentious, making living together and connecting very difficult. This person may be independent and autonomous but is not emancipated emotionally. The parties are negatively fused. Parents and young adults are unhappy about the antagonistic quality of the relationship.

FAILURE TO LAUNCH—INDEPENDENT—DISCONNECTED (SEE QUADRANT 3 ABOVE)

The third version of FTL is the young adult living outside the home and responsibly independent but refusing to have a relationship with their parents. Sometimes, this estrangement occurs because the parent has cut all communications with the young adult. These estranged relationships between parents and young adults are some of the more heartbreaking situations. Both parents and young adults suffer and carry the wounds of this breach throughout their lives. To learn more about this tragic growing trend of estrangement, see Josh Coleman's book, *Rules of Estrangement: Why Adult Children Cut Ties and How to Heal the Conflict.*[5] Some young adults who perceive a continuing relationship with the parent as toxic and damaging to their emotional well-being may choose not to have contact with the parent.

FAILURE TO LAUNCH—MIXED

This "mixed" type acknowledges that young adults often move from one quadrant to another, creating confusion for parents. Sometimes, the young adult may be quite hospitable, considerate, and cooperative. At other times, the young adult may be argumentative, abusive, and uncooperative. This unpredictable tendency is a common complaint from parents. It reflects young adults' ambivalence about allowing themselves to depend on their parents when trying to assert their independence. When they feel too dependent, they may withdraw or attack the parent as one who can't tell them what to do. For parents, this is like trying to dance with your young adult, and they keep changing the music and the dance steps without notifying you. This dynamic begins in adolescence but extends well into emerging adulthood and is frustrating and challenging. To be fair, sometimes parents change the dance steps and move closer to take care of the young adult, then back off, and send a message that the young adult is on their own. Such actions by the parents can create confusion for the kids. The challenge is finding the music within that enables us to move close and hold on when needed and back away when required.

THE LAUNCHED YOUNG ADULT (SEE QUADRANT 4 ABOVE)

Young adults launch when they are responsibly independent and relate amiably to their parents. The young adult may live at—or away—from home but pursue a positive relationship with their parents. If living at home, the young adult contributes to the household by paying rent and other costs, helping around the house, and being responsible for their needs (e.g., laundry, cleaning the room, car expenses, and the like). If living outside the home, the young adult and parents have regular adult-to-adult contact. These categories are not necessarily mutually exclusive, as described above, and this young adult may temporarily fall into Quadrant I. For example, many parents will help their young adults living outside the home with educational expenses, wedding costs, a down payment on a home, or an unusual expense (e.g., a medical bill). There may also be times when the young adult temporarily returns home to save for her wedding, as my daughter did in her last year of college. These temporary actions by parents don't necessarily indicate a failure to launch.

YOUNG ADULTS WITH SPECIAL NEEDS—AN EXCEPTION

It is important to note that unique circumstances may limit young adults' progress toward responsible independence through no fault of their own. These young adults may have severe mental or physical disabilities interfering with their progress toward independence and self-sufficiency. A disability is not a basis for "failure to launch." These young adults could also fall into one of the three FTL categories above. Despite these limiting factors, most young adults, even those with severe disabilities, strive to be independent. Parents should support this endeavor. Parents with whom I have worked, where there are special needs, worry about how their young adults will survive if something happens to the parents. It is even more reason to help these adult children attain as much independence and self-sufficiency as possible.

THE LAUNCH CODE REVEALED

The launch process starts with letting go as the toddler ventures forth under the parent's watchful eye. With the secure relationship of the parent and child, the toddler ventures forth to the room's outer edges, glancing back to be reassured his parent is still there. During adolescence and young adulthood, these kids move out to the edges of a much larger world but will still glance back in different ways to ensure the parents are still there. In the first semester of my older daughter's college experience, she called me one Saturday morning to tell me she and a friend were over at a boy's apartment until four in the morning. She may have expected a reaction of shock or disapproval, which she didn't get. Maybe she was disappointed. I was sound asleep when this occurred. There's something to say for *out of sight, out of mind*. From the toddler stage to young adulthood, the parent is trying to manage the process of letting go with love. The diagram below illustrates the practices on the left circle that parents need to adopt to do their best to launch adult children in the right way. Chapters Two through Seven describe these practices in the circle in more depth so you can assess how you are doing and learn how to do better.

PARENTS LETTING GO MODEL

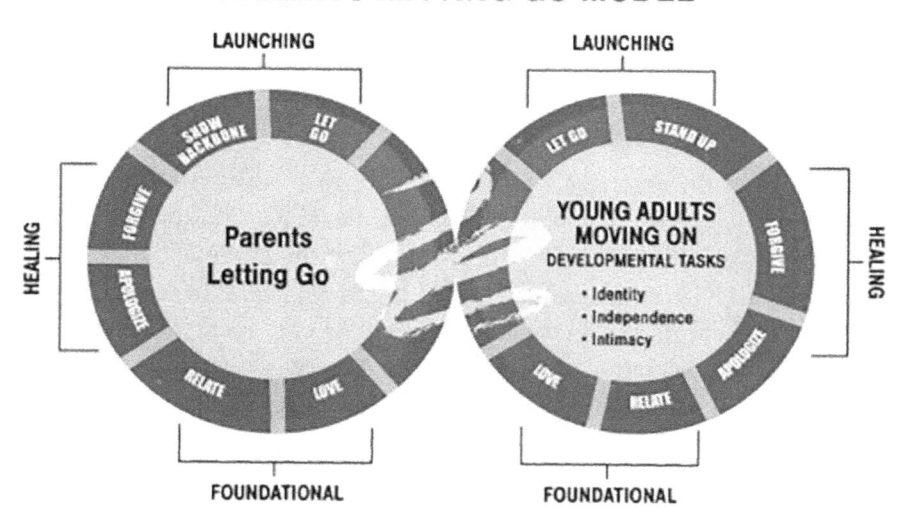

Parents Letting Go (left circle): LAUNCHING — SHOW BACKBONE, LET GO; HEALING — FORGIVE, APOLOGIZE; FOUNDATIONAL — RELATE, LOVE

Young Adults Moving On (right circle) — Developmental Tasks:
- Identity
- Independence
- Intimacy

LAUNCHING — LET GO, STAND UP; HEALING — FORGIVE, APOLOGIZE; FOUNDATIONAL — LOVE, RELATE

The Launch Code refers to the comprehensive model illustrated above, which describes six practices that parents need to implement or strengthen to create the best platform to launch a young adult. As you learn more about these six practices and complete the self-assessments in each chapter, you will be able to identify areas that you need to strengthen. Parents who successfully launch their young adults implement the practices on the left circle in the graphic above. The first two areas are *foundational* and involve securing the young adult's emotional safety by demonstrating unconditional love and showing understanding and an ability to build a strong and sustainable relationship with the young adult. The second two practices are *healing* actions on the part of the parents to reduce the extent to which the young adult or the parent experiences hurt, anger, resentment, or guilt that keeps the relationship stuck in an unhealthy way. These involve the practices of apology and forgiveness. The last two practices are essential to the launch stage. In *show backbone*, parents set boundaries, say no, and compel young adults to stand independently. And the final launch practice for parents is to say goodbye and truly *let go*. Chapters that follow will highlight one of the launch practices for description and discussion.

The circle on the right describes the essential tasks of the young adult during the launch process. The squiggly white lines indicate a healthy and positive engagement between the parents and young adults as separate entities. These practices are arranged in a circle, and not steps, because we continue to have opportunities to demonstrate them throughout our lifetime. When should we stop expressing unconditional love, saying we are sorry, offering forgiveness, and saying no as well as yes? The reality is that letting go and saying goodbye, as described in the last chapter, is something we must do every day. These practices of the launch code offer us a way to engage our young adults in ways that enable us to love and let go.

Parents must embrace and exhibit certain qualities to implement the launch code successfully. Although the practices provide a code to the launch process, the launch will not succeed unless you have the right "mindset" and "heartset." A sincere desire to love and let go of your young adult is more important than the strict adherence or execution of the launch code. Your impact and the ultimate launch success will suffer if you cannot embrace the following qualities as part of the journey. Even if you botch the launch code practices but demonstrate the qualities below, you will still positively impact your relationship with your son or daughter. The *journey* to build a positive relationship with our young adults and to let go is as important as the *outcome*. In addition, modeling the following traits enables us to implement the code successfully and invites our young adults to mirror them back to us. Relationships are inherently reciprocal—we get back what we give.

DO YOU HAVE THE "RIGHT STUFF" TO LAUNCH YOUR YOUNG ADULT?

Thomas Wolfe popularized the term "right stuff" when he studied the Project Mercury astronauts and subsequently wrote a book by that title. It refers to special qualities these astronauts demonstrated to endure the challenges of space travel. Parents face demands and pressures that require certain qualities and attributes to launch their young adults successfully. As I describe the different practices of a successful launch, I will lift up further attributes that parents need.

Rate the extent to which you demonstrate the following qualities in your relationship with your young adult on the following scale:

0	1	2	3
No demonstration of the quality	Some demonstration of the quality	Demonstration of the quality	Strong demonstration of the quality

_____**Transparency and Vulnerability**

Parents need to be honest and open when approaching their young adults. It involves risk by disclosing feelings of inadequacy, ambivalence, and mistakes. Often, parents present a picture of sailing through young adulthood that is only partially accurate. Vulnerability becomes most important in the practice of apologizing for parenting mistakes.

Many of us have never heard the words "I'm sorry" from our parents. We model and invite our young adults to do the same when we exhibit these behaviors. We then can connect at a deeper level. Brené Brown, a popular writer and speaker, says *vulnerability is the language of intimacy*. If you haven't watched her TED Talk on YouTube, please do.[6] Watch it with your young adult and discuss your reactions to it.

_____**Empathy and Compassion**

Compassion is "an empathetic awareness of another's distress with a desire to alleviate it." Empathy involves feeling another person's emotions. Listening deeply to what the other person is saying, thinking, and feeling is essential. Such listening is especially true if your young adult experience differs from yours. Listening with empathy and compassion requires an ability to understand the world of the young adult. I help parents understand that they may be the *target* of their young adult's anger and frustration, but they are not the *source*. The source is their young adult's failure or frustration with their life and feeling of dependency.

_____Openness

An essential approach to the launch is a commitment to openness. It requires a willingness to learn and a desire to challenge our notions of what is best for them. When we are open to change, we are available for personal growth. To become a better parent, you must become a better person. We need to change *first*. Changing first may be hard if the young adult is failing, contentious, or shuts us out, but we must be the bigger person. Change is embedded in the family life cycle and required of parents and young adults. Both parties must be flexible to accommodate a new stage of development.

_____Patience

The most important advice I give to parents is to be *patient*. At eighteen or twenty-five or even thirty, the way they are today is not how they will be five or ten years from now. "This too shall pass" should be a mantra repeated routinely. Most young adults envision their future in conventional ways—career, financial independence, marriage, and a family. They may trip and stumble, progressing in spurts in ways we didn't predict, but the vast majority eventually find a way to right themselves.

How did you score on these traits? If you have some lower scores, be willing to stretch yourself as you move forward to apply the launch code. We're all a work in progress. We need to change and grow to foster this in our kids.

Future Chapters

I recommend first strengthening your knowledge of the foundational practices described in chapters 1 and 2. Ignoring these would be like trying to open a safe by skipping the first two numbers. Without success in these two areas, displaying a backbone will be experienced as rejecting or controlling. It won't work. Likewise, if there are underlying feelings of guilt, hurt, anger, and resentment, spend time in chapters 3 and 4. Unresolved emotions, as described above and addressed in chapters three and four, lead to disabling behavior. Chapters 5 and 6 bring together love and backbone, and chapter 7 addresses the need to say goodbye and let go.

KEEPERS

My friend Terry Paulson, a leadership consultant, motivational speaker, and humorist, likes to have people identify "keepers."[7] These are vital points, recommendations, and ideas that a person takes and applies after hearing a lecture or reading something like this book. At the end of each chapter, I will offer an opportunity to capture your keepers. Identifying, describing, writing down, and communicating these to another parent or friend as soon as possible is the best way to lock in the learning. Why don't I start the list of keepers in this chapter? You can add yours to the list.

1. I need to remember that launching young adults in the right way means helping them become independent and self-sufficient while maintaining positive relationships.
2. I need to examine my beliefs and challenge any irrational thoughts I might harbor about controlling, fixing, or, in other words, taking responsibility for my adult child's actions.
3. _____
4. _____
5. _____
6. _____
7. _____
8. _____
9. _____
10. _____

CHAPTER ONE

LET GO WITH LOVE

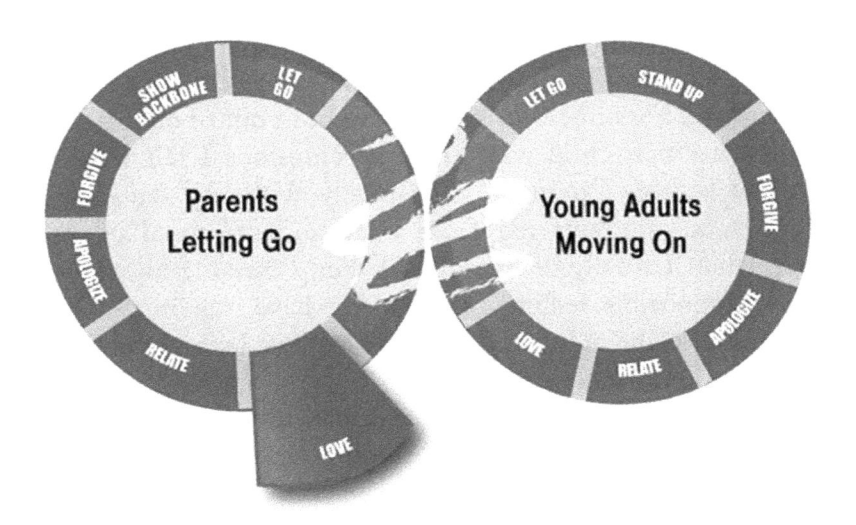

"Would you cry if I died?" An angry young adult asked this of his burly father in a hushed and hesitant voice as they sat in a therapist's office. The father, none too happy to be taking off work, brought his son to family therapy because of a court order. He was angry and disappointed by his son's behavior. The father, not known for expressing feelings other than anger, paused, then leaned toward the son and said, "There are not enough buckets in the world to hold the tears I would cry if something happened to you."

My colleague, Diane Dovenberg, shared this experience with me in the Wilder Child Guidance Clinic cafeteria where we worked. As she described the scene, tears welled up in her eyes as they did in mine. My tears spoke to this scene and the story of my relationship with my father—more on that later. Every child longs to hear a message assuring them they matter and are loved unconditionally. Knowing and experiencing this parental love is fundamental to the healthy parent and child relationship and to a successful launch.

WHAT'S LOVE GOT TO DO WITH IT?

Unconditional love for our children is the cornerstone of all other actions supporting their development. It is expressed in caring about our child's happiness without concern for how it benefits us. It is unselfish or sacrificial love, known as *agape* in Greek. Our young adults should not have to be someone other than themselves or fulfill our aspirations to earn our love. For our children, it is love born out of our attachment.

When my first child was born, the emotions I felt were ones I never knew before. Connecting positively with my daughter took a while because she suffered from colic and screamed relentlessly. However, when I finally did bond with her, I became aware of deep, protective, responsible feelings I could not have imagined. This love is simply because she is my child. As parents, we love our children for their being and not only their doing.

Even if our children engage in unspeakably horrible actions, our love perseveres. For example, Sue Klebold, the mother of one of the Columbine mass murderers, spoke of her inability to stop loving her son even in the face of atrocities.[1] Unconditional love—and the expression of that love—for our offspring override tendencies to see life in dualistic terms, whether "good" or "bad," whoever they are and whatever they do.

As Brené Brown says. We are wired to express love. She writes, "A deep sense of love and belonging is an irreducible need of all women, men, and children. We are biologically and spiritually wired to love, be loved, and belong. When these needs are unmet, we don't function as we were meant to. We break. We fall apart. We numb. We ache. We hurt others. We get sick."[2]

Expressing that hardwired parental love isn't just paramount for the young adult's well-being; it is equally important for the parent to communicate it for themselves. I have witnessed this truth time and again in my practice. One such instance included a young man named Ben and his mother.

> *Ben was a sixteen-year-old boy in one of my day treatment programs for delinquent adolescents with substance abuse problems. His mother was frustrated with his ADHD and oppositional behavior. In one family therapy session, she reached over and slapped him on the back of the head. With tears in her eyes, she told her son how much she loved him and how frustrating it was for her to be a good mother to him. Even though it was against her better judgment, she let him go to live with his father because she was at such a loss regarding how to help him.*
>
> *A few months later, she called to tell me that Ben was doing well at his father's, attending classes, and had recently obtained his driver's license. About a month later, she called again. After saying hello, she paused, and her voice betrayed a deep sadness. She said that Ben drove through an intersection, was hit broadside, and killed. It was almost too painful for her to report, a parent's worst nightmare. This mother would have to live the rest of her life without a future that included her son. One consolation was that she had the knowledge that she told him how much she loved him before he died.*

Unconditional love for a young adult needs to be both felt and expressed. When the relationship between the parent and the young adult is strained, critical, or contentious, expressing unconditional love is even more important. In such cases, the young adult may doubt the parent's love. When was the last time you said—verbally or in writing—how much you love your grown child? It's so important to them. It's so important to us. If not now, then when?

UNCONDITIONAL LOVE FOR THE YOUNG ADULT

What Unconditional Love Is

The model below clearly illustrates the integral role unconditional love plays in the process of launching. On each side, we can see the steps for both parties. The white wavy lines refer to continued positive communication and interaction between parent and young adult, allowing both to experience full autonomy. Isn't this the goal we all should desire: a relationship of closeness and freedom for parents and young adults?

PARENTS LETTING GO MODEL

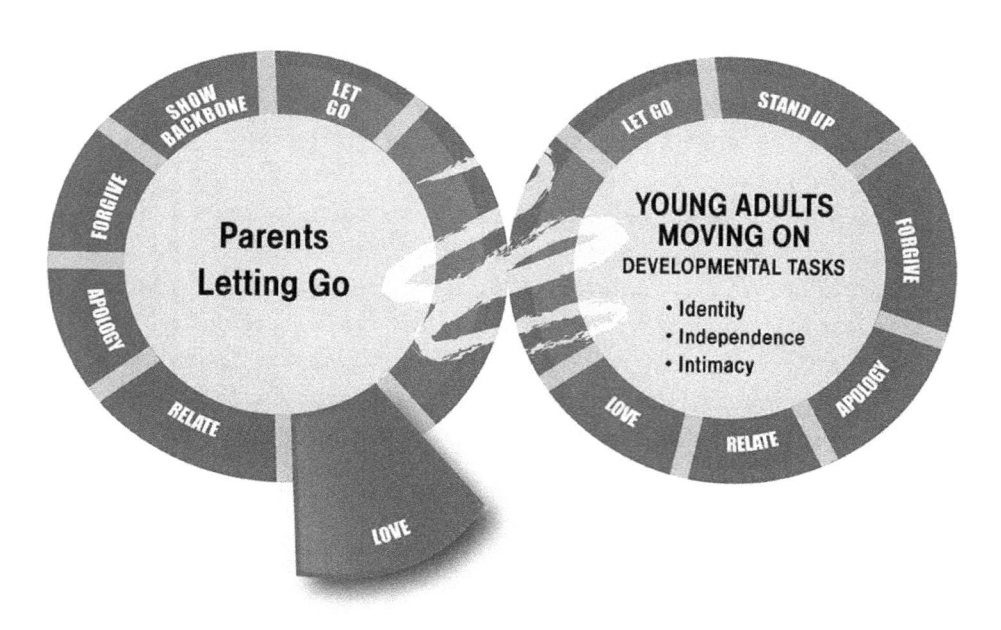

Parents Letting Go (segments: SHOW BACKBONE, LET GO, FORGIVE, APOLOGY, RELATE, LOVE)

Young Adults Moving On — Developmental Tasks:
- Identity
- Independence
- Intimacy

(segments: LET GO, STAND UP, FORGIVE, APOLOGY, RELATE, LOVE)

There are many ways unconditional love supports healthy development in young adults, preparing them for a successful launch. First, as described above, it is essential to their security. Unconditional love provides the necessary secure attachment. Secure toddlers venture from the mother to explore a new world. Failures of attachment lead to problems with behavior, managing emotions, and dealing with change and new situations. Toddlers who have not experienced healthy attachment can cling to the parent, withdraw, or exhibit angry behaviors.

Second, adolescence, which has extended into young adulthood, is the second separation stage in the parent-child relationship. The types of behaviors displayed at the launch stage are often older versions of attachment problems in infancy. These problems include, among others, clinging, demanding, rejecting, blaming, withdrawing, and so on. Although a parent can't go back and redo an earlier failure of attachment, it is possible to seek connection to the young adult through love at any age. In so doing, the parent creates a "safety net" or firm foundation so the adult can muster the courage necessary to let go and embrace the responsibilities of adulthood.

Third, parents continue to provide a *guarantor* relationship to young adults, vowing to be there for them throughout their lives. Even if they are in their darkest times, experiencing despair and loneliness, our young adults can survive on their own if they know we love them. In this way, as in their childhood, our love for them is life-sustaining and lifesaving.

Fourth, unconditional love is also the antidote to the experience of shame. Shame is the sense that one is defective or flawed—a reject. In a therapy session with a mother of a twenty-one-year-old living at home without a job, this mother said that her son constantly states that he is a loser and never finishes or succeeds at anything. Parents' unconditional love means their children have worth—they matter. This message nullifies the tendency to think of oneself as a "loser" or some other self-denigrating label. They need to know they have inherent worth or value. Identity starts with a sense that you have unique merits reinforced by a parent's love. Identity begins with a sense that you deserve to be alive and have someone who values you no matter what.

Finally, in addition to being the secure platform and antidote to shame, abundant research demonstrates that unconditional love and a warm, nurturing parental environment impact a child's mental and physical health. Living in a loving environment positively affects cardiovascular health, appropriate weight, brain development, and intrinsic interest in education. Perception of parental love or rejection accounts for 26 percent of children's psychological adjustment and 21 percent of adults' psychological adjustment. A Harvard study followed

268 graduates and concluded that "happy and successful lives are rooted in good relationships with parents."[3] One could say the same about the successful launch of the young adult.

Some of you who are reading this may believe, for various reasons, that you have not done as much as you could have or made inevitable mistakes in raising your young adult. In this case, I guess you can't join the "perfect parent club." One parent said that "parenting is an inherent guilt trip." Whether or not we have exhibited warm, nurturing, and unconditionally loving behaviors in the years a young adult grows up, it's not too late.

How do I know this? If you have a pulse, you still have time. Showing our unconditional love and emotional support can contribute to their health and well-being as they move across the threshold into adulthood. It's never too late for us to express these sentiments or too late for the young adult to receive them. There is hope for parents dealing with shame, guilt, alienation, and rejection regarding their young adult children. In future chapters, I will discuss two practices that can heal the pain we may feel about ourselves and our parenting or the actions of our young adult children. But before we move on, let me set the record straight about unconditional love and unconditional approval.

WHAT UNCONDITIONAL LOVE IS NOT

It's not a feeling that fluctuates with the behavior or interactions with a young adult. It's a mindset that we still love our child no matter what. Don't mistake hurt, anger, resentment, fear, or other such feelings for lack of unconditional love. When the young adult's behavior elicits these feelings, it's essential to understand that the underlying intention of the young adult is to find happiness or purpose in life. Although they may not admit it, they are likely hurting inside when they lash out at us or act inappropriately.

Their actions may also belie the inner struggle of wanting to be independent and yet feeling uncomfortably dependent on their parent. If this is the case, attacking or criticizing the parent makes them feel less dependent. When we feel hurt, angry, or rejected by our young adults, we must find ways not to take this personally. I know; it's easier said than done. It may help to see some pictures of the young adult as an infant or child to reconnect and recover the positive emotions we have lost. It can also help us remember our struggles and conflicts with our parents to experience the compassion and empathy necessary to connect with our kids.

Unconditional love does not mean unconditional approval. Parental love is about the personhood of the child. A parent can show love while setting limits, expecting changes, and saying no. There are instances when the most loving and sacrificial act is to say no. We demonstrated this act of love when they were young and wanted to touch the stovetop or play in the street. Sometimes, love means not giving in to whatever they want and instead acting in their best interest by doing what we believe is right. Giving into pressure when they ask for money to buy illicit drugs is not an unconditionally loving act. Love must be disconnected from the behavior of the young adult. It is important that we don't say, "I love you, but…" Such a statement—which many of us make—links our love to their behavior. As a rule, we should keep "I love you" and expressions of disapproval of behavior separate.

True "tough love" is not harsh love. Rather, it is the experience of standing our ground when we know what is in our young adult's best interest, even while knowing that they may struggle and suffer.

> *The father of a nineteen-year-old male with a warrant for his arrest, a history of substance abuse and dealing, and an unwillingness to follow rules of living at home made a tough-love decision. He packed a bag for his son and took him to a local young adult shelter. It was a painful action for his parents. They had tried numerous times to help their son change his behavior and be able to live at home, to no avail. The loving action was to say, "Son, you have to face the consequences of your behavior, and we will no longer be able to protect you or intervene."*

Parents suffer in this necessary tough love act of saying no. In a future chapter, we will explore how parents can bring love and backbone to the launch process. Most stories involving difficulties between parents and their sons don't necessarily involve the acting-out behavior described above. Nonetheless, these stories speak to the pain in relationships with parents. My story is one of these.

LOVE TO LET GO: MY STORY

At the age of twenty-five, I began to face the anger and resentment I felt toward my father. Although I was independent behaviorally and financially, living over twelve hundred miles from my parents, I was not emotionally independent. If you live with various painful emotions toward a parent, you are not emotionally separated and healthy. Such unresolved feelings creep into other relationships, particularly in my case, relationships with authority figures. Fortunately, I was in a graduate program in counseling psychology. I knew unresolved feelings toward my father would be detrimental to my work as a psychologist, not to mention my relationships in general.

Although my father was a good person and never abusive to me, the relationship had become estranged over the years. Each of us pulled further away from the other. My infrequent visits home were typically characterized by some degree of conflict or reaction on my part to something my father would say, particularly if the tone or message was critical. On one visit, my mother asked why I didn't talk to my dad more. Incidentally, mothers often play the role of promoting a better relationship between fathers and sons.

In this instance, I responded to my mother's question with anger and defensiveness: "Why doesn't he talk to *me*?" After making this comment and storming out of the kitchen, I started walking down the alley and found myself sobbing. The anger was sitting on top of an unexpressed hurt and feeling of rejection. These emotions illustrated my longing for an intimate relationship with my father that didn't exist.

On a subsequent visit home in my early twenties, I proudly arrived, sprouting a sorry excuse for a beard. When my father saw this, he refused to speak to me. At the dinner table, I would have to ask my mother to ask him to pass the butter. Later, reflecting upon my father's behavior, I realized this reaction must have been what he experienced or observed growing up. His father, great-grandfather, and other relatives were all of Amish descent, and according to the Amish tradition, they shun a child or community member if they violate the norms. Shunning involves a withdrawal of fellowship from a member who violates specific standards. Essentially, they act as if you don't exist.

I'm still not entirely sure about what precipitated his shunning of me, but I can guess that it had something to do with growing a beard. Have you ever seen Amish men? They have beards. This rejection by my father on such a small matter and the fact that he had never told me he loved me left me insecure about his love and our relationship. I thought if I ever did anything really egregious and ended up in prison, he would never come to see me and essentially disown me. Although, like most young adults, I viewed the gap between my father and me as primarily his fault, I decided to take the initiative to address this problem for my well-being.

The process I took to heal involved two steps, and it could be the same if a parent took the initiative. First, I sat down and wrote a letter to my father detailing my many grievances with him over my twenty-eight years with him. As I did this, I indicted my father for not reaching out to me emotionally, criticizing me, and rejecting me on more than one occasion. I connected to the underlying hurt and sense of rejection at some point, and tears came to my eyes. I ended the letter with a statement of my forgiveness for his failure. A level of empathy preceding this forgiveness arose out of understanding the limitations my father experienced with his own father. In my father's old-school world, men didn't express feelings of love to their children. This realization is what put me on the path to forgiveness. It's hard to forgive when we can't put ourselves in another's shoes. Empathy is the path to forgiveness. I needed to let go of the hurt and resentment, and I could do that by expressing my feelings and embracing forgiveness. However, I acknowledged that I was part of the problem during the act of forgiveness, particularly in my young adult years. Simply completing this cathartic writing exercise of letting go of my resentment, experiencing empathy, and embracing forgiveness freed me from the hold these thoughts and feelings had on me. Just writing the letter was for me and not something I needed to share with him. As such, it went to the shredder.

As Rabbi Kushner, author of *Why Do Bad Things Happen to Good People*, says, "forgiveness is the gift you give yourself." It was a gift to release emotions and thoughts, keeping me negatively fused to my father. On the other side of the relationship between parents and children, the emotions that parents need to release include guilt, regret, mistakes made, and failing to be the parents we want to be. In further chapters, we will explore how parents can let go of these and other negative feelings that bind us to our young adults in unhealthy ways. Now that I had released my underlying hurt by writing the letter, the second step of my healing process was to express my love for my father. This task was a more difficult task than I had thought it would be for several reasons. One was that my father had never told me he loved me. This increased the levels of doubt, insecurity, and vulnerability if I were to express such a sentiment to him. There is often a risk of being rebuffed when reaching out to share a desire for closeness with a parent. A parent might give a potentially devastating response such as, "If you love me, then why don't you act like it?" It's no less intimidating for some parents to express love if this is something they have never done. I had never told my father I loved him. Part of me wanted to protest and say, "He should be the one to initiate this communication." For me, the expression of love broke an unspoken rule in my stoic family; such verbal expressions were not the norm. Yet, I decided not to wait.

On one of my visits, I drove my father to the airport for a business trip. I remember my hands being sweaty on the steering wheel as I rehearsed what I would say. I decided not to say it to him in the car. It felt a little too confining and uncomfortable. Neither of us could escape the scene if it didn't go well. As I helped him pull his luggage out of the car trunk, I said to him, "Dad, I just want you to know I love you." There was an immediate release of emotion because I no longer felt the burden of defensiveness and reactivity. You may ask, how did my father respond? Was it like the burly father described at the beginning of this chapter? I'd like to say he reached out, embraced me, and said he always has and always will love me. Unfortunately, he gave what I had come to experience as the classic two-headed parent reply of his generation: "Your mother and I love you too." Not exactly what I wanted, but I had determined that regardless of his response, I needed to communicate my love to him. It was a no-strings-attached risk, a risk I took as a young adult but one we need to take as parents. What he did or didn't say did not diminish the freedom I felt in sharing my feelings for him. When I flew back to my home in Minneapolis, I wrote him a letter describing my experience of working through my feelings for him and my uncomfortable but sincere effort to express my love for him. Shortly after, he acknowledged the letter and expressed his love for me in a phone conversation.

The story has a bittersweet ending. Sometime after our reconciliation, my dad died unexpectedly of a heart attack. I got a tearful call from my mother saying that my dad was gone. He was sixty-six. He had no cardiac risk history and was not a smoker, a drinker, or overweight. We were all in a state of shock and disbelief. In attending the funeral, I found myself sobbing not only for the loss of my father but for the loss of the years of closeness we never had. Sometimes, we grieve what we never had more than what we had. While, thankfully, we had time for reconciliation and closeness in my father's final years, we could have enjoyed it during my growing-up years. One regret I have is that I didn't apologize for my adolescent and young adult behavior that was detrimental to our relationship, and I wish I had. Although this is a father and son story, it could be any combination of parent and young adult child. It could be your story as a parent.

Now that you've read my story, think about your young adult life or remember your experience with your father or mother. Hearing stories from the young adult's perspective helps you empathize with your son or daughter. Next, I'd like you to note that the process I used to address the gap between my father and me is the same process I suggest for parents. Either party can move to close an emotional gap and set both parties free. My story shows how, when it comes to parent and young adult relationships, a healthy launch requires moving closer together to gain emotional separation.

When describing this process, I use two words interchangeably. *Differentiation* or *individuation* are psychological terms that describe the young adult's healthy emotional and behavioral separation from the parent. Neither the parent nor the young adult can attain the desired state of connected autonomy (differentiation) if there is emotional dependence or a contentious or alienated quality to the relationship. This point is true, even if the adult child is behaviorally autonomous. The young adult must resolve childhood abuse, mistreatment, neglect, or other failures of their parents to move to a point where hurt or resentment doesn't poison their lives and relationships. It doesn't require the parent to change any more than the parent requires the young adult to change to feel more loving and accepting. Parents must face their shortcomings and mistakes in parenting, admit them, and apologize. Young adults must confront the source of their hurt, anger, and resentment and let it go to allow feelings of love to emerge. The process of reconciliation and closing the gap to let go can start with either party. In the case of my father and I, I was the initiator. He responded in kind, enabling me to experience emotional separation and an intimate connection to him in the short years we had before he died. I know this is not always the case; parents and adult children suffer when such reconciliation doesn't occur.

My story displays a longing for closeness to my father and the distance and alienation I experienced in my relationship with him as a grown child. Although, of course, both mothers and fathers must find a way to love and let go, it should also be noted that my experience—both personally and in my practice and research—is that the emotional connection between sons and fathers is often somewhat more challenging than between sons or daughters and their mothers. My mentor at the University of Wisconsin, Carl Whitaker summed up the challenge of fathers and sons when he said they "are a sorry lot because they have such difficulty connecting emotionally."[4.]

There are four lessons, in particular, I'd like you to take from my launch experience. First, expressing and affirming love between a parent and young adult is a freeing experience and necessary for both sons and daughters and their parents. Second, the gap can be closed by either generation initiating the process, but it's essential to do it without preconditions or preconceptions. Third, relationships are reciprocal; when one moves to close the emotional gap of the relationship, there is an invitation for the other to do the same. Fourth, we never know how much time we have left to reconcile with our young adult children. We must summon the courage to do so before it is too late.

PARENTAL LOVE SUPPORTS THE LAUNCH PROCESS: MY RESEARCH

My relationship challenges with my father and my desire for emotional separation led me to pursue a PhD in counseling psychology at the University of Wisconsin. Against my advisor's advice, I pursued a dissertation focused on healthy separation from parents. Most literature on helping teenagers and young adults become more independent and self-sufficient focuses on parents backing off and permitting more freedom. Parents are encouraged to help young adults move out of home, get a job, go to school, be self-supporting, and so on. My hypothesis involves another dimension—love as equally crucial to letting go. To provide proof of this, I decided to test it. As my subjects, I chose two groups of older adolescents on the verge of separating from their parents.

The first was a group of adolescents enrolled in a drug treatment program through the juvenile justice system; essentially, they were abusing drugs and exhibiting delinquent behavior. The second comparison group was a group of adolescents with no drug abuse or delinquency problems. I wanted to measure the two groups' perceptions of the extent to which their parents showed love and supported autonomy. My biggest challenge was finding an instrument to measure this healthy state of separation or differentiation. I contacted a well-known psychiatrist named Murray Bowen[5], who often referred to a differentiation scale he had to see if I could use such a scale. He wrote back and stated that the scale was subjective and that differentiation was too complex to measure. Fortunately, I found a professor in psychiatry at the University of Wisconsin-Madison, Dr. Lorna Benjamin[6], who had developed an instrument to measure these two parental qualities at the heart of differentiation. Dr. Benjamin's instrument enabled me to measure *love* and *support for autonomy* by parents separately and together.

When parents' support for autonomy was measured separately from showing love, I found that the delinquent group scored higher. These delinquents were more like free-range chickens who were allowed to go where they wanted and do what they wanted. When the two measures were combined—parental support for autonomy and showing love—the nondelinquent group's scores were significantly higher than the delinquent group. The nondelinquent group saw their parents as significantly higher on behaviors that reflected love and support for autonomy, such as encouraging a separate identity, listening, confirming their fundamental goodness, displaying congeniality, soothing, calming, and affirming competence.

Careful research often proves obvious. My study demonstrates that the best approach to launching a young adult necessitates a parent's love. Specifically, at the beginning of the launching stage, parents of healthy or "normal" adolescents combine love and letting go. In the case of the delinquent group, perceptions of parents giving considerable autonomy but a lower proportion of parental love correlated with family conflict, drug abuse, and delinquency. Such behaviors don't bode well for a successful transition into adulthood. I share my research to demonstrate that simply granting more freedom is insufficient. Love is essential to building a successful launch pad. Too often, advice is given to just back off or detach, but my experience and research would suggest that parents need to stay involved and express love and support for autonomy.

In the diagram below, you will find essential parent launch behaviors with corresponding desired young adult behaviors. These correlate with positive emotional separation (differentiation) and are adopted from the work of Lorna Benjamin, cited earlier. Since relationships are inherently reciprocal when parents reach out in love and a desire to support autonomy, the chances of the young adult responding similarly increase. In my case described earlier, my reaching out to my father in love led to him responding in kind. As you look at the diagram, ask yourself how much your actions align with healthy parent behaviors that show love and support autonomy.

Parent Behaviors	Young Adult Behaviors
Expressing unconditional love	Showing love and caring for parents
Encouraging separate identity	Establishing a separate identity
Expressing a belief in the young adult's competence	Demonstrating competence
Listening and carefully considering the young adult's views	Sharing, assertive, and self-disclosing without defensiveness or passivity
Demonstrating empathy	Showing concern and empathy for parents
Nurturing, soothing, and comforting expressions	Responding positively to parents' calming and comforting expressions
Showing trust and ability to count on young adult	Exhibiting trust and ability to count on parent
Being welcoming and friendly	Being welcoming and friendly

When asked to describe a healthy, intimate relationship or marriage, Carl Whitaker says it requires a high degree of "I-ness" and "we-ness." [7] The same is true of the parent-young adult relationship. Although these may seem contradictory, the challenge is to manage the dynamic. Sometimes closeness is emphasized, and distance or allowance for independence is emphasized. When not managed well, it may feel like the parent and young adult are dancing to different music. One moves closer, and the other moves further away. An emphasis on either to the exclusion of the other could jeopardize the relationship and the launch process. Therefore, creating distance or separation from the young adult is insufficient to lead to healthy emotional separation. This chapter focuses on the "we-ness" side of the parent-young adult relationship. Later chapters focus on supporting the "I-ness" side of healthy relationships. We desire both in our relationships with our young adult children.

I have one final point about expressing unconditional love. Don't assume your young adult knows you love them if you haven't verbalized it. Many parents who are not demonstrative in their love assume the young adult knows they are loved, and the words do not need to be said. The sincere verbalization of love fills in the "silence" that can create doubt in the young adult's mind. It's especially true if the relationship is strained, as in the case of my father, or the young adult who has acted irresponsibly, as in the case of the young adult described at the outset of this chapter. Erase all doubts of your love, for your sake and theirs.

LOVE TO LET GO: YOUR STORY

What is the story of launching your young adult? Have you covered the base of ensuring they know they are loved unconditionally? Like most parents in my survey, you would likely believe you have communicated unconditional love to your young adult, and they would not doubt it. You may be right. In a recent survey I completed with over one hundred parents referenced earlier, a large majority (91%) believed they communicated their unconditional love for their young adult in words and actions. So, my story may not resonate with a lot of parents or young adults. Although I did not survey the young adults to ask if *they* thought their parents had successfully communicated their unconditional love, my experience tells me that their perception might be somewhat lower.

Below is a self-assessment questionnaire measuring how much we demonstrate unconditional love. The questions are based on the model I used in my research, which was developed by Lorna Benjamin and the work of Sue Johnson. Sue Johnson (2008) has written a book describing the emotionally focused marital relationship that is linked to underlying attachment needs.[8] These attachment needs are the basis of the desire for "we-ness," which is important to intimate relationships, including parents and adult children. The questions below assess our ability to both love and let go. Please take the assessment and see if you can identify areas where you could improve.

UNCONDITIONAL LOVE ASSESSMENT

Answer the following questions, rating the extent to which you believe these characteristics are true. Use the following rating scale:

0	1	2	3	4	5	6	7	8	9	10
completely not true				somewhat true, and false				completely true		

1. Your young adult can get your attention; you are emotionally available to them. _____
2. You tune in, listen, and understand them. _____
3. You tell and show them that you think they are important to you. They matter. _____
4. You show acceptance of their feelings without ignoring or being judgmental. _____
5. You allow them to have different beliefs, values, and perspectives. _____
6. You show unconditional love for them regardless of their achievements or shortcomings. _____
7. You allow them to develop and have their own identity. _____

8. You allow and support their freedom and independence while staying connected to them._____
9. You allow them to make mistakes and fail while showing love and acceptance._____
10. You show a willingness to listen, consider, change your mind, and otherwise be influenced by them while maintaining your values and beliefs._____

Are you willing to find out? Invite your young adult to complete the questionnaire in Appendix A to learn about their perceptions of your love for them. Tell them you are trying to learn how to be a better parent. Propose that you meet to discuss their responses at a time and place outside the home (breakfast, lunch, coffee, etc.). The home can feel too much like it involves a parent-child dynamic. You want to foster a more adult-to-adult connection. Indicate that you seek to understand them and learn how to be a better parent.; build a closer and stronger relationship with them. Assure them you will not share their responses with someone else unless they give permission. Finally, communicate that you will do your best to practice good listening and allow them to "pass" on any question(s) they feel uncomfortable answering.

It's crucial to honor these conditions so the dialogue you begin fosters improved communication. Note also that each question in the young adult version includes a follow-up question. This second question will help you learn how you can improve. In other words, in each case, you will ask them to suggest specific actions you could take to do better. It would be best to ask the question as written because it will cause your young adult to search their mind for ideas of what you can do differently. Don't ask questions that lead to a yes or no response. Instead, ask open-ended questions that get your young adult to think more deeply and respond with meaningful suggestions. That approach will lead to more valued dialogue over time. See the next chapter to understand the importance of this line of inquiry.

Find those with the most significant gaps in your self-assessment versus theirs. Discuss their suggestions in the follow-up question. If they didn't make any suggestions, ask them for a few ideas of how you can narrow the gap between your answers and theirs. Specifically, ask for ideas for how to do better with that item. Chapter 2 provides guidance on how to ask for feedback and suggestions for improvement. Commit before you leave the discussion to work on one or more of their suggestions. Taking the quiz is likely not threatening, although possibly revealing your responses to your adult child might be uncomfortable. However, moving beyond your estimates of their answers to inviting their participation can be difficult and intimidating to you both. It involves being vulnerable and committing to being honest and open to learning to be a better parent. You will find the risk is well worth it. Understand that this exchange process is as important as the content in building a closer relationship.

Note: If both parents were available to the young adult, the recommendation would be to have a one-to-one conversation to review your and their responses separately. Each parent and young adult must find the path toward greater love and autonomy. I'd avoid the double-team or two-headed parent interview approach.

Don't be afraid to use your young adult's preferred or common communication vehicles to connect with them, particularly if they are not living at home. A study at the University of Kansas (Metz Howard, 2014) points to the value of multiple communication channels.[9] The study looked at college students' various forms of communication—landlines, cell phones, texting, instant messaging, Snapchat, email, video calls, social networking sites (e.g., Facebook), and online gaming networks. College students average around three different preferred channels of communication. The study found that adding a communication channel can significantly improve the relationship with your young adult. Sometimes, having physical distance, either by living away from home or talking on the telephone, can increase self-disclosure. One parent said, "I have had more in-depth communication with my son through email once he went away to college than I ever got when he was living at home." My follow-through with my father via a letter and phone call was instrumental in closing the emotional gap between us. Even after you've given them multiple options for responding to the questions, they still may refuse to participate. Their refusal may suggest a more significant gap in your relationship and an even greater necessity of communicating your unconditional love. We must take the lead and communicate love to them regardless of their willingness to respond to the survey. This step can help them move toward us even though their response timetable may differ.

PARENTS, TAKE THE HIGH ROAD. IT'S LESS CROWDED.

Parents are responsible for stepping up and closing the gap between them and their young adults. You may be facing an angry, rejecting, blaming, withdrawing, or otherwise challenging young adult. Their behavior does not excuse us from acting in love. We may naturally feel inclined to back away, defend, or point out the shortcomings of our young adults and all we have done for them. It is a natural feeling and action since, as noted above, relationships are inherently reciprocal. "You mistreat me, then I will mistreat you." This pattern describes the state of negative enmeshment. You are fused or enmeshed through negative emotions. You don't have to stay there.

How will the relationship change unless we try to shift the relationship and interactions toward a more positive end? Why would you think their behavior would change if we stay defensive, angry, and rejecting our young adults? This approach reflects the popular definition of insanity, continuing to do the same thing and expecting different results. Is it easy to shift toward a more loving approach? No, it isn't easy. However, we as parents need to take the first step, modeling and working toward having a relationship in which we express love freely. Paradoxically, we initiate moving closer so we can let go. After all, we decided to have children and experience the hardwiring bond in our relationship with them. For our sake and theirs, we need to show it. We must walk the talk; our actions must reinforce our verbal communication of unconditional love. I'll offer suggestions for such steps toward the end of this chapter, but first, let me highlight some attributes we need to cultivate to increase our ability to let go of love.

DO YOU HAVE THE "RIGHT STUFF"?

Demonstrating unconditional love and the other practices that help parents with the launching process requires specific attributes. In the

Introduction, we discussed the qualities of vulnerability, empathy, openness, compassion, and patience. These attributes are crucial to building a better relationship with our young adults. In her writings and TED Talks, as mentioned in chapter 1, Brené Brown (2010) describes vulnerability as *the language of intimacy*.[10] Intimacy involves risk. We can't expect to connect to our young adults unless we soften our hearts and risk vulnerability. Putting yourself in their shoes by imagining your parents asking you these questions as a young adult can help you engender empathy and compassion. It's hard for me to imagine how difficult the conversation with my father would have been if we had attempted to discuss our responses to these questions.

Spend a little time thinking about expressing these qualities in the messages and actions that communicate, "I love you unconditionally." When approaching your young adult with love, there must be congruence or coherence between your heart and your head. If you believe it is the right action to express unconditional love to your young adult, but you're constrained by anger, resentment, hurt, disappointment, and other emotions, the message will not land. In the following chapters, we will discuss the importance of changing one's heart and letting go of such emotions so that the "I love you" transmission is unrestrained and impactful.

Beyond the attributes listed in the Introduction, it helps to adopt *a grateful heart*. If you have a contentious relationship or have experienced many disappointments with your young adult, gratitude may be difficult. We need to remind ourselves of the gift our child represents and how it felt to hold them in our arms at birth. A grateful mindset helps us maintain balance when it seems the young adult is failing or exhibiting irresponsible behaviors. It's easy for our minds and attention to gravitate to problems, failings, mistakes, and other sources of pain, but gratitude helps us keep perspective.

The challenge is finding our young adults' gifts and positive qualities. Take some time to look back through old pictures or movies of your child and reconnect with the feelings and thoughts of the strengths and character traits you admired at that time. As these young adults go through tough times, they need to know we are so grateful we have them and that they matter. We win the right to be heard when we recognize them as special, unique, talented, and loved. As Epictetus said:

*He is a wise man who does not grieve for the things
he has not but rejoices for those he has.*

BARRIERS TO EXPRESSING UNCONDITIONAL LOVE

Now that I've made a case for reaching out to our young adult children with unconditional love and the other attributes referenced above, we can tackle a common challenge in the launch process: resistance. Both parents and young adults may resist the process. Several things can stand in the way of expressing unconditional love even though we believe it is right. First, some parents feel so hurt and rejected by their young adults that they find it hard to be loving. In this case, we must remind ourselves to separate the behavior from the person. We should recognize that these young people try their best—sometimes in strange or inappropriate ways—to establish their identity, independence, and need for intimacy. In a word, they are trying to find "happiness."

As I said, sometimes going back in your memory and seeing the little boy or girl you held when they were infants can help. You can reconnect with feelings of love and attachment. You will find your heart softening by expressing love accompanied by appropriate acts of kindness. Although expressing unconditional love can change your heart, it's not primarily for you; it's for them. It may require you to override your hurt feelings and instead bring up your hardwired desire to love them. Reaching out to them without expectations of a payoff or specific response is our responsibility as a parent.

A second barrier may be your own experience in growing up. It's not unusual for my clients to speak of not hearing messages or seeing actions of unconditional love from their parents. One mother who was abused as a child stated, "I never heard either my father or mother tell me I was loved, so how can I express this to my children?" My response to this client was that she doesn't get a pass because she didn't get something from her parents or because her parents were abusive. We can learn what not to do from our experience with parents as much as we can learn what to do. One client grew up with an alcoholic father who beat him regularly. He said he learned what he never wanted to be or do as a parent and has treated his kids, both young adults now, with unconditional love and affection. Beyond learning what not to do as a parent, those from abusive homes often have experienced love and affirmation from an aunt, uncle, grandparent, teacher, or another influential adult. For example, the mother mentioned above, who never experienced unconditional love from abusive parents, received unconditional love through an aunt and grandparent.

Third, our attitudes and feelings can become barriers to expressing unconditional love and ultimately letting go of our young adults. If we are angry, blaming, rejecting, punishing, and demanding, it will be hard to move toward expressing the necessary unconditional love that will affirm and emancipate our young adults. We must let go of feelings that ultimately bind us and our young adults in a negative state. These feelings and accompanying actions trigger similar emotions and reactions from the young adult, driving the relationship into a negative downward spiral. Such emotions characterized my relationship with my father in my early young adult years. You may have reasons to be angry with your young adult for inappropriate treatment of you. However, holding on to these negative feelings without expressing the underlying emotion is damaging.

Fourth, parents raised in stoic, but not abusive, environments where expressions of love were lacking may find it hard to extend a message of unconditional love toward their young adults. These parents may feel it's a sign of weakness to admit this enduring love for their child. It may feel too vulnerable. Or they may think the young adult will try to use this admission to extract specific concessions. Neither my father nor the "burly father" described at the beginning of this chapter learned to express this unconditional love verbally. But in both cases, the love was there. What if we overcome these barriers and reach out to our young adults, and there's no response, or the young adult refuses to acknowledge or accept our sincere desire to close the emotional gap? Such rejection can happen. We need to remind ourselves it is something we must do regardless of the response; otherwise, it becomes a conditional expression of love. It's also important to remember that our communication timing may differ from our young adult's timing to hear the message or respond. It's an opportunity to practice patience and let go.

WILL MY ACTIONS MAKE A DIFFERENCE?

Most attendees at my workshops want to know how to help their young adults; however, this is often code for "How can I get them to change?" This underlying drive to help your young adult change ignores the underlying false assumptions I outlined in the Introduction. We must remember that the only person we can change is ourselves. My goal is to help you feel less guilt and fear and sleep better at night, knowing you are being the best parent you can be. Will this transform the relationship with our young adults? The answer is yes. Your mindset and actions will be different, and if one party changes, the relationship changes. You will change even if the young adult has cut off all contact. However, shifts in relationships are complicated. It can be awkward if we change without communicating our desire to do so. The results may not be pretty. It's like altering our dance step midstream without telling our partner. Your young adult may become more resistant initially or be confused by the difference in your approach.

Our goal is to improve how we relate to our young adult children regardless of their responses. Our positive efforts to change are much more likely to elicit the behaviors we desire in them. But if you express love with the belief that this will impact the actions of your young adult or they will reciprocate (a hidden agenda), you are not acting unconditionally. The relationship will change as you relate differently. Love breeds love, and kindness breeds kindness. In some cases, a young adult has become estranged and alienated from the parent and has chosen to have no contact or not respond to any of the parent's efforts. This is their choice as adults.

Estrangement, as this condition is labeled, is heartbreaking. In his work, *Rules of Estrangement*, my colleague, Josh Coleman, discusses these types of situations. What If you make all the necessary efforts to employ the practices outlined in this book to launch your young adult and continue to be rebuffed? Ultimately, you must acknowledge your powerlessness to change your young adult—or the relationship—and grieve the loss. At the same time, a parent should never stop reaching out, even if it's only with a birthday card or present, or a holiday greeting. Continuing such gestures, practicing patience, and understanding their reconciliation timetable may differ from yours can help cope with this loss. If you are experiencing estrangement from your young adult, I suggest you read Dr. Coleman's book and visit his website: https://www.drjoshuacoleman.com.

EXPRESSING UNCONDITIONAL LOVE: OUR CHARGE

I recommend writing about our unconditional love for our young adults and then delivering this message in person. In my case, I did the opposite, shared with my father in person, and followed with a letter describing my need to reach out to him in love. Preparing to write such a letter takes some time to reconnect to feelings you experienced when your adult child was an infant or young child. Recognize that the little boy or girl is still there but in a grown-up form. To this end, pull out old pictures and movies and observe your child and your interactions with the child. In addition, review materials and awards you have saved from your young adult's school and extracurricular activities. Make a list of the "being" qualities of your young adult. These are hardwired qualities such as personality, temperament, intelligence, capabilities, and demonstrated strengths. Add to their actions or "doing" qualities like learned skills, accomplishments, and achievements that have made you proud. Reread these occasionally to balance any current issues or behaviors that concern you. Finally, take some time to think about how grateful you are that this child has been in your life. Things may be rough right now, but keep in perspective there have been good times and connections worth remembering.

Write a letter to your young adult with the first draft for your benefit. Approach writing the letter with empathy and compassion. Put yourself in their shoes as you read that draft. Suggested themes:

- o   What have you appreciated about your young adult over the years?
- o   What has made you proud of them, particularly areas of personal strengths such as care for others, persistence, humor, friendliness, etc.?
- o   How have you benefited from having them in your life?
- o   What have you learned from them that has helped you?

- Describe the ways you love your child.
- Describe your unconditional love for your child from your heart. You can use guidance from this book and others you have read, but be sure your love is sincere in your voice.
- Reassure and promise that your unconditional love will be there no matter what.
- Apologize if you believe you have made mistakes. If there are mistakes that your young adult still holds onto, write specifically about them. See future chapter on apology.
- Forgive your young adult for behavior they identify as mistakes or failures. It is particularly important if you believe your adult child is stuck due to a sense of failure or guilt. Don't express your forgiveness to your young adult if the behavior is something only you believe needs forgiveness. Such an act could seem condescending. To be clear about how and when to forgive, see a future chapter on forgiveness.
- Express your hopes, desires, and aspirations for your young adult without being prescriptive. You want them to feel happy and fulfilled, at minimum.

Read the letter out loud to see how it sounds. Share the letter with your spouse, close friend, or therapist to ensure it is free of blame and accusation. Also, avoid saying " I love you, but" or "I'm sorry, but." The "but" in these statements negates the first part of the statement and will suggest that you don't love unconditionally and aren't sorry. See chapter 3 for further clarification of this point. After you have edited and discussed the letter, prepare to communicate this to your young adult. You can do this in writing; I suggest using the old-fashioned way of writing a personal letter. Even though our millennial and Gen Zers generations are very digital and media savvy, there is something about a handwritten note that sends a more personal message. One parent cautioned me that today's generation might not read cursive, particularly if our handwriting is like mine. What happened to penmanship? If you saw my writing, you may ask the same question. I typed out my letters to my kids but signed them. If you can muster the courage, the best approach is to take your young adult out to eat or take a walk, meet in the park, and so on. Next, read the letter to them. In my experience as a therapist with parents sharing such a letter, it can be quite emotional for the parent and sometimes for the young adult, but always impactful.

Here are a few excerpts from letters I collected from parents over the years:

> *I want you to know I love you. I always have and always will, no matter what has happened in the past or will happen in the future.*
>
> *You mean the world to me, and that will never change. I will always be here for you.*
>
> *Your traits of empathy, persistence, and intelligence will help you be successful in your drive for independence.*
>
> *I love you with all my heart—no matter what—unconditionally.*
>
> *I am so proud of you and all your accomplishments. You have such a big heart. I will always be in your heart, and just a thought away.**

*Notice the unique way this mother communicated her presence with her daughter. Most mothers would say the daughter will always be in the mother's heart. Instead, she said the mother will always be in the daughter's heart and "just a thought away." It's a way of saying I will always be with you.

Here's an excerpt from a parent of a young adult with a mental illness diagnosis:

> *You will be living with this (with the mental health problem) all your life, even after your dad and I are no longer on this earth. We realize we are part of the problem with our control issues and trying to steer you forward, and sometimes we see the light at the*

end of the tunnel, but you only see an oncoming train. There will always be good and bad days (in life), but we will always love you unconditionally and with all our hearts.

When you have prepared to communicate your unconditional love for your young adult, you need to approach them and indicate you want to share an important message with them. When you meet, discuss your goals and expectations of the meeting. Share some feelings and thoughts about them related to the past, present, and future. Ask them to listen (or read if sent) without interruption or comment until you have finished. Once you have finished reading or they have read what you wrote, indicate that you do not expect any specific response from them. The one exception is if you choose to send a letter. Then, you would ask them to let you know they got it.

Expressing love is the first practice parents must demonstrate to launch their young adult successfully. It is the cornerstone upon which the launchpad is built and rests. Without it, the structure would be unstable. It's a step in making the connection and letting go, which is necessary for a successful launch. We should never take this for granted or believe this step isn't required. Everyone of any age, parent, or young adult wants to know that they matter and are loved and that "there aren't enough buckets to hold the tears that would be shed if they died."

KEEPERS

What vital points, recommendations, and ideas will you take and apply from this chapter on unconditional love? As with chapter 1, I'll start the list of keepers from this chapter, and you can finish it with what you most want to remember, review, and apply. Jot them down, apply, and share them as soon as possible. Application is the best way to reinforce what we've learned.

1. To experience and know that one is loved unconditionally by a parent is essential to leaving the family in a healthy way. Love them to let them go.
2. Parents must take the initiative and communicate unconditional love through words and actions. Actions speak louder than words. In the context of this practice, love is a verb, not a noun. Do it; don't just say it. But also, don't just do it; say it.
3. _____
4. _____
5. _____
6. _____
7. _____
8. _____
9. _____
10. _____

CHAPTER TWO

UNDERSTAND AND RELATE

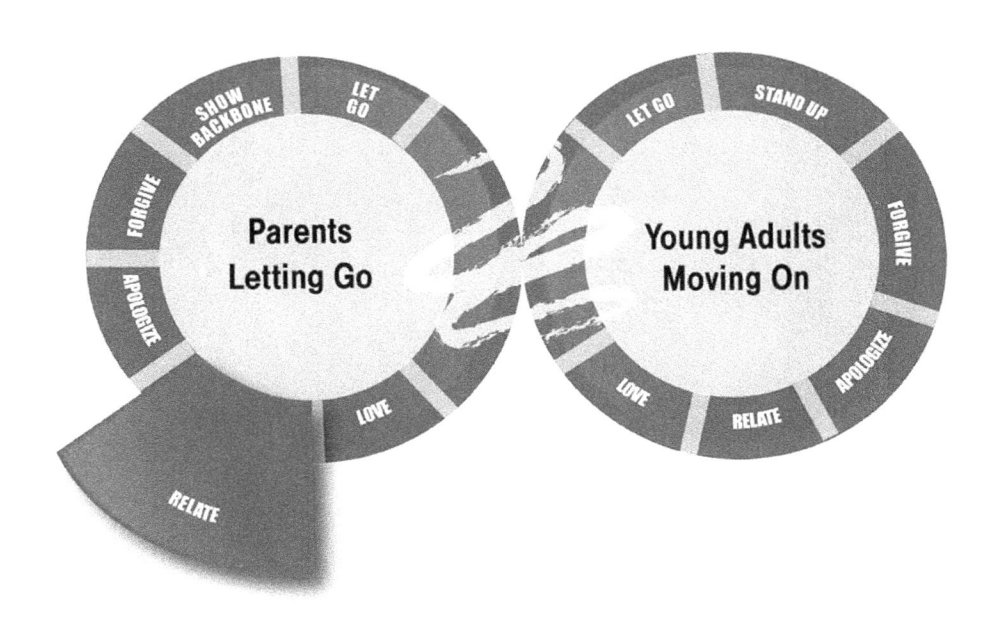

Romance fails us, and so do friendships, but the relationship of parent and child remains indelible and indestructible, the strongest relationship on earth.

—Theodor Reik

We can't skip over communicating unconditional love. Nor can we skip over the practice of relating in ways that strengthen our understanding of—and connection to—our adult kids. Contrary to the belief that we should back off from our young adults at the launch stage, we need to increase our efforts in ways that will smooth the transition. Let's be clear; I am not talking about increasing our caretaking behaviors contributing to greater dependency. We can move closer in understanding and relating to our young adults while giving them the space to gain emotional separation and independence. Show love and support autonomy.

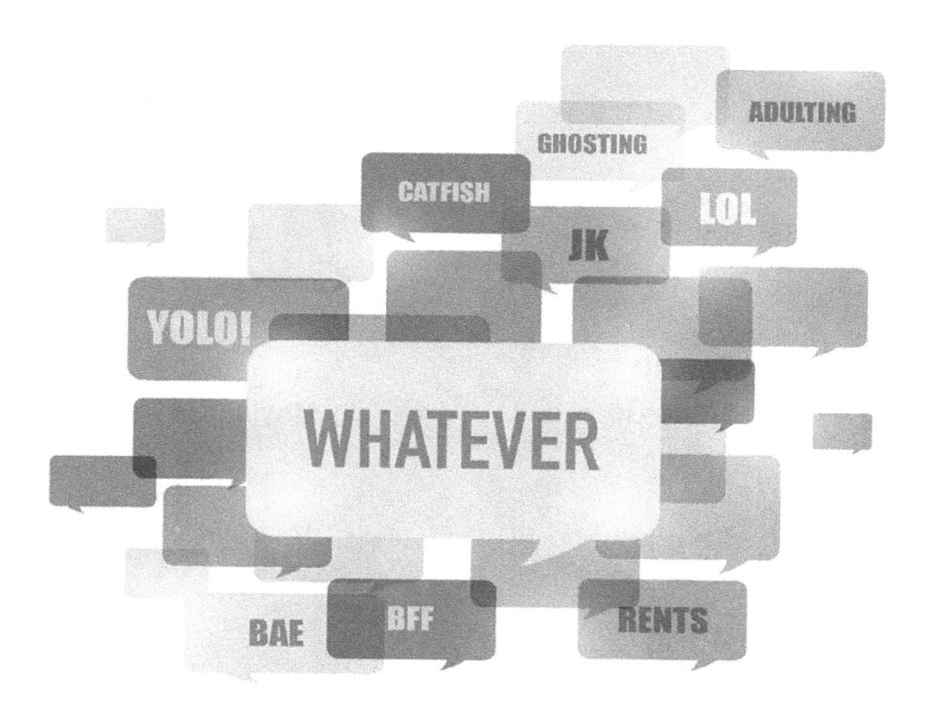

FROM LAWRENCE WELK TO RAP

Every generation of parents seems to disparage the younger generations, a phenomenon that goes back to antiquity. The sentiment is best characterized by phrases like, "What's wrong with kids these days?" Can you translate some of the acronyms and words of today's generation pictured in the image above? If you can, count yourself as "hip" or at least not "square." If you remember Lawrence Welk, you must be a boomer or a silent generation member.

I reflect on my time sitting in my family's den watching the Beatles for the first time with my parents. "You can turn them upside down and mop the floor with them," was a comment I heard. To the Lawrence Welk generation, the Beatles were hardly music. Fast-forward to the 2022 Super Bowl and the halftime entertainment. Rappers from the Los Angeles area performed the entertainment. Like my Lawrence Welk parents, I looked at the contemporary performers and wondered why anyone would view this as "music." My three young adult children thought the halftime entertainment was terrific.

We live in different entertainment worlds with different preferences. "Other" isn't bad. It's just different. We must remind ourselves of this fact when we can't appreciate something from our young adult world. Today's young adults, ages 18 to 29, stretch across two different generations—millennials born between 1981 and 1996 and Gen Zers or "Zoomers" born between 1997–2012. For an in-depth review of generational differences, please consider *Generations* by Jean Twenge (see bibliography).

Trends and findings about millennials and Gen Zers to follow come from a variety of polls and surveys.[1] As parents, we must try to transcend our biases to appreciate our kids' world. Many studies and books have described the millennial generation, and some are starting to show up related to Gen Zers. I want to highlight differences between millennials, Gen Xers, and boomers as sources of conflict and, more importantly, opportunities for dialogue and mutual understanding. We need to build bridges of understanding with our young adults if we wish to have a closer relationship with them and the ability to let go with love. St. Francis of Assisi's prayer is fitting when he says, *seek to understand before we seek to be understood.* Today's failure to launch experience differs from the one that occurred after the Second World War or even fifteen years ago, during the Great Recession.

When my father returned from flying bombing missions over Germany, he had no home. Since my mother lived with her parents, he moved in with them. This disrupted the normal process of being married and living independently, but forty-eight percent of young adults, including my parents, found they had no choice. They first had to find work to support a separate household. It's a stretch, I know, to call this a failure to launch, but it was a time when young adults felt stymied in their quest for independence.

During the great recession of 2007, many young adults felt they had no choice but to live at home. There were no jobs, and they were saddled with college debt. Some kids during that period were willing to deliver pizzas, but many believed that their financial investment in college required them to obtain employment in their chosen field. Fast forward to the early 2020s, and you have a different failure-to-launch experience, with fifty-two percent of young adults living at home, according to the Pew Research Institute.[2] Like the 1940s and the disruptive impact of the war on the emancipation process, today's young adults have faced the effects of a recession and the pandemic on their quest for independence. One in four college students returned home during the pandemic, and some have gone back.

Data on the rise of depression and anxiety in young adults suggest that many have become apprehensive about moving out, taking jobs, or returning to work. Unlike the Great Recession's failure to launch, today's young adults have more economic opportunities, and nearly two jobs are available for every unemployed person in the United States. Unfortunately, the pandemic has taken a toll on young adults.

> *Sarah, a single mother of a thirty-seven-year-old daughter, contacted me because her daughter was out of work, struggling with depression, and drinking too much. She wondered how her bright young daughter, a successful athlete in high school and a college graduate, had become so disabled. She had been laid off during the pandemic from a serving job at a restaurant and was living on unemployment and the stimulus check. By the time the money had run out, she had become depressed and lost all confidence in herself and relied on subsidies from her mother to survive.*

The failure to take steps toward independence is both a result of depression and a contributor to depression. We have to concurrently find ways to get them help for depression and anxiety while encouraging them to move toward greater self-sufficiency.

WHO ARE THESE EMERGING ADULTS OF TODAY, AND WHAT IS THEIR EXPERIENCE?

As discussed in the Introduction, there is a trend in the literature and research to label the stage of life between adolescence and full adulthood as *emerging adulthood*. Jeffrey Arnett coined this term to describe a young person between eighteen and twenty-five.[2] Arnett has since defined emerging adults as those between 18 and 29. The parents of these emerging adults are the focus of this book. To address the failure to launch segment, I'm emphasizing the ages of eighteen to twenty-nine. But understand there are thirty and forty-some adult children who haven't launched.

Taking time to describe today's young adult population enables you to understand your young adults' habits, views, behaviors, and values. It's always dangerous—even incorrect—to take broad-based statistical research and such findings and apply them to one case. For example, my forty-two-year-old son is, by some criteria, a millennial. Yet he eschews being labeled that way. He has a strong work ethic and is an achievement-oriented, hardworking physician who dissociates himself from the general finding that millennials don't have a strong work ethic.

This chapter will help you approach your young adult with a broad understanding of their generation, but I caution you from assuming these findings apply to your son or daughter in every case. Let me start with some information on millennials, followed by those related to Gen Zers and some discussion of their similarities and differences. The following highlights and themes regarding millennials and Gen Zers come from various sources.[3]

MILLENNIALS AND THEIR PARENTS

Let's take a closer look at millennials. Millennials are the first generation predicted to earn less than their parents. My oldest daughter grew up in a traditional colonial-style home in the suburbs, certainly not wealthy by any stretch of the imagination, but comfortable. My wife and I were in our late forties when we achieved this standard of living.

In contrast, my adult daughter never envisioned living at an economic level different from what she experienced growing up. Even though she and her husband both work, they are burdened by child-care costs, college loan debt, and a mortgage. Discretionary funds don't exist. Twenty percent of all millennials live in poverty. While millennials' average college debt load is nearly $40,000, their average salary is $47,034. Given these facts, it isn't surprising that over sixty percent of millennials rely on their parents for some financial support. There's not much left after paying college debt, housing, and a car payment. Buying a house seems out of reach for many millennials and Gen Zers.

Millennials approach work differently than we do. They are the first generation not to list "work ethic" as one of their top values and may change jobs frequently to achieve a better work-life balance. They change jobs on average seven times during their twenties. Often they don't commit to a career until their thirties. I talked to a friend who hired a young woman a few years ago, and after two weeks on the job, she came into his office and announced that she would be gone every Tuesday from noon to one thirty for a yoga class. She followed this assertion with a promise she would make up the time later in the day. She was not requesting, merely relaying this necessary change to her schedule with the assumption of her boss's accommodation.

Can you imagine this happening twenty-to-thirty years ago? Many would quickly move to label this as "entitlement." However, before we get caught up in what has become almost a cliche characterization, I'd argue that these young adults may be more intelligent than us in how they approach work. Many of our generation and parents toiled in lifelong jobs despite disliking their work. Whatever the boss required, it was delivered. Parents felt pressure to provide for the family and thought quitting an unfulfilling job was risky.

Millennials also have a different approach to marriage and family life. Today, fifty-two percent of millennials live with one or both parents. Undoubtedly, this has grown with the pandemic and virtual learning, but the numbers were high before the pandemic. In one 2019 Census Bureau study, New Jersey rated highest in eighteen-to-thirty-four-year-olds at home with forty-six percent. In my survey of parents in 2021, thirty-seven percent of parents said that COVID-19 adversely affected the parents' efforts to launch their young adults. Millennials and Gen Zers desire to live closer to their parents but are also known to travel more than their parents. When my wife and I made it to Europe for the first time, my kids had already traveled to Europe, Asia, and South America.

It should be noted that sixty percent of parents enjoy having their young adults living at home. Millennials have fewer conflicts with their parents than past generations and have regular contact. In 1986, about half of the parents spoke to their children once a week. Today, sixty-seven percent of mothers and fifty-one percent of fathers say they have contact with their adult child almost daily.[4] Here's some good news for those of us in our retirement years. More than sixty percent of millennials end up taking care of their boomer parents in their homes. Today, sixty percent of first-time caregivers are Gen Zers and millennials. So, young adults are stepping up to take care of aging parents. My youngest daughter, a millennial, has already offered to take my wife in when she can no longer live independently. Unfortunately, the same offer was not made to me, but that may be because Mom will likely outlive me. Not to be outdone by his younger sister, my son didn't offer to take us in but said he would find us the best nursing home money could buy. He may be right; he isn't a millennial.

On the issue of marriage, much has changed over the past generations. In 1960, the median age of first marriages for males was twenty-three, and for females, twenty-one. Today, the average age of first marriage for young men is thirty and twenty-nine for young women. At the ripe old age of thirty-two, my son whined about how all the attractive women were married and then found a great match through an online dating service. Online services, or apps, are the most popular way to find a partner now. We relied on friend "referrals" or even work connections. Some other interesting findings regarding millennials are that they have less sex than Gen Xers or boomers and have fewer sexual partners. Forty-four percent of millennials are married. However, rates decline as cohabitation increases.

There are some sources of conflict, but there are also opportunities for understanding. Millennials are the least overtly religious generation. Thirty-eight percent are labeled "nones" because when asked what religion or church they claim, their answer is none. Gen Zers are continuing this trend, with almost half indicating they are nones. Whereas seventy-six percent of baby boomers claim to be Christian, only half of the millennials identify as such. This trend has undoubtedly led to some interesting Thanksgiving dinner discussions. Many of the men in my church-based book club have expressed their disappointment and concern about their young adult children not attending church as if that is the hallmark of a Christian or person of faith. The new generations are leaving the church and not returning when they have children, as past generations have.

On the other hand, millennials say they are spiritual but not religious. One way to think about the distinction between spirituality and religion is that the former is internally generated, and the latter is externally generated, characterized by dogma and rituals. Also, millennials are more service-oriented than past generations. Most have donated money, goods, and services and want to make a positive difference in society.

Other disconnects between the generations exist because of changes in technology, science, and events such as 911. Forty-one percent of millennials don't have a landline, and this is likely much higher for Gen Zers. They are technologically savvy, with ninety percent having a social media site and one in four posting a self-video. I admit I am a technological dinosaur and am made aware of this daily as various electronics seem to break down. Often, I call my son when I have a problem, and he likes to remind me it's not the computer; it's an "operator error." Another interesting statistic is that, unlike older age groups, thirty-nine percent of young adults have a tattoo.

MILLENNIALS AND GEN ZERS

The current young adult population cuts across two generations—millennials and Gen Zers. Does the question arise as to how different Gen Zers and millennials are? My experience leads me to believe that Gen Zers will likely continue the trends seen with the millennials, but here are some differences. Pew argues that, on critical social and policy issues, Gen Zers look like millennials. Some unique aspects of Gen Zer's experience are essential to consider. First, they don't remember 9/11 or the recession that affected the millennials, but they continue to be affected by the pandemic. As a result, they are more practical, realistic, and careful in their approach to work and financial security. An eighteen-year-old son of one of my clients wants to know how to start a 401k even though he doesn't currently have a job. Another eighteen-year-old wants to skip college, go to work, and buy an apartment building. Gen Zers are more pragmatic, pessimistic, and individualistic, whereas Millennials are more idealistic, optimistic, and team-oriented.

Whereas millennials transitioned into the digital age, Gen Zers are true digital natives who have not known a time without cell phones or computers. They continue a trend toward more racial diversity and increased education of the millennial generations. They live on social media, spending fifty hours a week online or on their phones, and prefer YouTube and Snapchat to Twitter or Facebook. Their parents are more likely to be Gen Xers. They are a generation that has become comfortable with gender-neutral terms. Like millennials, they want to make a positive difference and have become more politically active and interested in social justice. [3]

Are there any surprises about these descriptors and trends related to millennials and Gen Zers? Do they present conflicts for you and your young adult child if the statistic is accurate for your child? If you are a boomer, it's a different world than ours, and likely if you are a Gen Xer parent. The challenge for us is to find a way to understand this new world and how we can communicate across our differences. If you are cringing at some of these differences, take a deep breath and repeat the mantra: differences aren't necessarily bad. Your reactions to them pose a more significant threat than the differences themselves, sending you down the road of believing that one is right. This road leads to a dead-end. I admit that some differences can strain family relations, but they also afford an opportunity for understanding and personal growth.

> *Judy, a middle-aged schoolteacher, contacted me with urgency as she was adjusting to an announcement her college student son had made recently. He said, " I have known for some time that I am gay but wasn't ready to disclose this until now." Judy arrived at my office with a stack of books on homosexuality. She was searching for answers. Was his homosexuality something she caused? How should she respond to this news? She was over the initial shock but was now trying to wrap her head around*

this change. Over several counseling sessions with her and her husband, they were able to dive more deeply into understanding homosexuality and begin to adjust to this new reality. She made great progress because of her openness and love for her son, which was never at risk.

In such circumstances, young adults must appreciate their parents' angst about these types of announcements. In turn, parents must understand and appreciate the difficulty the young adult may have telling parents about this newly discovered sexual orientation and its accompanying challenges. Although these dissimilarities between our generations and the next tap into strong, long-standing beliefs we may have as parents and challenge us to adjust our perception of them and their future, love must win the day. As such, it's important to remind ourselves, as discussed in chapter 2, not to say, "I love you, but…." Rather than saying phrases like," I love you, but" we should say ones like, "I'm struggling to understand and appreciate this change, but no matter what, my love for you hasn't changed." Our kids need to hear this reassurance from us, and we need to say it.

GENDER CHALLENGES AND THE PLIGHT OF YOUNG MEN

Books could be written about the differences between young men and women in the emerging adulthood stage. Much valuable research and writing in this area is being done by the Society for the Study of Emerging Adulthood. Check out the work of Jeffrey Arnett, a founder of this society, in the bibliography at the end of the book. My approach and book emphasize what parents must do to let go in a spirit of love. Concerning parenting young adult males versus females, my comments come primarily from my observations and clinical experience. I want to acknowledge that further study is warranted to test some of these observations and conclusions. We have a monumental task of understanding our young adults.

It's fair to ask about differences between sons and daughters, which may play a role in the launch process. Although it's possible to describe some differences between sons and daughters, generalizations or applications to your situation can be challenging. The reason is that multiple factors influence how sons and daughters react to the challenge of independence, complicated not just by the factors described above. Add another layer of complexity to sex roles and the growing trend for teens and young adults to explore and adopt different gender identities. The following example is becoming more common in US Households. How would you handle this?

> *"I'm nonbinary," announced a senior high schooler one day as she ate dinner with her parents.*
> *"What's that mean?" asked the parents.*
> *Three months later, this same young woman decided she was transgender.*
> *"What's that mean?" asked the parents. Fortunately, these parents have been reassuring in their love for their daughter, who now wants to be addressed as "they" or "them," and their parents are scaling a steep learning curve to understand this new or different young adult living in their house.*

Before I discuss the unique plight of young males, it's important to note that focusing on improving young men's status takes nothing away from women. We should celebrate and continue to push for women's rights and achievements. It's indisputable that women have lagged behind men in many areas of education, work, and society because of discriminatory practices and other factors. Wages continue to reflect this bias. However, the trend began to shift in the nineteen-sixties and accelerated after the turn of this century. Laws against discrimination (Title IX), the women's movement, and birth control enable young women to be more independent, self-sufficient, and successful.

On the other hand, young men are falling further behind. As I recently described on my website blog, our boys are in trouble. According to Pew Research, cited earlier, of the fifty-two percent of young adults living with their parents, the majority are males. In my clinical work with parents of young adults, eighty percent of the parents have concerns about a male adult child. In his book *Of Boys and Men*, Richard Reeves speaks most passionately and eloquently about the plight of boys and young men.[5] He reports that more young women enter and graduate from four-year colleges than young men, almost reversing the trend in the nineteen seventies. A more alarming statistic is that males drop out of four-year degree programs at a higher rate than females. According to a *Wall Street Journal* article, men drop out of school at an extremely high speed, accounting for seventy-two percent of the enrollment decline at colleges and universities. This trend doesn't bode well for future male employment. More ominous findings Reeves reports are the statistics related to what he calls "deaths of despair."

The young adult population is at the most risk for opioid overdose, with males accounting for seventy percent of this tragedy. Suicide is the second leading cause of death and is increasing for young adults ages 18–29; men are three times as likely to commit suicide as females. Depression, anxiety, and other mental health conditions have been increasing for both male and female young adults. Most young adults I meet have mental health concerns—depression, anxiety, ADHD, social anxiety, and so on.

Females typically have better social support because they tend to be more relational and generally have more friends to whom they can confide. Males are not known to reach out to friends regarding personal problems, but according to Reeves, nearly half of the young men were willing to do this in 1990. Now, the percentage is 22 percent. [6]

Males are dropping out of college and out of the workforce. In the book *Men Without Work,* Nicholas Eberstadt describes the number of men who have dropped out of the workforce has tripled since 1965.[7] At a time when there are two jobs for every person out of work; there is a growing segment of our male population who is not motivated to pursue one of these jobs. My concern is that this pattern may begin in the teen and young adult years and that some of these failures to launch young men will become what Eberstadt calls NILFs—not in the labor force.

I can tell you parents of late twenty-year-old adults are hitting the panic button when their daughters and sons are still at home. These are adult children who live at home, both males and females, with no clear direction or interest in moving out or seeking employment. Reeves and Eberstadt are economists, and both sound the alarm regarding the phenomena of failing young male adults and offer structural or societal solutions. Still, they overlook the most influential factor in the trajectory of these teens and young adults: the influence of parents. One news release study out of UCLA, August 8, 2018, found young adults are more likely to share personal concerns with their parents than their peers.

Both males and females have suffered as a result of the COVID-19 pandemic. In many cases, the home became a place of comfort and predictability unavailable in the outside world. As a result, it became easier to go to one's room, get on Facebook, or, more likely, Instagram or TikTok, or for males to get online and play video games, than venture out searching for a job or an educational opportunity. Young women at home may end up in contentious relationships with their mothers and somewhat distant relationships with their fathers. Moms are often seen by their daughters as critical of hair, makeup, weight, and body art. On the other hand, some young men and women can withdraw and minimize contact with their parents. Parents often comment on how much time their son or daughter spends in their rooms.

Within the confines of this book, I can't suggest specific differential actions for males and females, or other dimensions referenced above. I confidently state that embracing the assumptions in the Introduction and strengthening the practices described in this book will make a positive difference in the launch process with whatever gender the young adult adopts. Accepting that we can't control our young adults, are not responsible for their behavior, and are not responsible for fixing them are important mindsets to embrace. Understanding the young adult of today and showing that compassion and love are indispensable to assisting with the launch process. And when would we not want to show love, build a closer relationship, apologize, forgive, show backbone, and ultimately let go?

A WORK IN PROGRESS: THE YOUNG ADULT

Both young adults and parents face challenges and circumstances in their lives. Young adults between eighteen and twenty-nine try to establish themselves in their careers and as individuals. In other words, they are discovering what they do and who they are—their *identity*. The former is a Western understanding of identity linked to abilities and achievements. But identity also involves our being, inherited characteristics, and genetic hardwiring. Parents need to call out and affirm this later source of identity—personality, temperament, aptitude, and unique qualities—not just focus on the achievement side. We quickly identify and reinforce the qualities and characteristics we want young adults to exhibit. Inadvertently, my parents almost drove me to law school by repeating I would be a good lawyer because I constantly argued. A solid sense of identity is essential to the separation and launch process.

A second crucial developmental task is gaining *independence*. This task is accomplished by establishing oneself as a self-sufficient adult, but it involves more than financial independence or moving out of the house. As described in the introduction and chapter 1, young adults must also achieve a healthy emotional separation from their parents. Parents can facilitate this natural drive toward independence, impede it by actions that maintain dependence, or foster an antagonistic quality to the relationship.

A third developmental task of the young adult is forming *intimate relationships* outside the family. Again, parents play an essential role in sustaining a bond with the young adult while supporting the development of relationships with others, perhaps even with a significant other. Parents who resist the young adults' drive to seek intimacy outside the family or attempt to interfere or control this process can jeopardize the young adults' launch. Continued constraint in this manner increases the chances of damage to the relationship, as the young adult feels anger and resistance. The result can be young adults cutting all ties with their parents. For example, some parents I work with don't like the person their son or daughter chose as a life partner. Still, it's necessary to find a way to, at a minimum, be considerate and kind to your young adult's intimate partner and at least try to find something positive about them. More on this subject in chapter 7.

In addition to these life-stage tasks, the young adult's physical development occurs in the brain. Historically, we believed in treating young adults as full-grown adults when they reached the age of eighteen. Our society operates with this assumption because they can get a license, vote, and join the military. However, some neuroscience research has concluded that the young adult's brain is still developing into the mid-twenties. The prefrontal cortex is the specific area of the brain that is the last to reach full development. This brain area contains the executive function responsible for logic, planning, problem-solving, and related tasks. During the late adolescent and early young adult stage, the amygdala, the source of fight and flight drives, and the hypothalamus, the source of the regulation of emotions, can overpower the prefrontal cortex. This "overpowering" leads to overreactions, large emotional fluctuations, and risky decision-making. Add to this sky-high testosterone levels in young men or increased estrogen and progesterone in women, and a potentially explosive situation exists. When I was nineteen, living in Ocean City, New Jersey, I took on the dare from one of my friends to jump off a bridge over the bay leading to the mainland. It was thirty or forty feet high and over a canal where boats passed. Did I jump without checking for a boat below? Yes, but now I know I only had half a brain. Would I do it now? No way! In fact, I now have a fear of heights.

The implications of understanding brain development in late adolescence and young adulthood are twofold. First, this knowledge can explain some of the emotional volatility and risky behavior that young adults exhibit, although this is not to excuse such conduct. Second, these young adults need some of the imposition of the fully developed adult brain to inhibit some of their risky behavior. I mean setting boundaries and limits for actions such as driving over the speed limit, using dangerous drugs, jumping off bridges, and so on. Incidentally, most young adults get through this stage unscathed despite questionable decisions, and as such, we need to remind ourselves that *this, too, shall pass.*

Let me discuss one additional challenge for parents and children, which is personality or temperament. There is one question I have received numerous times when working with families over the years. Frequently, when parents request help from me to launch their young adult, they have other adult children who are launched and doing fine. "Why is this one child not responding to my parenting as the others in my family, they ask?" The answer is the title of a book by Stella Chess, first published in 1965, *Your Child is a Person.*[8] She highlights the challenges of encountering different temperaments, defined by every person's unique hardwiring. Oppositional temperament, either long-standing or surfacing in adolescence, can be challenging for parents to manage. And, of course, we have practically an epidemic of attention deficit disorders among children, adolescents, and young adults these days. What's the lesson in this for parenting? One size of parenting doesn't fit all types of temperaments.

Understanding temperament and developmental tasks can help us navigate the launch process. Understanding is the starting point for building the relationship we need to have to launch our young adults successfully. Take a minute to go to appendix A and complete the questionnaire: How Well Do We Know Our Young Adult? This quiz will give you an idea of your current understanding of them and their lives. You can reality-check your answers by asking your young adult to answer the questions. Assuming you couldn't answer all the questions about your young adult and want to understand them better, the next session on three skills will give you the tools to accomplish this. As you master these techniques, you are guaranteed to become a better person and parent even if your young adult fails to respond as you would like. Remember: the successful launch process involves doing as much as possible to build a positive relationship with our young adults while recognizing they have half the say in this endeavor.

A WORK IN PROGRESS: PARENTS

Let's not forget that a parent's temperament, personality, parenting style, and developmental challenges further complicate the approach to parenting. Divorce can add another layer of complexity, especially if the divorced parents continue in a contentious relationship. It's not unusual to have parents, divorced or not, take bad cop/good cop roles or compete for the affection of the young adult. So many factors make simplistic guidance impossible. Understanding the complexity of the young adult and the parent's development and personal characteristics at the launch stage should challenge us to be humble learners without all the answers.

Complicating the young adult development process are the development challenges of middle-aged adults. Our progress, or lack thereof, on the following tasks can significantly impact adult children's development.

1. Expanding opportunities for the young adult's independence—car, job, travel, and so on.

2. Reallocating responsibilities among grown children and expecting them to step up if at home and take on more responsibilities.
3. Rearranging physical facilities and resources—when a young adult leaves, opening up a room for other children, a home office, a workout area, or the like. When my oldest daughter left for college, the younger daughter immediately moved into her room, much to my older daughter's indignation.
4. Widening the family circle to allow for the exit of the young adult and welcoming of new members—significant others, marriage partners, and grandchildren.
5. Maintaining open communication and collaboration across the generations.
6. Deepening existing adult friendships as well as acquiring new ones.
7. Developing a new adult-to-adult relationship with your launched adult child.
8. Grieving the loss of the family unit and a member. Sadness and loss are inevitable corollaries of letting go.
9. Revising the marriage relationship without a child focus—a chance to reconnect with a spouse that can feel like dating again.
10. Assisting aging and ill parents of the husband and wife.

Which one or more of the above tasks is especially challenging for you at this time, and how might it affect the launch and letting go process? Launching the young adult requires both parties to work on or through their essential developmental tasks.

THREE SKILLS TO STRENGTHEN THE RELATIONSHIP

There are three skills described below that will help you understand and relate to your young adult and strengthen your relationship. They are listening, inquiring, and requesting feedback and feedforward. These are important not only to engendering a better relationship with our kids but also to the influence process. These are skills I used extensively in my days as an executive coach at 3M. In chapter 6, I will discuss the role of parents as a "coach" to their adult children. By applying these skills, we are paving the way for our kids' transition into adulthood while sustaining, if not improving, the relationship with you. Furthermore, we are laying the foundation for a future adult-to-adult relationship and friendship. As with any tools or techniques that improve relationships, they are only as good as they are put into practice.

LISTEN WITH THE THIRD EAR

Want to Get to Know Your Young Adult? Listen With the Third Ear

What could I possibly mean by the "third ear"? The expression comes from Theodore Reik, a psychoanalyst and author of a book of that title.[9] It refers to the ability to listen to a person's underlying needs and emotions and not just words. Sometimes. We must pay attention when our young adults raise concerns or miss what they are trying to communicate. But listening is far from a passive behavior. It takes a desire to understand and attend to the speaker, being present, and being willing to check out what you heard to ensure understanding.

> *Several participants in my workshops for parents commented on how valuable the session on listening was. It highlighted their shortcomings in listening and how to correct these and tune in to their kids. This section of the workshop was one of the most highly rated.*

Some of you who have been through courses on listening at work or in other settings may think you can skip this book section. I would put myself in that category since I have taught listening skills to parents in three different parenting programs and consider myself a "black belt" in listening. Unfortunately, I don't always practice what I preach, to which my wife and kids would attest. Effective listening requires intention, attention, time, desire, and skill to be an effective listener. In our hyperkinetic world, authentic listening is in short supply.

UNDERSTAND AND RELATE

How Well Do You Listen?

Rate your listening skills with your young adult from 0–10 on each of the following items, with "10" being the highest rating you can give yourself and "0" being the lowest. The highest score possible for the whole assessment is 100. You can earn a "pass" on this section if you score 100. If you are brave enough for a reality check, ask your young adult to rate your listening skills—see appendix A. If you are really brave, ask your spouse to rate your listening. Unfortunately, I know what answer I would get from my spouse.

LISTENING SELF-ASSESSMENT

0   1   2   3   4   5   6   7   8   9   10
Not True at All   Completely True

As their parent, I:

_____ 1. Don't interrupt them when they are speaking.
_____ 2. Don't think about what I will say next when listening to them.
_____ 3. Don't finish their sentence.
_____ 4. Maintain eye contact and don't allow interruptions such as phone calls, checking my cell phone, or other parties to interrupt our conversation.
_____ 5. Routinely describe what I hear them saying to ensure I understand.
_____ 6. Ensure an important conversation is finished, and if not, I propose another time to come back to it.
_____ 7. Don't try to fix or tell them what to do instead of listening.
_____ 8. Pay attention to not only the content of what is being said but also to the emotion communicated through tone, words, or body language.
_____ 9. Ask for clarification if I'm not sure I understand what they are saying.
_____ 10. Listen to understand and not judge.

Total Score:___

How did you do? Circle some skills you may need to practice, and let's discuss some ways to sharpen our listening skills.

NONJUDGMENTAL LISTENING SKILLS

Nonjudgmental—or active—listening means you do not put your opinion into the process. There is a time to voice your thoughts on the matter, but it should come after you have listened and obtained confirmation from your young adult that you heard and understood them. Think of listening as occurring at different levels. The first level is *attend*. If you are not attending by exhibiting behaviors such as walking away, trying to listen while watching TV, or using your cell phone, you give a nonverbal message that you don't want to listen. As an executive coach, I often hear direct reports complain that their boss had an annoying habit of checking their iPhones while listening to them. Eye contact or full attention is essential.

After attending, you need to *hear* or be aware of what the other person is saying. Hearing is an auditory competence, but it doesn't mean you have understood the person. It simply suggests that you heard the words.

Listen to understand is the next step. In this part of the process, you try to understand thoroughly what the other person is saying. You can repeat the words you think you heard or summarize them and ask if you heard them correctly. You may believe you know what the other person is saying, but you can only be sure if you check for understanding.

Finally, when an emotion is expressed, just stating the content of what you heard is not enough to gain confirmation of the message. You must *listen with the heart* (employ the third ear) or *understand* the emotion expressed. Reflect or summarize the emotion as well as the content. Fully listening to content and emotion sends a message to our young adults that we care and genuinely want to understand and know them. Don't we all want to be understood and known without judgment? Still, when our kids express some heartfelt emotion, we must don our listening black belts and match them with heartfelt listening, top of the ladder. When we listen with the third ear for the message coming from our child's heart, we make a profound, intimate connection. All conversations do not require the listening found at the highest rung on the ladder (below). Below is a graph showing the progression from attending to deep empathetic listening.

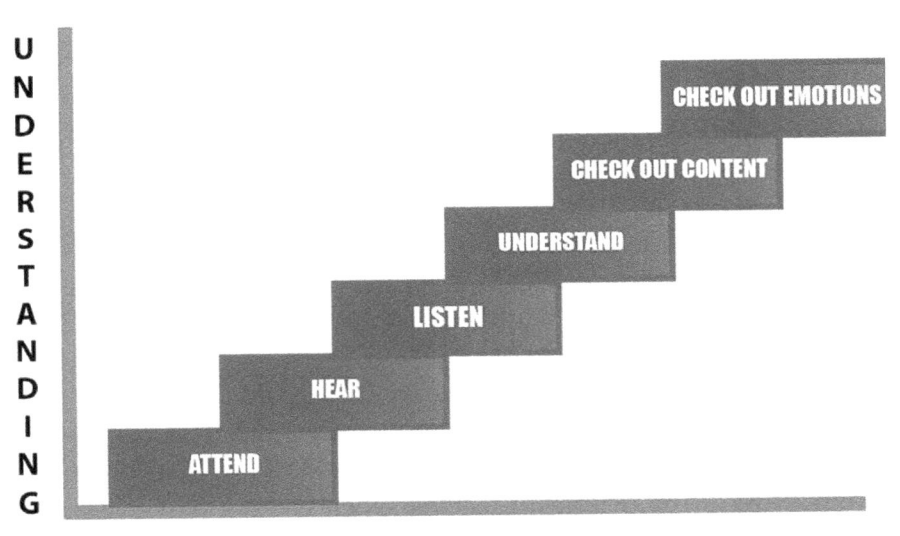

UNDERSTANDING (y-axis) vs. EMOTIONAL CONNECTION (x-axis), stair-step from ATTEND → HEAR → LISTEN → UNDERSTAND → CHECK OUT CONTENT → CHECK OUT EMOTIONS.

IMPORTANCE OF NONVERBALS

Ray Birdwhistell, an anthropologist, found that 30–35 percent of the social meaning of a conversation between two people involves the chosen word.[10] This leaves room for the nonverbals and tone to support, contradict, or add clarity to the meaning of the words. When asked how their day was, a college student could say, "Fine," with a different tone or body language that signals a different meaning. One version of *fine* may be said positively and signal a good day. Another version of *fine* said with a tone of resignation may signal, "The day sucked, and don't bug me."

We need to listen beyond words. When listening at the verbal and nonverbal level, maintain eye contact, don't check your phone, and be conscious of posture. Lean forward, adopt a pace and tone that matches your young adults, and ensure you are not interrupted. On that latter point, if you get a phone call or someone walks in and wants to talk, arrange to connect with them later.

PRACTICE QUIZ: HOW WELL DO YOU HEAR, LISTEN, AND REFLECT?

Here are some comments made by a young adult and possible parent responses. Choose the one that best reflects effective listening.

A. Young-adult response to the question: What was a difficult challenge in growing up? "When we moved, I was going into ninth grade and felt like everyone was staring at me." Parent-response options:
  1. When we moved, you didn't like the new school?
  2. You shouldn't have been upset about that. You know we had to move because your father's job changed.
  3. You felt uncomfortable when you started ninth grade at a new high school, and people were staring at you.

B. Young-adult response to the question: What makes you happy? "I like to smoke weed and listen to music to mellow out when I am at my friend's house." Parent-response options:
  1. How far do you think smoking pot will get you in life?
  2. Where have we gone wrong? How will you be successful in life if all you do is smoke pot?
  3. Do you feel like smoking pot and listening to music helps you relax? (Possible extended question: Do other things help you relax?)

C. Young adult response to interview question: When you think of making a difference in your life or having a purpose, what comes to mind? "I don't know; make a lot of money." Parent-response options:
  1. It sounds like you haven't thought a lot about it, but you know you want to make a lot of money.

2. Make a lot of money! Do you think that will make you happy?
3. You should be thinking about what you need to do with your life. The answer is not going to drop in your lap.

How did you do? Regarding effective listening, the best answers would be A-3, B-3, and C-1. It may be hard to hold back from giving your opinion. Remember that the more critical long-range goal is building and deepening the relationship. There is a time to share your input or opinion. However, this is best done in a separate conversation. Jumping in with your idea or opinion during a conversation where you must check for understanding can shut down the conversation altogether. One caveat: young adults often confuse "listening" with "acceptance" of what the other person is saying. Our kids can say, "You don't understand," but the issue may be that you have heard them but don't agree with their perception or request. Disagreeing with something your young adult says doesn't excuse you from checking out what you heard before sharing your perspective. You may wonder when the parent gets to talk or if you can ask any questions when listening. Let's go to the next skill.

ASK-INQUIRE

There is an art to learning how to ask questions. Questions, mainly those you invite to clarify what your adult child is saying, are essential to listening. Since our goal in this chapter is to describe ways to build a deeper and more caring relationship with our adult kids, our questions should serve this goal. As such, here are some guidelines. First, be sure the question is relevant to understanding your young adult. Second, is the question sincere? Do you want to know the answer to help you understand better? Third, will the question lead to your child feeling more comfortable and supported by you or threatened and defensive? Finally, try to use open-ended questions.

On the latter point, asking questions that cause the young adult to search for answers or ideas is important versus delivering a yes or no response. To avoid the one-word response of yes or no, or "I'm fine," ask for two or three ideas or thoughts they might have. Listen to the difference between these two questions and how you would answer them: "Can I be helpful in some way?" versus "What one or two things could I do that could help you?" It would be easy for your young adult to say "nothing" in answer to the first question, but they are more likely to respond at least with one suggestion to the second. The inquiry can continue, if not be a further conversation, by asking some leading, open-ended questions. Here are some open-ended questions that can invite further discussion and understanding.

- Can you say more about ... ?
- Can you clarify what you mean by ... ?
- Can you tell me how you feel about ... ?
- Can you tell me how you experienced ... ?
- Can you help me understand ... ?
- Can you say or explain that in a different way so I'm sure I understand ... ?
- Can you give me an example ...?
- Can you give me one or two ideas ... ?

WANT TO GET TO KNOW YOUR YOUNG ADULT? ASK.

The following is a set of suggested questions that you can use to interview your emerging adult. They center around the three I's: identity, independence, intimacy, and intention. The answers to these questions will help you understand your young adult and identify gaps in your perceptions. Remember: the questions are *suggested* ones. You can pick and choose, but take some from each category. Maybe start the first session by selecting just ten. Order the questions from the least threatening or uncomfortable for you and your young adult to those that might be more challenging. Indicate to your adult child that the interview and questions will increase your understanding of them and improve our relationship. Assure your young adult that you will not be judgmental or use the information they share against them now or in the future. You will also not share this information with others unless they permit you. Here they are:

UNDERSTAND AND RELATE

The Past

1. What are one or two of your fondest childhood memories?
2. What things did you like to do when you were younger?
3. What were one or two of the most difficult challenges you faced growing up? How did you meet those challenges?
4. What important qualities or unique characteristics did we share with you growing up?
5. What were the unique or special qualities of your childhood?
6. What were the things we did as parents that you liked or found most helpful during your growing up?
7. When you look back at your childhood, what are one or two of your most important achievements?
8. What were your greatest disappointments or regrets in your childhood?
9. What do you wish you could do over again?
10. What do you want me, as your parent, to remember most about you?

The Present

1. What do you most like about yourself?
2. What do you most dislike about yourself?
3. What one or two things are going well for you?
4. What are one or two of your most difficult challenges?
5. Who are the people, friends, to whom you feel close?
6. What makes you happy?
7. What do you most appreciate about us as parents?
8. What things in your life upset you or cause you to be worried?
9. What different actions would you like us to take that would be helpful to you?
10. On a scale of 1–10, how satisfied are you with your level of independence? (10 = very satisfied and 1 = very dissatisfied)? What one or two ideas do you have as to what we could do to support your independence?

THE PARENT'S LAUNCH CODE

The Future

1. What are the most important tasks you need to accomplish in the next five years?
2. Where do you hope to be living in five years?
3. What strengths or resources do you have to help you accomplish these tasks?
4. Will you have a partner or be married in five years?
5. What one or more things could interfere with your accomplishing these five-year goals?
6. How would you like to see our relationship change in five years?
7. What are your most essential strengths or skills to help you succeed?
8. In what ways do you think you will be different in five years?
9. What one or two actions can we take to support your five-year plan?
10. When you think of making a difference in your life or having a purpose, what one or two ideas come to mind?

*Note: In chapter 6, I will describe how I use a five-year planning strategy, including an interview with the young adult to help parents partner with their adult children.

Offer to answer any of these questions regarding your life. *Be honest, open, and vulnerable.* These are the most engaging qualities you can bring to the relationship. Be aware and willing to share your own young adult experience. Be honest or pass if you don't want to discuss a topic. It's okay not to talk about your sex life or drug usage during your young adult years, but understand you must give them the same consideration. Don't lie or make up something. Young adults are quick to pick up when someone is not authentic. One parent in my workshop used these questions to build a deeper relationship with her daughter and commented as follows:

> *The interview questions and process were worth the price of the entire workshop.*

DEBRIEFING WITH YOUR YOUNG ADULT

Ask your young adult these questions after the interview and note the answers that will help you continue to improve your understanding and relationship.

1. What did you find most helpful about the interview?
2. What one or two things did I do that were helpful?
3. In what ways did you see me trying to be a better listener?
4. What one or two ways could I listen better?
5. In what ways did I show that I understood you?
6. What one or two ways could I better understand you?

Ask your young adult if they would like to meet again over lunch or dinner and what ideas they have regarding using the time. Afterward, your young adult could come up with questions for you—turnabout is fair play. Identify some subjects to discuss ahead of time. Or talk about whatever comes up with a promise that you will focus on nonjudgmental listening. Consider beginning a ritual of talking over a meal at your favorite restaurant. This activity is a bridge leading to an adult-to-adult relationship with your young adult. Maybe at some point, they will even buy that restaurant meal.

RESISTANCE

It's common to have the young adult hesitant or even refuse to do the interview with you, especially if the relationship has been contentious. You can't force the young adult to respond to your request, but here are some suggestions. First, offer to treat them to breakfast, lunch, or dinner. Getting out of the house and eating together will provide more of an adult-to-adult venue for your conversation. Second, offer reassurance that your intent is not to challenge, judge, or criticize any response they give. Suppose you have a history of not listening, interrupting, or adding your opinion before they complete their thoughts. In that case, you may suggest that if you don't listen nonjudgmentally, you will give them five bucks each time you slip. Practice your nonjudgmental listening before you start. It could cost you if you don't. Finally, offer lots of options when requesting an opportunity to interview them. They can answer some questions, all the questions, do it now or later, in person or otherwise—phone, email, and so forth. Ask them for ways to understand them better if they refuse to do the interview. Let them say no, and then step back and try to communicate via email or text your desire to learn and understand them better and give them options. Using written communication may cause them to pause before saying no. As stated in chapter 1, please don't be afraid or hesitant to use your young adult's preferred or common communication vehicles to connect with them.

SUMMARY OF PRINCIPLES RELATED TO LISTENING AND INQUIRY.

1. Recognize that we all need to be understood.
2. It is essential to understand your emerging adults to have and maintain a relationship with them.
3. If there is a history of asking questions, failing to listen, or becoming judgmental, you may need to apologize and indicate a commitment to do better.
4. Adopt a learner's stance. Then you will have a role similar to a student—one who asks questions and listens carefully to the answers to learn.
5. Listen with the heart for feelings/the head for content is a route to true understanding and intimacy.
6. The only way you and your emerging adult know you understand them is to check out what you heard. "Is this what you are saying?"
7. It's important to block or bracket your inner noise or thoughts and focus on what the other person is saying. You can do this if you stay focused on the message you are hearing and how you will summarize or reflect on this to ensure understanding.
8. You can also check to see if you get what they say by asking, "Do you believe I have heard and understood you?"

9. Make time to talk. If you have another commitment when a vital conversation begins, make an appointment for the rest of the discussion.
10. I have found getting out of the house, going for a walk, or driving together fosters more open communication than direct eyeball-to-eyeball talks at home.

FEEDBACK AND FEEDFORWARD

If your young adult participates in an interview process, try to understand them better, or if not, you can develop and use a third skill that involves asking two simple questions. This nonthreatening approach increases your credibility and positive emotional connection to another person. *Like better listening, implementing a specific form of feedback and feedforward will improve your relationship with your kids at any age.* I used these two forms to effectively elicit information from my daughter and improve our relationship when she was in tenth grade. My mentor and friend, Marshall Goldsmith, a leading leadership expert and executive coach, offers these two questions as an effective way to learn about and engage another person (Goldsmith, 2014).[11] You can hear him describe this technique he uses with business leaders at the back of the book in notes to this chapter—see YouTube link. Although he primarily describes this process as relating to leaders in business settings, he states one can use this within the family. He testifies to the success of this technique with his family.

The approach involves asking for feedback on one or two things you are doing **right** as a parent and "feedforward" on one or two suggestions of how you could **do better**. Your young adult is more likely to offer suggestions for improvement than give you critical feedback. Well, maybe not. But it's worth a try. You will notice that a *feedforward* request is embedded in the "future" interview questions above. Have something to write on to capture their responses.

Steps in the Process

1. Ask the young adult to describe two or three behaviors you do that are helpful to your relationship with them and that they want you to continue. Jot these down.
2. Ask them to describe two or three behaviors you do that are helpful to their moving toward greater independence. Jot these down.
3. Then ask for "feedforward." Specifically, ask your young adult to share two or three behaviors they would like you to stop or start that would help build a better or closer relationship with them. Jot these down.
4. A second feedforward question is: What two or three behaviors could I do or stop doing that would help support their efforts to become more independent? Jot these down.

Now's the challenging part. In each instance of receiving feedback or feedforward, you need to say two words—and only two words, "Thank you!" Please don't comment, "Oh, I know I do that," or try to defend or clarify, "Well, the reason I do," or evaluate, "Oh, that's a good idea." Just say, "Thank you!" After saying thank you, indicate your desire to continue to do the positive things your young adult has said you do. Beyond this, indicate you will commit to continuing to do what your young adult told you he liked that you did. Also, pick at least one but preferably two feedforward suggestions and make a commitment to carry these out in the next weeks and months. Commit to the ones you believe will help and that you are willing and able to do. You don't have to do all the requested suggestions.

Follow up periodically to see if your young adult has observed you carrying out your commitment. Follow-up is critical because the goal is to change your behavior in ways that will change your young adult's perceptions. The only way the perception will change is if they observe the behavior. Checking in and asking them regarding observations of your changes leads to perception change and, ultimately, to a more positive relationship. Here are the steps in the process.

THE PROCESS OF FEEDFORWARD

| Parents ask for feedback and feedforward | → | Parent commits to change in behavior | → | Young adult observes behavior | → | Parent checks to see if change is observed | → | Young adult acknowledges change - alters attitude |

THE IMPACT OF "FEEDFORWARD"

If you follow the process above, your relationship with your young adult *will* change, not just because you committed and demonstrated the actions they requested but because they observed these changes. The goal is to change behavior and their perceptions. Changing perceptions is most important if you have a contentious relationship with your kids or they are acting irresponsibly. If you commit to working on changing this behavior, and they give you feedback you are changing, your young adult's perception will change, and they will warm up to you. Their perception will stay the same if they don't notice the difference. You have to ask them to observe your behavior and ask them for specific indications of the change to which you committed. I will give you a real-life example of a failed feedforward effort on my part.

My wife said I was constantly complaining about my aches and pains. I didn't believe she was accurate, but I decided to try to change, so I committed to myself that I would not complain about any ailment. Weeks passed, and I knew I had not said anything about physical aches and pains. One day, after about two months of no complaints, I came in to wash my hands and noticed I got a blister from raking leaves. My wife asked me what I was doing. I told her I was washing my hands and had a blister.

A week later, feeling quite proud of my silence regarding my health complaints, I asked her how she thought I was doing in not complaining about my aches and pains. She replied that I hadn't done so well, adding that I had complained about a blister just the week before. I had dedicated several months of consciously reduced whining about my discomforts, and all that hard work had gone unnoticed. Instead, she looked for something that would align with her perception of me and pointed to the blister. This lack of change in perception in the face of contradictory data is called "confirmation bias" in the scientific literature. Essentially, we recognize data that fit our perceptions and ignore anything that doesn't support these. Now, if I had approached this differently, each week asking my wife how I had done the week before, her perception would change. As she recognized that my whining behavior changed week after week, she would gradually adjust how she saw me.

This story shows how it is critical to check in routinely with your young adult about executing your agreed-upon feedforward actions. Incidentally, as illustrated in my example above, one change your young adult may ask is that you stop doing something. We can all do better as parents. Our young adults want a better relationship with us but also want to push for their independence. These two drivers of their behavior can lead to conflict and contentious relationships. We can change the quality of our connection with our young adults by expressing unconditional love, listening nonjudgmentally, using open-ended questions, and engaging our young adults with feedback and feedforward. We need to change our approach to change the relationship for their sake, our sake, and for a successful launch. When we change, the relationship will change. Keep in mind that relationships are inherently reciprocal. Although your change commitment should not be contingent on your adult child's change, there is a greater likelihood of a change from them if you change first.

When it comes to change, be the first!

DO YOUR REPORT CARD

Throughout this book, I recommend that parents take responsibility for their actions. It helps if you recognize that your young adult can choose whether or not to have a relationship with you. Therefore, how will you measure your progress if you can't evaluate your parenting skills—listening or otherwise—based on your young adult's response? A report card is a good tool.

UNDERSTAND AND RELATE

MY REPORT CARD

Many parents tend to judge their efforts to understand and connect to their young adults by the responses they get. Expecting specific responses to questions about your parenting can be a trap. Our young adults can hold any opinions about our behavior regardless of our good intentions and best efforts. Remember myth number one, the belief that we can control them. Changes by them are one data point or factor in determining how we are doing, but they are not the most important in the short run. The key is that you have reached out, and continue to reach out, in love with a desire to understand and improve your relationship with them. Look in the mirror and ask yourself, "How did I do with my goal of attempting to express love and understanding? Where can I improve?"

Here are suggestions for a self-report card with suggested actions. Feel free to take any learnings from this book that you want to apply and drop them into this chart.

SAMPLE PARENT "SELF" REPORT CARD

My actions to increase understanding and relationship	What did I do today relative to this goal?	What positive impact did it have on my young adult? (don't expect)	What feedforward (suggestions) did my young adult give?	Any additional actions I will take on this goal?
I have learned something new about my young adult				
I have tried to ask open-ended questions for understanding				
I have used nonjudgmental listening				
I have used good nonverbal communication				

THE PARENT'S LAUNCH CODE

I have asked for feedback and feedforward				

KEEPERS

Finally, *give yourself credit*. Parents are the most self-critical people I know. Focus on what you are doing "right" rather than what you are doing wrong or on your young adult's unresponsiveness. If you have read the introduction and chapters 1 and 2, written notes to your young adults, completed an interview using listening and inquiry skills, and engaged them with feedforward, congratulations. Keep it up. Continue to reach out to your young adult, no matter what, because your deepest desire, and theirs, is to have a loving connection. The drumbeats of guilt continue no matter what the age of our children. We need to let go of the past, concentrate on what we have the power to modify, and forge ahead with sincere efforts to have the best relationship we can have with our kids. In the next two chapters, we'll discuss how to let go of guilt and resentment.

As I've done before, I'll start the list of keepers, and you can finish the list. What vital points, recommendations, or ideas regarding understanding and relating will you apply from this chapter? What tips were helpful in this chapter, and do you want to remember, review,

UNDERSTAND AND RELATE

and apply them? Please jot down these thoughts, share them, and use them immediately. Application is the best way to stamp in learning.

1. Listening and understanding practices are foundational to the success of the other five launch practices.
2. Nonjudgmental listening and inquiry are bridges to connect to my young adult.
3. Appreciating and acknowledging the monumental developmental tasks of our kids engenders credibility.
4. Understanding our own development tasks provides a focus for efforts we can control.
5. _____
6. _____
7. _____
8. _____
9. _____
10. _____

CHAPTER THREE

APOLOGIZE

Words don't come easily, like sorry, like sorry.

—Tracy Chapman

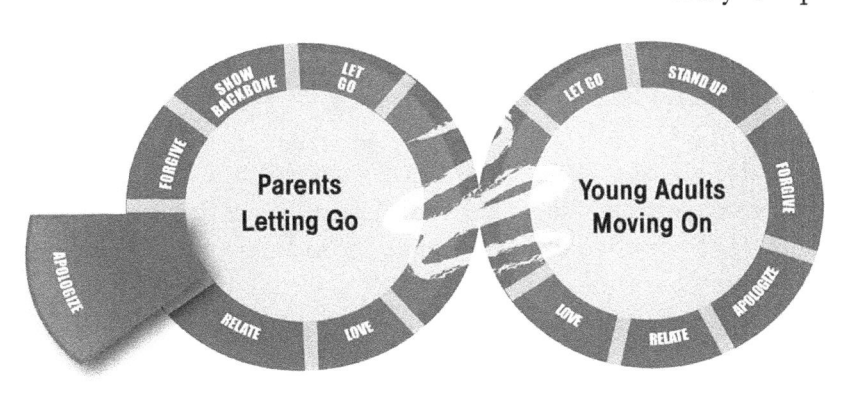

Leaning closer to her dying father, my client, a mother of two, strained to hear him as he tried to speak. She had been steadfastly caring for him during his lengthy battle with cancer. Inside, she wondered why she was so diligently tending to him since this man had been a terrible, abusive, and raging alcoholic father. She grew up in a home where the only predictable thing was his unpredictability. She never knew when the next drunken attack would come. With tears in his eyes, he spoke of his deep regret for his abuse and called out for her forgiveness.

My guess is that this deathbed confession and request for forgiveness is a scene that happens way too often. In the final hours before death, all those who hear words like these from a family member want to think they are sincere and not just the ill person's preparation to meet his Maker. Such apologies, genuine or otherwise, must be bittersweet. They beg the question: Why were these words not said many years ago when they could have made a difference?

Many who have had abusive, neglectful, or inattentive parents who did not live up to their responsibilities of loving, supporting, and protecting their children would like to hear an acknowledgment of these shortcomings and an apology. Can we live without these statements? Sure, many of us do. But an apology is a way of the parent saying: "It was not you; it was me." Since children have inherited imperfect parents, we are likely to have made mistakes with our kids, too. We don't know how much these mistakes may still leave emotional wounds on our children. Why would we wait if we can apologize for our shortcomings and help heal these wounds?

OPPORTUNITIES TO APOLOGIZE

As parents, we can sometimes hurt our children through hurtful, abusive, or inappropriate actions. Sometimes, we don't live up to our standards for what we believe makes a good parent. In these cases, a sincere, heartfelt apology to our adult children can do much for us and our young adults. It can be a key to letting go by both parties and enable us to free ourselves and our children. Otherwise, these past actions and unpleasant memories keep us fused negatively to each other.

Guilt and remorse can cause a parent to withdraw from the parenting role. We try to compensate for the past by compromising expectations, making excuses, ignoring inappropriate behavior, failing to set clear boundaries, and not enforcing consequences. We can't expect our young adults to respect our efforts to be better parents if we don't take responsibility for our past mistakes and shortcomings.

For the young adults, hurt and resentment keep them bound in anger with us, showing up in overreaction to our parenting efforts, distancing, and withdrawal. In such situations, parents and young adults can't let go and attain the level of connected separation indicated in the graphic above. The circle on the left represents the parent, and the right indicates the young adult. Three failures of separation can occur when past issues are not addressed and resolved through apology and forgiveness.

In the next chapter, we'll get into the specifics of forgiveness as the second healing practice. We'll describe three failures of separation (negative enmeshment, positive enmeshment, and disconnected). We can address these launch failures through a parent's willingness to apologize.

Negatively enmeshed

NEGATIVE ENMESHMENT

Young adults harboring resentment toward their parents due to their perceptions of parents' treatment remain bound in negative enmeshment. *Enmeshment* may sound like psychobabble, but to be clear, it just means being stuck, entangled, and ensnared. Both parents and young adults can exhibit enmeshment behavior. It's not just a young adult problem. The practices in this book help parents avoid or address enmeshment and move to a healthy state of loving separation. The wavy dark lines illustrate that the relationship is contentious.

Attacks on parents indicate negative enmeshment. These attacks can involve blaming, accusations, excusing of behavior, and claiming parents' actions caused failures in their own lives. This internal young adult mindset will affect their relationships with friends, potential partners, and bosses and how they approach responsibilities. One young adult I saw in my practice said, "My mother never loved me as much as my siblings, never gave me the attention I needed." Such indictments relegate the young adult to a life of victimhood and failing because they harbor a built-in excuse for failing.

The diagram above shows this state of enmeshment where the connections between the young adult and parent are negatively charged. This kind of relationship was what I experienced with my father.

Positively enmeshed

POSITIVE ENMESHMENT

Some young adults and parents experience a state of *positive* enmeshment. Stuck together through positive emotions, as illustrated by the wavy white lines. In this state, young adults cannot contradict or challenge their parents. They do not believe they can be themselves without risking rejection. In this situation, they have difficulty making decisions independently, constantly seeking parental approval. As for parents, they are positively enmeshed in supporting—if not controlling—their young adults, holding on too tightly out of anxiety or beliefs the young adult can't make it on their own.

Parents also may hang on too tightly because they fear the loss of closeness to their children. The parent binds the child emotionally and behaviorally to them and forestalls the launch process. When this occurs, the apology of the parent may need to be more in terms of overinvolvement, overcontrol, and overdependence on maintaining a closeness to the young adult.

Disconnected

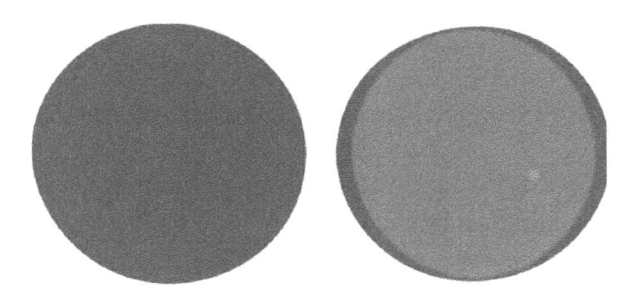

DISCONNECTED: THE ESTRANGED YOUNG ADULT

This relationship pattern is perhaps the saddest situation, occurring when the young adult cuts off communication with one or both parents. I have several parents experiencing this cutoff from their young adult children. Two of these parents have been told why; the third had her young adult daughter go off the grid and has not communicated with her mother in over four years.

A colleague of mine, Josh Coleman—found at drjoshuacoleman.com—specializes in helping parents with this problem. At times, issues with the parent, either from the past or present, lead the young adult to believe they would be better off not having any contact with the parent. You can imagine how heartbreaking this estrangement is, particularly when the young adult gives no explanation. In these situations, both parties suffer; such a cutoff, with its accompanying grief and loss, causes ongoing pain. The lack of communication or any contact limits the parents from apologizing in a way that could be healing and lead to reconciliation.

> *A mother of an estranged daughter, whom she has not heard from in four years, tells me it's too painful to reach out with a card or flowers and have no acknowledgment. The father continues to send flowers and cards on birthdays and holidays, and she thought she might ask him to add her name. In one of our sessions, we discussed how the pain of this loss might feel worse than the death of a child because you can't grieve or obtain any closure.*

THE GIFT OF APOLOGY

An apology is a gift we give our adult children and ourselves:

1. An apology can diffuse the anger and hurt that keeps the young adult enmeshed.
2. When a parent owns and apologizes for hurtful behavior, it becomes hard for the young adult to continue to harbor resentment. As such, it reduces the inclination to excuse the child's present behavior because of some past offense.
3. When a parent says they are sorry, it validates the young adult's feelings, even if the parent disagrees with the child's perception. As a result, the shame caused by the young adult's belief that they are at fault or inherently defective can diminish.
4. We never stop being teachers; when we apologize, we are modeling and teaching that we realize we make mistakes.
5. Apology addresses our guilt over failures, mistakes, and shortcomings as parents. We show them we can take responsibility, be vulnerable, and apologize. Although we can't apologize with the secret hope they will reciprocate, we have at least taught them how they could come back and apologize for any hurtful actions.
6. You demonstrate vulnerability, which, as stated in the earlier quote from Brené Brown, is the language of intimacy.
7. It creates the possibility for forgiveness. There is no guarantee it will happen, but it is unlikely without an apology.
8. We become a better parent and a better person by 'being first" to try to mend a strained or damaged relationship.

Take the high road; it's less crowded.

DO WE NEED TO APOLOGIZE?

The answer to the question is, not if we have been perfect parents! I imagine a conference for perfect parents. As you slowly crack the door to glimpse the speaker, you soon realize the stage is empty. You open the door further and discover that the auditorium is also empty. It's okay to join the imperfect parent club; many more are at that auditorium down the hall. You'll be in good company. In my workshops, I offer a chance for any parent who believes they have been perfect to opt out and get their money back. So far, no one has taken me up on this. To acknowledge our parental imperfections, check any of the statements below. If you can identify with any of these statements, congratulations! You are a member of the imperfect parent club. Furthermore, you have identified opportunities to use the practice of apology to bring healing to you and your young adult.

_____I have regrets about my parenting.
_____I know I said or did wrong things.
_____I believe my parenting contributed to my children's problems today.
_____I wish I could have a do-over for some situation or time in the past.
_____My young adult believes I did or didn't do something in the past that has led to hurt and anger toward me.
_____I expected too much or too little of my child.
_____I did something unintentional that has caused distance and hurt between my child and me.
_____I failed to protect or intervene in a situation with my child, leading to distance and hurt between my child and me.
_____I got divorced.
_____I didn't give my young adult enough time or attention when they grew up. I was too busy.
_____I was not as affectionate as I should have been.
_____I was inconsistent in my parenting.
_____I was overly critical.
_____I yelled, hit, or spanked out of anger.

_____I was depressed or anxious and couldn't be there emotionally for my child.
_____I drank alcohol in my early pregnancy before knowing I was pregnant and thought I damaged my child.
_____I should have kept my promises.
_____I was overprotective and didn't allow my child to make mistakes and learn from these.
_____I was overindulgent, did too much for them, gave them too much.
_____I didn't tell my child I loved them enough.
_____I didn't encourage them in their interests or aspirations.
_____I always criticized them, and they could never live up to my expectations.

I suspect I got your attention with the quiz above since it's hard to believe you didn't check one or more of these items. I sure did. You may feel annoyed with me for calling attention to your shortcomings, but please be assured that I am not trying to add to the guilt you may feel as a parent. The positive news about taking such a survey is that we all fall short of perfect parenthood. The intent is not to browbeat you for parental mistakes but to invite you to use this awareness to let go and bring healing to you and your young adult.

DOES YOUR YOUNG ADULT THINK YOU SHOULD APOLOGIZE?

Do you have the courage to ask your young adult what apologies they would like to hear from you? Sometimes, what we think should be a basis for saying we're sorry differs from what our kids may think. Some actions may call for an apology our kids don't remember or hold against us. Or there may be incidents we are unaware of, but they hold against us. When I think about things I regret as a parent, I remember when my son was maybe three or four years old, and I was holding his younger sister and trying to comfort her. My son kept coming up and bugging me for something he wanted. I told him to stop bugging me and swept his legs out from under him with my feet. I still vividly remember the shocked look on his face as he landed on the ground. And how ashamed I felt. The memory of this encounter was something I needed to address, and I took the time to apologize to him in writing and in person. He indicated that he didn't remember this event, but I still needed to apologize for failing to be the parent I wanted to be.

Are you willing to learn what your young adult might believe about your failures, shortcomings, or hurtful actions in their growing up? In appendix A, under chapter 3 on Apology, are questions you can ask your young adult to learn of opportunities to say you are sorry. I wouldn't blindside your young adult with this set of questions, because you may get a defensive or uncooperative response. Indicate you want to address any past parenting actions you have done or not done that have never been addressed. Tell them you are sincerely interested in discovering any past mistakes and want to take responsibility for them. Then, ask your young adult if they would be willing to respond to some questions. Before approaching your young adult with the questions, here are some suggestions and reminders. Invite them to meet outside your home to answer questions about your parenting over the years. If they balk at a meeting, ask them if they would answer the questions through text or electronic media. Texting may not be the best vehicle. While face-to-face is the optimal venue for this type of communication, as I've said before, getting their perceptions and input is most important—whatever mode it may be delivered.

Listen nonjudgmentally. This form of listening was discussed in chapter 2 and may be worth revisiting. It means listening for understanding and clarification. Check out what you have heard at the level of content and feelings.

WHAT CONSTITUTES A GENUINE APOLOGY?

Let's start with a definition.

Apology: A statement of remorse, regret, and responsibility for:
• Having done or said something wrong • Not being able to do or be something • Having offended another intentionally or unintentionally

THE PARENT'S LAUNCH CODE

The hard work for us parents is to say we are sorry without any qualifications or expectations.

A genuine apology is sincere and respectful, expressing understanding, empathy, and responsibility. Apologies need to originate and emanate from the heart. We say we are sorry because we care about our young adults and feel it is the right thing to do. It must be heartfelt. Now, please take a closer look at the elements of an apology. First, it is a statement of remorse based upon a heartfelt understanding of the impact of your actions on another. Second, it is a statement of regret because you believe your actions had a hurtful effect. It is crucial to be sincere and contrite when expressing remorse and regret, or it will not be well received. Your tone and body language need to match your words. Third, it requires taking responsibility for unkind communication, decision, or action. In Lewicki's research on an apology, the most critical element is the willingness of the offender to take responsibility for their actions.[1]

The apology should start with identifying what we have done wrong regardless of what the other person did or said. We take responsibility for "our part," no matter what. You don't have to say it was *all* your fault, but it's important to take responsibility for what you said or did that was offensive. Acknowledge you can't change the past but are committing to try to eliminate the offending behavior in the future. Stating you will make amends or improve your conduct is the best—if not only—way to demonstrate your genuineness.

When it comes to parents' past actions, they must give the young adult space and time to consider and decide whether or not to offer forgiveness. Apologizing with expectations or hopes of forgiveness could be perceived as contrived. If you don't receive an expression of forgiveness and are upset, hurt, or resentful, you should reconsider your motives for apologizing. The main work you need to do as a parent is to admit and make amends, as possible, for past grievances. If you receive a pardon, that's icing on the cake. Lewicki's work with college students cited above found that the request for forgiveness is the least essential element in an apology.

WHAT TO AVOID IN AN APOLOGY

Avoid saying, "I'm sorry, but, if, or however." Such a statement essentially negates the "I'm sorry" part of the sentence. As an executive coach who spoke at 3M, Marshall Goldsmith, described this contradiction when apologizing. It was hard for me to implement this practice in my marriage. As a prospective lawyer, I was used to defending myself routinely as a child and finding someone—or something—else to blame. Just saying "I'm sorry" and taking responsibility for my part in the problem without qualifiers left me frustrated and vulnerable, but doing this has made a big difference in my marriage. My example illustrates how important apology is not just in parent-child relationships. Be aware of the "buts" like these:

- Sorry ... but you had a part in this
- Sorry ... but we all make mistakes
- Sorry ... but you're not perfect
- Sorry ... but it was an accident
- Sorry ... but I was trying to be helpful
- Sorry ... but you shouldn't take it so personally
- Sorry ... but (other)

Avoid the "if" statements that are nonapologies, such as, "I'm sorry if you didn't understand," "if you felt I was condescending," or "if you were offended."

Blanket apologies are less effective than those that specify the parent's actions. They include apologies such as, "I'm sorry I was such a bad parent" or "I'm sorry for everything I ever did wrong as a parent," which will also appear insincere. It is better to identify your specific contribution to a difficult time and take responsibility for it. Acknowledging a pattern in the mistreatment of your child is appropriate. For instance, "I'm sorry I was so critical of you and led you to believe you could never please me." By the way, this perception that a young adult has never been good enough is prevalent. The pattern is often generational and something the parent experienced growing up. It is a gift to break this generational pattern, apologize, and tell your adult child that you love them (unconditionally) and accept them the way they are. Why would we withhold such a gift?

Saying, "I'm sorry you feel ... or I made you feel ... or that you took this wrong ... or that you misunderstood me" are not genuine statements of regret, but instead, blame the other person. They are underhanded apologies.

"I would say I am sorry, but I didn't mean to say or do something" is not an apology. It's an excuse. The receiver's actions and perceptions are the crucial basis for an apology. The intention is not the critical factor.

Giving a partial apology isn't enough. It is like someone swore at you and then slapped you but only apologized for swearing. This oversight leaves the victim feeling you aren't taking full responsibility for his actions. Research from *The Journal of Personality and Social Psychology* reported in *Psychology Today* shows that such partial apologizers feel worse than full apologizers.[2] The partial apologizers introduce a new type of dishonesty by trying to avoid or cover up the full extent of their offense.

Saying, "I did the best I could as a parent," does not work. This veiled apology absolves the parent of responsibility for the child's treatment in growing up. Unless we are perfect parents, we could have done better. Such a statement could imply that it was the child's fault. The implication is that something else went wrong, and the parent is not responsible because they did their best.

Saying you're sorry to the wrong person is not helpful either. For instance, you may tell a spouse you are sorry for something you did to your child but not tell the child. Worse yet is asking the spouse to apologize on your behalf.

Saying you're sorry without any behavior change is just an excuse for continuing to do something offensive and is insincere. Continuing the actions that prompted the apology renders the statement ineffective. Saying sorry doesn't give one a free pass for repeat offensive or abusive behavior.

WHY DO WE RESIST APOLOGIZING?

Because it is hard! As the Tracy Chapman song says, "I'm sorry are words that don't come easy." **Parents may think that admitting mistakes erodes the image of being competent and correct.** They also believe an apology could undermine the child's confidence and compliance with parents' future expectations. When children are younger and of school age, they may idolize their parents and believe they can do no wrong. However, there comes a time when the child begins to see the flaws and shortcomings of the parent. The child realizes that the parent can make mistakes, fail to meet promises, and do things that contradict the parent's messages or values. This failure can lead to the child questioning other parental statements or actions and, ultimately, losing the sense of the parent's credibility. Men tend to have more difficulty apologizing as compared to women.[3]

As I observed my father's relationship with his father, I was aware that his father needed to be correct and most likely never apologized to my father. My father never apologized to me when I was growing up; if he did, I do not remember and think I would have. This unwillingness to apologize is an "old school" type of thinking—that if I apologized, I would lose my credibility or control. The lack of apology in the face of clear actions deserving an apology can lead to rebellion or, at a minimum, a credibility problem addressed above.

Parents may feel that admitting mistakes and apologizing implies they have failed as parents. Having this belief is unfortunate for two reasons. First, it's important to distinguish between errors or failures and *being* a failure. The former constitutes guilt, and the latter constitutes shame. Shame reflects a belief that you are fundamentally flawed. At some of our worst times, we may feel so bad that we wish we had not even become a parent. This reaction is confusing a mistake with *being* a mistake. Please don't go there; this irrational thinking can lead to a dark place. None of us are mistakes, but we all make mistakes. On the other hand, guilt can be helpful and constructive in identifying ways we could have made better choices. These less-than-perfect decisions reflect our *im*perfect humanity. As such, they are an appropriate basis for an apology. Far from being a sign of failure, apologies open a channel for intimacy.

Some people believe that apologies are a sign of weakness. This view is pervasive in the world of politics and business. Such admissions of mistakes have risks. When I was leading a health promotion initiative at a local company in the late nineties, I failed to screen certain distributed materials that contained numerous errors. I asked to appear before the human resources operating committee to acknowledge my mistake and apologize. I felt emotionally naked in front of the committee, but my apology was well received. However, it didn't add to my brand as a strong leader. At no time did I see anyone make such a public apology in my twenty-six-year career at the company. If I had to do it over again, would I do the same thing? Yes. Sometimes, you need to do what you know is right. As a parent, acknowledging mistakes is the right thing to do.

We must value relationships over our pride. Resistance to apology may arise from pride and a belief that the other person is also to blame. Apologizing for one's part in a mistake does not excuse the behavior of the other person involved. It's just saying: "I'm taking responsibility for my part in what went wrong." To resist acknowledging one's failures because, in your view, the other person did something to contribute to the problem will either cause one to resist admitting wrongdoing or lead to an "I'm sorry but" non-apology. As parents, we need to be the first to apologize. It takes *courage,* Brené Brown says to admit our imperfections, but this vulnerability is the route to a deeper connection to our kids.[4]

Some worry that an apology may excuse current behavior or be used against the parent later. Or your young adult may take the opportunity to dredge up other past actions deserving of an apology. Yes, this risk exists, but facing up to past adverse events that bother your young adult is a good thing; it can free both parties. If the apology relates to some ongoing behavior that the parent acknowledges and indicates a desire to change, then the parent must ensure that the behavior changes.

> *Once, I was coaching an executive at 3M on changing inappropriate leadership behavior—overreacting. He would overreact to something he heard from a customer that turned out to be untrue, and then he would have to go back and apologize to his direct report. His human resource manager observed this leader's*

behavior and apologies and said: "We will know George has truly changed when he no longer has to apologize." Sustainable change validates an apology.

Those adults who never heard an apology from their parents may find it difficult to apologize to their children. In some people, conscious or subconscious resistance may be due to never hearing "I'm sorry" from their parents. They never had a parent admit wrongdoing, so why should the adult child receive one? Parents can choose not to be constrained by the past. We can learn what *not to do* from the failures of our parents as well as what *to do* from their successes. I have not let the experience of my father failing to apologize to me constrain me from apologizing to my kids. Why not push through this resistance and break the generational pattern you know hurt you? Be sure to reach out to your kids even if your parents never apologized to you. Be the one who changes this generational pattern.

WHY APOLOGIZE IF I DON'T BELIEVE I DID ANYTHING WRONG?

I recently talked with my son and mentioned that I didn't believe in spanking and, as a psychologist, know the research on contraindications for this. But I did say the one time his older sister lied to me, I sent her to her room and told her to prepare for a spanking. I'm unsure if the actual spanking ever occurred, but the impact paled compared to waiting in her room for the chastisement. After I recounted this one-time use of corporal punishment and how this was inconsistent with my beliefs, my son said, "You spanked me once." I was shocked to hear this and asked him to tell me when. He could describe the specific setting and the fact that my mother was visiting. I immediately apologized to him and said that I regretted this action.

In this case, I did not doubt the accuracy of his memory even though I could not recall it. I then asked if there were other times when he may have experienced hurtful criticisms or actions on my part that still bothered him so I could apologize for them. I am embarrassed to admit this spanking and have no memory of the event, but sometimes, our recollections don't match our children's. A lack of memory is no excuse for failing to apologize.

Likewise, believing that what we did was not wrong but hurt our child does not excuse us from apologizing. Two fathers told me that what they did was for their son's good, but the sons did not receive it that way. Perceptions are an adult child's reality and interpretation of our actions. An apology in such situations acknowledges that my intention may have been honorable, but my actions were not perceived as such. We need to recognize when our actions are not helpful. "I'm sorry for what I did or said that was not helpful or hurtful" would be an appropriate apology. You're not apologizing for your intention but rather for the unintended impact of the actions.

Apologizing is the loving and right thing to do that will set us free as parents, free our young adults, and help restore the relationship. It's the loving thing to do because it says no matter what I did or didn't do or what I experienced as a child, I want to love you and take responsibility for my parenting. It's important to understand that listening and trying to understand your young adult's position and apologizing are not admissions that the other person's perception is entirely accurate. Saying I love you and am sorry does not mean you agree with your young adult's perceptions. Your memory may differ, but you are sorry that your actions were harmful.

Apologizing sends a message that love and the relationship
are more important than being right.

THE IMPACT OF AN APOLOGY

Apology Changes Us

If you apologize to your young adult, you will find a difference in your heart and actions, but you may not see a change in them. The critical question is not: "Have they changed?" The more important question is: "Have I changed?" Although saying "I'm sorry" is a gift to your child, it also represents a gift you give yourself. It's important to note that saying we're sorry is designed to address our shortcomings as parents and let go of the emotions that keep us bound in negative ways to our children. It's about positive change within ourselves and opening space for the love these kids need without the interference of emotions and memories that cause us pain.

We should act differently after apologizing since we won't have the burden of unaddressed issues and events of the past. When we have not said sorry, we are susceptible to defensiveness and reactivity that can color our words, body language, and tone. By failing to apologize, we risk freeing our young adults and ourselves from the past and jeopardizing our relationship in the future. One parent who saw a change in the behavior of their young adult daughter after writing a letter of apology wondered if it was the impact of the apology or the conscious effort of the parent to change their behavior. Likely, it was both.

Apology May Not Change Them
Several possible responses by your adult child may occur.

- Your young adult may excuse you or say there is no need to apologize. In such a case, indicate you need to say you're sorry even though they may not believe there is a need.
- The young adult accepts the apology.
- The young adult accepts the apology and offers forgiveness.
- The young adult receives your apology but does not acknowledge it.
- The young adult uses your disclosure of an offense you described to blackmail you. Since you did _____, you should now do _____.
- Your young adult uses your admission as a basis for excusing their behavior now or in the past.
- The young adult does not acknowledge your apology and refuses to communicate with you.

APOLOGY WHEN YOU ARE ESTRANGED FROM YOUR YOUNG ADULT

Estrangement or alienation, as discussed earlier, describes the cutoff relationship between parents and their young adult children. It is painful and widespread. The Council on Contemporary Families co-chair Joshua Coleman calls this breach in parent-young adult relations a "silent epidemic."[5] I would refer to Dr. Coleman's book as the authoritative work on this subject. Sometimes, something is done or said that is so offensive, hurtful, or rejecting that the young adult can't let go. The impact of such a parental offense is particularly true in situations of physical or sexual abuse. So, what can you do?

First, try to find the source of the rift between you and your adult child. Ask for help understanding what has led to the distance and what you can do to close this gap.

Second, once you have established the harmful action, take responsibility for the incident without the "buts" or qualifications described above. Third, if the above steps fail to lead to reconciliation or a better relationship, you may offer to bring in a third party to help understand you and your young adult. In this regard, you could ask your member of the clergy, a close friend of the family, or perhaps a family therapist. Fourth, start with recognizing that your adult child may not want to be associated with you; there is nothing you can do to change this. This continued estrangement can be doubly painful if there are grandchildren involved.

But no response or lack thereof should be an excuse to respond in kind by cutting them off. We may only be able to send cards or gifts on holidays and birthdays or infrequent texts or emails sharing something positive about our feelings and memories of them. We love our kids no matter what, and we must continue to take the high road of reaching out in love. We long to connect to our kids regardless of age or what may separate us. Assume your adult child is also suffering since they long for that same connection.

IS THERE A TIME WHEN PARENTS SHOULDN'T APOLOGIZE?

First, don't apologize if you are not ready just because you think you "should" or to make yourself feel better. If you don't feel remorse and some level of empathy, your apology will likely be insincere. In such cases, you should talk to your young adult and try to understand more about what they experienced and why it hurt them. You also should put yourself in their shoes and consider why an apology makes sense.

Second, do you always have to apologize for communications, decisions, or acts your young adult finds offensive? The short answer is no! Sometimes, we must make the tough call, set limits, establish constraints to ensure safety and say no. To illustrate my point, I'll give you an example of setting limits from my experience as a parent. My two daughters saw me as overprotective well into their late teens. When they lived at home, I restricted their driving or going with friends to nightclubs in downtown Minneapolis. We lived in a suburb of the Twin Cities, and there were regular reports of violent incidents in Minneapolis's entertainment district. I make no apologies for being overprotective. As a psychologist, I was aware of the statistics related to the sexual abuse of girls up to eighteen. Research conducted by the Centers for Disease Control (CDC) estimates that approximately one in four girls are sexually abused before age eighteen.

Third, be thoughtful about why you apologize and the impact. You should not apologize to get something off your chest. It should be kind and sincere and something that your child would likely see as an appropriate action on your part. The AA tradition step eight involves "making a list of all persons we have harmed and being willing to make amends to them." But step nine reads, "Make direct amends to those people, whenever possible, except when to do so would injure them or others." You can ask whether this apology and possible effort to make amends would be helpful or hurtful. For instance, if you had been abusive and made efforts to face it, but your child wants to move on and not hear about this, you need to respect this desire and not dredge up the specifics of this offense to feel better. A good rule of thumb is to err on the side of apology. The upside of apologizing to our kids is more significant than the downside and will help us be better parents and people.

> *Joe, a twenty-eight-year-old male, continued to harbor resentment toward his parents. He believed they did not support and help him enough when he experienced bullying during childhood. He shared this source of resentment with his parents, who each apologized to the son in person, and the mother wrote a heartfelt follow-up letter. This action paved the way for this son to let go of resentment and move out while still maintaining a caring relationship with his parents.*

THE QUALITIES WE NEED TO APOLOGIZE

First, it takes a **willingness to be vulnerable**. You put yourself out there without any assurance of a receptive response. Saying I'm sorry is humbling, particularly with our children. Second, it requires **honesty** to confess what we have done. Our children at any age can detect if we are not being honest and sincere or faking our confessions. Third, we must gain **the recognition that we all make mistakes**, not to excuse our behavior but to admit we are human. This belief humanizes us in the eyes of our young adults. We're also very tough on ourselves, so saying sorry is a way of letting go of excessive self-blame and guilt. Fourth, it takes **love and compassion**. Apologies require love because we want to secure our relationship with the young adult. In addition, understanding and empathizing with our young adults and their pain enables us to feel what they feel. There is healing for both parties in such a heart-to-heart connection. Fifth, it takes a **willingness to be first**. We can't wait for our young adults to offer us an apology for what they have done or for them to ask for an apology from us. We are the parents; we brought them into our lives, and we need to take risks, take the high road, model, and be first.

Be brave, be vulnerable, be first!

AN APOLOGY EXAMPLE

If you are convinced of the value of an apology to your young adult and want to let go of unhealthy attachments for your sake and theirs, you will need to decide how you want to do it. This decision may depend on your young adult's availability and receptivity and preferred style of communicating something so intimate. One way your young adult may not be available is that they have died. In such a case, I still believe there is value in saying sorry, maybe at the gravesite, to help you let go. The most effective way to communicate an apology is to meet with your son or daughter outside the home to share your apology with them, whether written or not. The following is a letter I wrote and shared with my young adult daughter in which I address some of the mistakes and failings during my parenting. My daughter received my admittance of remorse graciously, and although I did not expect or receive any absolution, it was the right thing to do. It reads:

> To my daughter,
>
> I wanted to reflect on my parenting of you as you were growing up and even now as you are forty-four years old. I have many fond memories of our relationship, particularly in the early years, especially when you were our first-born and only child. I was so proud of you and showed you off to my friends. You made funny faces and recited "Little Boy Blue" at age two. As the years passed and two other children arrived, our relationship changed, and my time and attention dispersed. I'm sorry I didn't do a good job staying connected to you during this time. You were a happy, expressive, bright young girl who deserved more attention. I was the one that dropped the ball on connecting with you, and I am sorry.
>
> In middle school, you spent more time with friends and focused on things outside the family. When you began to have trouble taking geometry and algebra in eighth grade, you began to doubt yourself even though we had affirmed your intelligence, as had all your teachers. Your experience had told you that you didn't have to study and could get straight A's. When you began to falter in this eighth-grade course, you

questioned your ability and resisted my encouragement that you could and should be doing better. My mistake is that I should have sat down with you and discussed the need to study and prepare as the answer, not a lack of ability. I always thought of you as bright and thought academics should come easy. I realize now how saying that put undue pressure on you to perform, and when you struggled, you doubted yourself. That doubt and loss of confidence are my fault and not yours. I should have picked up on this problem and been more engaged in helping you learn to prepare for school rather than communicating that you were so bright you could do well by just showing up. I'm sorry.

When you were worried about your mother and her health issues, I thought you could get through this on your own. I saw your anger at your mother and didn't pick up the underlying fear you had about her condition. I now recognize how upsetting and scary it was for you to see your mother struggling. Again, I failed to pick up on this, move closer to you, take you to breakfast, spend time with you, and be reassuring. I wasn't there for you emotionally when you needed me, and I am very sorry. It was my fault you did not have the attention and support you needed at that difficult time.

I can't go back and have a do-over, or I would do what was right and step up to meet your needs. If there are things I can do now or as we go forward as two adults to make up for these failures or be more sensitive and emotionally available to you, please let me know. I'm sure there are other things I did or did not do that you may still think about with some sadness or pain. Please know that I am open and receptive to hearing about these and won't blame you or defend myself. I will listen to what I could have done differently and take full responsibility for my failure. I have plenty more of "I'm sorry" available and want to be sure that I have owned and addressed all of these you need to hear.

APOLOGIZE

I love you dearly, have always loved you, and always will. I would appreciate it if you could forgive me for these things, I didn't do for you. That said, forgiveness is your choice, and I don't have to have this, particularly if it's hard for you to do now or in the future. But know that you're listening and acknowledging my desire to apologize for my failures as a father are enough.

Love, Dad

ARE YOU READY TO CRAFT YOUR APOLOGY?

Review the following components of an effective apology and consider including them in your communication. If you draft a written apology, go back and see if your communication contains these elements:

- A heartfelt appreciation and remorse for your actions impact on your young adult
- An expression of empathy and compassion
- A sincere statement of regret—the "I'm sorry"—for the impact of your actions on your young adult, whether intended or not
- An expression of responsibility without any qualifiers, explanations, or excuses—you take responsibility for your part no matter what your young adult said or did
- An offer of amends as appropriate and possible to repair the damage to the relationship

KEEPERS

What vital points, recommendations, and ideas will you take and apply from this chapter on understanding and relating? Why don't I start the list of keepers and have you finish the list with what you most got out of this chapter and want to remember, review, and apply? Please jot these down and use them as soon as you can. Application is the best way to stamp in learning. Here's my starter list. Highlight any you wish to keep and apply or add your own.

1. It is never too late to apologize to your young adult. Why wait?
2. An apology consists of a sincere statement of regret.
3. Apologizing is not for wimps! It takes courage, strength, and vulnerability.
4. Apologizing and admitting mistakes are ways I say and model that I care.
5. Apologizing as a parent sets us and our young adults free.
6. There are right and wrong ways to apologize.
7. _____
8. _____
9. _____
10. _____

CHAPTER FOUR

FORGIVE

*Resentment is a poison in our lives and those we love.
Forgiveness born of love is the antidote.*

—The author

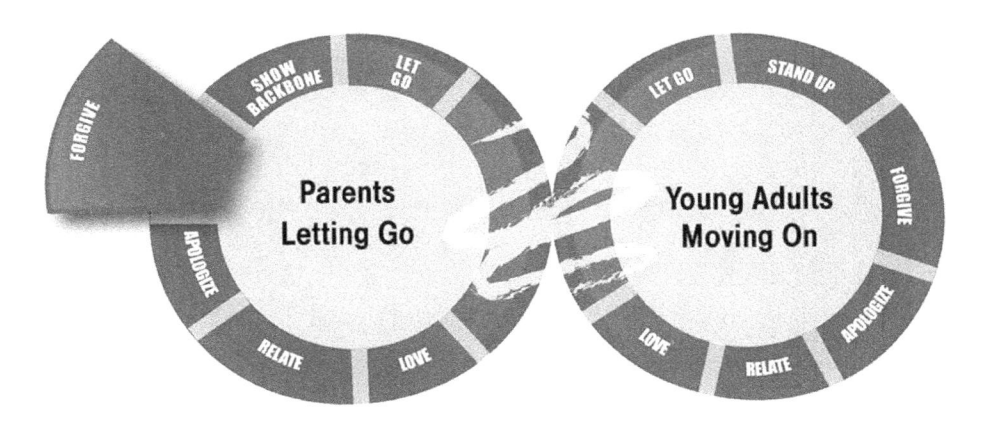

October 2, 2006, was a typical day in Nickel Mine, Pennsylvania. Children had said goodbye to their parents and made their way to the West Nickel Mines Amish School. Twenty-six children ages six through thirteen attended the school. Charles Carl Roberts IV, a milk truck driver with two children of his own, drove to the schoolhouse. After telling the adults and boys to leave, he tied up the

THE PARENT'S LAUNCH CODE

ten girls who were left. He then said he was angry with God and needed to punish some Christian girls to get even. He shot eight of the ten girls before taking his own life. Five of the ten young girls died, including one named Anna Stoltzfus. As I read the paper the following morning and saw Anna Stoltzfus's name, my hair stood on my neck. Anna was the name of my youngest daughter.

Like many others hearing about this incident, I was horrified and wondered how this could have happened. Not to mention, they were a group of young children of Amish heritage who eschew violence. But the story didn't end there. That afternoon, the grandfather of one of the girls expressed forgiveness toward the killer, Charles Roberts. Amish neighbors visited Roberts's widow and her children to comfort them the same day. At the funeral for Roberts, the Amish outnumbered the non-Amish. It's hard to imagine how the parents of these Amish children could show such forgiveness and compassion shortly after such a horrific tragedy.

There are two lessons from this incident. First, resentment is a cancerous poison that eats away at one's soul and can even lead to murder. Second, forgiveness fueled by compassion heals and is the only antidote to such resentment. Whatever the situation, forgiveness is a vital practice for healing to begin. Forgiveness is true for parents who need to open their hearts to their young adults, themselves, and, in some cases, others whose actions have been harmful. The healing code for launching includes apology and forgiveness, which enable parents to let go of negative emotions binding the parent negatively with the adult child.

The last chapter focused on apology, and I shared how guilt, shame, and regret for past actions can bind parents to their kids in unhealthy ways. The practice of apology is the healing antidote to this binding emotional state that frees our adult children and us from the control of past shortcomings and regrettable actions. Similarly, holding a grudge, holding onto rage or anger or bitterness, keeps us negatively bound to our kids and can cause us to act in ways that impede the letting go process. As apology frees the parent from guilt and regret, forgiveness frees the parent from resentment. In this chapter, we will explore the need for and importance of forgiveness in two areas of parenting. It's interesting that there is much more writing and research about forgiveness than apology. Parents need to forgive their adult children for past and current actions damaging the young adult, the parent, or the relationship. Such actions may involve your young adult not living up to their potential or acting out in ways that have left parents distressed and distraught.

> *In a counseling session, a mother reads her letter of apology for her anger and critical remarks toward her nineteen-year-old. She sobs as she reads her letter and wonders what happened to her bright young boy, an Eagle Scout, who is now facing multiple criminal charges. This young man's actions toward both parents, especially the mother, were abusive and inconsiderate. His refusal to not bring drugs into the house and to smoke pot at will in his room showed a callous disregard for his parent's wishes.*

Removal from the home, in this case, is, at best, a short-term solution. Neither the problem nor the anger, frustration, and resentment dissipate by physical distance. What can help is forgiveness. Forgiveness starts at home. We first need to apply the concept of forgiveness to ourselves, especially if we have guilt regarding our parenting and have formally apologized to our young adults. Whether we experience forgiveness from our adult children or not, we need to forgive ourselves and our belief that we are responsible for such actions. Before we can embrace the practice of forgiveness, we need to start with an understanding of forgiveness, followed by identifying faulty assumptions.

UNDERSTANDING FORGIVENESS

Before moving to the application of forgiveness as an essential practice to release resentment, let's spend some time defining this practice. Forgiveness *is the voluntary process by which someone undergoes a change of attitude (heart) regarding an offense and lets go of feelings such as resentment and vengefulness.* There are different aspects to a genuine act of forgiveness. They include the following:

- A change of heart or one's feelings toward the offender
- A decision or choice to forgive the offender
- An action or communication
- A change of behavior toward the offender

> **Other definitions of forgiveness by writers and researchers.**
>
> "Forgiving is an act of mercy toward an offender who does not necessarily deserve mercy. It is a gift to our offender for the purpose of changing the relationship between ourselves and those who have hurt us."[1]
>
> "Forgiveness is an exercise in compassion and is both a process and an attitude."[2]
>
> "It is a decision, an attitude, a process, and a way of life."[3]
>
> "Forgiveness is the gift we give ourselves." (Numerous authors have used this phrase, but I would add it is a shared gift we give our young adults as well.)
>
> "Forgiveness comes when we let go of the feeling of resentment by surrendering our vision of the self as victim."[4]

Within the context of our parenting role, forgiveness means demonstrating love and compassion by letting go of memories, thoughts, or feelings about ourselves or our children that bind us in unhealthy ways and cause us to suffer needlessly. We need to forgive ourselves and our children because "sorry" isn't enough.

WHAT FORGIVENESS IS NOT—FAULTY ASSUMPTIONS

- Accepting, excusing, or condoning the behavior of another.
- Justice. You may pursue justice, but forgiveness does not require justice.
- Reconciliation. This may happen but shouldn't be the primary source of motivation.
- Requiring the offender to admit or confess the offense.
- Only for the benefit of the offender.
- Dependent on a feeling.
- An action without a change of heart.
- Something you do for a person other than the offender.
- Something you do to forget the offense.

It is essential to neither expect nor require something from the offender since this can keep you in a victim position. Understand and approach forgiveness because it is the right thing to do and because it has many benefits.

When it comes to forgiveness, don't expect, don't require, and don't delay.

THE BENEFITS OF FORGIVENESS

Forgiveness is a gift we give ourselves. It allows us to move out of being victims of someone's actions. We are responsible for our feelings, thoughts, and actions. The extent to which we hold onto anger or resentment toward someone keeps us negatively attached to that person. We keep carrying them around in our heads like a bag of garbage. One study from the *Journal of Social Psychology and Personality Science*[5] supports my assertion. In it, Erasmus University students who practiced forgiveness were compared to those who did not. In contrast to those students who did not forgive, the first group experienced less slant on a hill they were asked to climb, and when required to jump, they could jump higher. The message is clear: forgiveness lightens one's load.

Several years ago, while sitting in church, I found myself ruminating about a service vendor who had cheated me and thinking of how I could get back at this person, possibly by suing him. As I struggled with this and said a short prayer asking for guidance, the thought of forgiveness came into my mind. I remember the immediate relief I felt as I embraced this option and experienced how my ruminating resentment seemed to melt away. One certainly doesn't have to be spiritual to apply forgiveness to someone we perceive as having wronged us. However, we know that every significant religion embraces the concept and practice of forgiveness. Christians will recognize the *admonition*—to forgive others to experience God's forgiveness. Forgiveness helps us to let go.

Holding on to the object or impact of an offense by another reinforces our anger and resentment. There was a time when we thought the best approach to anger was to vent. We were encouraged to punch a pillow or a punching bag. In contrast, Carol Tavris has shown through her research and writing featured in her book *Anger: The Misunderstood Emotion* that focusing on anger, or its source, increases one's attachment to that emotion.[6] The more we obsess about an offense, the more a feeling gets lodged in our brains. There is some evidence that people who cannot cease ruminating about an offense are more likely to commit acts of aggression against the perceived offender (McCullough et al. 1998).[7] By way of illustration, as I write this, I think of an incident involving a physician who returned to the hospital that fired him with an assault rifle. He started shooting, killing at least one person. His firing happened two years earlier, suggesting he had ruminated about being let go until he worked himself up and acted out violently. This tragedy underscores the point that the more we mentally revisit unresolved resentment, the more we reinforce this neural pathway in the brain. Similarly, trying not to think about an offense can also wire the thought into the brain. Try not to think about bananas. What just happened? A banana appeared in your imagination. Forgiveness overcomes the problem of ruminating, as well as trying not to think about an offense against you.

> *He who seeks revenge should remember to dig two graves.*
> —Confucius

> *When I worked in a youth service capacity in the early seventies, a young person came to my house in tears. He had just received news that his older and only brother had been killed in Vietnam. The report was heartbreaking to the family. The father quickly shifted his sadness to anger at the government's decision to go to war in Vietnam. He seethed with rage that his surviving son and family members began to avoid him. Within a year of his namesake son's death in Vietnam, this father, with no known health conditions, died of a massive heart attack. I sensed that his heart couldn't handle the rage and resentment he harbored and just gave out.*

Resentment is like drinking poison and then hoping it will kill your enemies.
—Nelson Mandela

Relationships are inherently reciprocal. The Golden Rule—*do unto others as you would have them do to you*—speaks to this tendency toward reciprocity. So, if we hope to have a better relationship, if not a reconciled one, we must start with forgiveness. There is evidence that the practice of forgiveness benefits other relationships. It is associated with more volunteerism, charity donations, and altruistic behaviors.[8] Forgiveness is good medicine. According to the Mayo Clinic and other sources, forgiveness yields better health.[9] Forgiveness leads to improved relationships, decreased anxiety and stress, lower blood pressure, lowered risk of depression, and a more robust immune response. Robert D. Enright and Everett Worthington have extensive research documenting the psychological benefits of forgiveness (see the bibliography for these writings). If the arguments for forgiveness are so widespread and clearly help us become better parents and people, why is it so hard to do so, especially with people we love?

BARRIERS TO FORGIVENESS

There are many impediments to forgiveness, or it would be more widespread. Confession, apology, and forgiveness are in short supply in politics and business. If we have a car accident, we are advised never to admit fault to the other driver. When companies are sued, they circle the wagons and build a defense without acknowledging any wrongdoing. We aren't inclined to apologize or forgive at a societal level. But at a personal level, what holds us back? The following are some reasons people resist forgiveness and suggestions to help counter them. Sometimes, we get caught up in anger and retribution. Revenge repels others. Sometimes, we think we have been unjustly treated, and the other person should apologize first. We remain a prisoner of our resentment if we wait for an apology.

Some may believe that forgiveness, like an apology, is a sign of weakness. Gandhi says, "Forgiveness is a sign of strength, not weakness." At times, we may hold back because we may believe that the person may view this as excusing or condoning their actions. Finally, parents may often hang onto guilt and thus not be able to forgive themselves. I worked with a mother who asked her daughter, a new driver, to drive to the store to pick up something with her younger sibling. They had an accident, and both died instantly. This mother continued to grieve and resist forgiving herself because she believed in doing so, she might forget her daughters. Forgiveness doesn't induce amnesia.

THREE PEOPLE WE MAY NEED TO FORGIVE

The need for forgiveness can arise in a relationship with three persons: us, our young adult children, and a third party. Because most of us are imperfect parents, there are opportunities to forgive ourselves. Our unresolved emotions may negatively affect our approach and interactions with young adult children. Sometimes, there is another person with whom we harbor resentment because we believe they have been abusive or neglectful. Such cases may involve your spouse, another child, an extended family member, someone known outside the family, or a stranger. We have become aware of child sexual abuse in the Catholic Church and Boy Scouts, but the perpetrator is often even closer to the family, such as a neighbor, relative, or friend.

Although forgiveness is a choice, it's challenging in such cases. Parents feel responsible, that they should have known and should have intervened. However, all forgiveness must start with us. How will we forgive our kids or a third party if we can't forgive ourselves as parents?

Knowing and owning one's feelings is the first step to change and heal. Identifying the need for forgiveness begins by paying attention to feelings we may have toward another and their actions. If you are unsure of your feelings that may require an act of forgiveness, please go to appendix A under chapter 4 to learn how to ask some questions that may help start a dialogue with your young adult about this subject.

START WITH SELF FORGIVENESS

The path to forgiving others, whether our young adult children or a third party, begins with our willingness to forgive ourselves. We start by acknowledging our flaws and our imperfect—or broken—world. Dr. David Schramm, a professor at the University of Utah, studied empty nesters and found that only 3 percent believed they were "excellent parents." [10] I'd like to meet that 3 percent! Maybe they represent that elusive perfect parent I have been trying to find. You're likely more honest if you don't see yourself in the 3 percent and you are in good company. According to Brené Brown, shame about our imperfections or failures holds us back from self-forgiveness and reaching out to others for support.[11]

In the previous chapter, we discussed the problem of imperfection in parenting and the need to address this issue through an apology. We can acknowledge and communicate our shortcomings and regrets to our young adults through apology, but this does not necessarily mean we have let go of the memories and emotions associated with our parenting. A further step for our healing and reducing the emotions attached to the past is forgiving ourselves. If for no other reason than a desire to be a healthy person, please consider forgiveness. We will experience the byproduct of such an action in the quality of our relationships with others.

> *Holding feelings such as anger and resentment is like holding onto a hot coal that you would like to throw at the offender.*
> —Buddhist saying

An Example of How Guilt and Lack of Forgiveness, Disabled a Young Man

> *I began working with a nineteen-year-old male's mother when I was a psychologist at Wilder Child Guidance Clinic in St. Paul, Minnesota. Her son was still in high school but attended infrequently, lived at home, and refused to get a job or move out. He had no learning or physical disabilities or mental health problems and enjoyed the good life, living off mom and dad with no real incentive to move out. The mother had two children, a son, and an older sister. The sister had left home shortly after high school and was doing well. The mother shared numerous attempts she had made to facilitate her son's launch, all to no avail. As we worked together, it became apparent that parental guilt was the culprit.*

When her son was a toddler, he fell down the stairs. Horrified, she believed she had caused irreparable brain damage. She rushed him to the emergency room, but there was no indication of a concussion or any injury to the brain. From then on, this mother's guilt caused her to treat her son as fragile and needed to be protected. When he didn't do well in school, she believed it was due to damage he had incurred from his fall. Excusing his irresponsible behavior due to her perceived neglect, she lost the ability to be firm and follow through on her expectations of him to move out. She had told me how she had apologized to her son for neglecting to prevent him from toddling down the cellar stairs. But apologizing wasn't enough to free her from the incapacitating guilt she felt as a parent.

The day arrived when this mother told her son he had to leave. As the son packed his bags and drove out of the driveway, the mother was tearful but remained firm. He didn't go far. For a while, he parked his car in his sister's driveway. Soon, he was encouraged to find another place to squat, and through some couch surfing at friends' houses, he finished high school and joined the military. Her inability to forgive herself for her son's fall delayed the launch process. She had to forgive herself and let go of the past to maintain firmness with her son. Only then could he move to responsible independence. We don't want to disable our kids by assuming they can't function or become independent adults because of past events or circumstances. This disabling can happen if we don't let go of the wounded emotions and memories of the past by apologizing to them and practicing self-forgiveness.

SELF-FORGIVENESS IS THE GIFT WE GIVE OURSELVES

In chapter 3, I outlined the kinds of behaviors that require apology. These behaviors that we regret require not only an apology but self-forgiveness. Is self-forgiveness really necessary? Just like an apology, forgiveness of self or others is always a choice. When we forgive others, we forgive the ones who have wounded us. When we forgive ourselves, we forgive the wounding of ourselves. Then, we are both the forgiver *and* the forgiven.

Here are some good reasons for self-forgiveness. First, it repairs a broken heart. We suffer from a self-inflicted wound of self-condemnation. It replaces self-hate with self-love and self-compassion. Second. It frees us from emotions that bind us in negative ways to our young adults. Our ability to be parents who are both loving and firm is compromised. We may jeopardize our ability to be firm with the expectations and limits we set. Third, it allows us to accept what we have done but not excuse it. We show compassion and mercy toward ourselves and model this behavior for our kids. We allow them to make mistakes, own up to them, and forgive themselves. Fourth, the practice of self-forgiveness opens the channel to self-awareness, self-disclosure, and ultimately to greater intimacy when we share this with others. Finally, forgiveness impacts our health and well-being. Although not a primary reason for this, letting go of guilt and forgiving oneself has numerous positive benefits. Forgiveness improves health, allowing us to heal depression, anxiety, anger, and stress. In short, it contributes to increased well-being and a better quality of life. For more on these benefits, see Robert Enright's *8 Keys to Forgiveness*.[12]

STEPS TO PARENTAL SELF-FORGIVENESS

The following section describes a process for self-forgiveness. I hesitated to describe this process in such a detailed way, but for some of you who are really suffering from the "guilty parent syndrome," these specific steps and questions can be helpful. If you have apologized and forgiven yourself, you may want to skim over this section. Sometimes, simply apologizing enables us to let go.

Step One: Face the Person in the Mirror

Self-forgiveness starts with facing the action that requires forgiveness. In this regard, ask yourself these questions:

- What specific action did I take that was hurtful or harmful?

- In what way was this action perceived as hurtful or damaging to my young adult?
- What are my feelings about this deed: hurt, sadness, remorse, Guilt, regret, shame?
- In what way have these feelings negatively affected my well-being?
- How have these feelings affected my relationship with my young adult?
- Have I apologized to the young adult for their actions that they believe hurtful?
- Have I apologized unconditionally and requested their forgiveness?

Step Two: Decide to Forgive Me

- I have made up my mind to forgive myself for my actions.
- I accept responsibility and communicate my responsibility for my actions.
- I am committing to letting go of self-blame, Guilt, and shame.
- I am apologizing to myself as a sign of self-compassion and self-acceptance.
- I am willing to pursue any appropriate and necessary amends.
- I have addressed and overcome the barriers listed in Step 1 above.

Step Three: Follow a Ritual of Self-Forgiveness

- Be sure you have apologized if it was an offense against your young adult and pursue amends that you and your young adult agree.
- Balance the actions you need to forgive yourself with a list and description of your positive qualities and virtues.* Avoid the dichotomy of believing you are either better than everyone else or the lowest of human beings. Take pride in the courage to be vulnerable and compassionate in pursuing forgiveness.

- Create a written or recorded message of forgiveness to yourself. It should be your specific actions, remorse and other feelings, willingness to be accountable, and desire to let go of self-blame, guilt, and shame. Expressing your apology to your young adult and you are also essential, as is your forgiveness.

Step Four: Live a Forgiving Life

- Refuse to return to ruminating about the event and your feelings. Realize it may take a while for your feelings of self-blame, Guilt, and shame to dissipate because they need to "catch up" to your actions of forgiveness and compassion. This lag is typical. Just don't go back and wallow in them. Focus on the forgiveness message.
- Identify what you learned from the experience, how you will avoid this same mistake, and how this may change your approach to life. Remember: the only real failures we face are failures to learn.
- Commit to living a life without resentment. Practice forgiveness at every opportunity, whether big or small. Refuse to maintain hurt, anger, or resentment toward others and yourself. As I've mentioned, Robert Enright's *8 Keys to Forgiveness* effectively communicates the importance of forgiveness. His section, "Developing the Heart of Forgiveness," is excellent.[12] Also, Joan Borysenko presents forgiveness as a lifestyle choice in her *Guilt Is the Teacher, Love Is the Lesson*. Another helpful book on this subject is by Fred Luskin, entitled *Forgive for Good: A Proven Prescription for Happiness*[13] (see recommended readings in the bibliography).

*If you are not a writer or desire some other approach or ritual to forgive and let go, consider reading *Radical Forgiveness* (chapters 25–30) by Colin Tipping. (See bibliography). Share your forgiveness message with a close friend or your young adult if they are supportive, understanding, and compassionate. Decide afterward what you want to do with the communication. You should preserve the forgiveness part and reread it occasionally if you slip back into self-blame. If you are finished with the self-blame and have indeed let go, you should shred or burn the communication.

FORGIVING OUR YOUNG ADULT

In chapter 4, we discussed how young adults' anger, hurt, and resentment toward parents keep them and the relationship negatively bound. We can say the same about a parent's hurt, anger, and resentment toward a young adult. In such cases, the relationship is tense and characterized by overreaction or withdrawal from the connection to avoid tension.

My father tended to find fault in my actions, even in college. When I returned from college on holiday, I remember saying I would not let him "get to me." I was determined not to react in anger. Shortly after arriving home, I raided the refrigerator with my arm on the door, and he said, "Stop leaning on the door." I reacted angrily, saying, "I'm not leaning on the door." Essentially, the unresolved hurt and resentment I was harboring toward my father surfaced quickly, and it seemed I was powerless to control it by conscious efforts to do so.

Similarly, if a parent is holding hurt, anger, resentment, guilt, or any other emotions identified in the earlier chart, that parent is at risk of overreacting or withdrawing. Such emotions keep the parent fused negatively to the young adult. Then the young adult, likely to react in kind, is bound to the parent. Under such circumstances, healthy emotional separation becomes difficult; the relationship continues to suffer, and other relationships are often negatively affected.

In this case, letting go of these feelings will free the young adult to move forward. Although, as discussed numerous times, we can't ensure or guarantee that our efforts to resolve our feelings will change our young adult's behavior, it's something we need to do. Remember: we must step up, be first, and take the high road.

Some Typical Actions of a Young Adult That Require Forgiveness

First, your young adult has undertaken a clear, specific act that has been destructive, offensive, or hurtful to you or others in which you had no part.

Substance abuse is something that fits into this category. Second, there was an act on your young adult's part that was destructive, offensive, or hurtful in which you played some role for which you are willing to accept and apologize. Third, your young adult has chosen not to have a relationship or any contact with you. It's an opportunity for forgiveness as well as apology.

WHEN NOT TO FORGIVE YOUR YOUNG ADULT

Not every offense requires forgiveness. If something happened accidentally or was of such limited impact or concern to you or your young adult, you don't need to forgive. You don't want to trivialize forgiveness. But if it is something you have tried to ignore and keeps surfacing in your thoughts or brought up by your young adult, this may be a sign you need to forgive.

There are other reasons that forgiveness may not be the right choice. First, you decide to forgive your young adult for not meeting some expectations you had of them, such as a particular career, choice of a mate, or retaining a particular religious orientation. Such forgiveness speaks more to your unresolved need to control. You brought them up to think independently, and you must accept they learned that lesson, especially when their thinking doesn't align with yours. This difference may be more of an opportunity for self-forgiveness.

Second, I have sat with several parents who have come to my office struggling with their son or daughter's announcement of their homosexuality. Earlier, I referenced a parent who indicated that her son disclosed that he was gay. She had to try to understand and accept this reality, as did the parents of the young college student who announced that she was nonbinary. Neither of these situations requires forgiveness, except the parents may need to let go and forgive themselves for their expectations of their young adult. As stated elsewhere, expectations are the root of all unhappiness.

Third, if you have an ulterior motive, such as hoping your son will change due to your acts of apology or forgiveness, it can backfire. Pursuing forgiveness as some quid pro quo doesn't work—I'll forgive you if you forgive me. Your motive will be seen as manipulative and could cause further damage to the relationship. You can hope for reconciliation, especially if the relationship is estranged, but it can't be the primary driver of your actions.

Fourth, you can't forgive with the hopes of forgetting the offense. Forgiveness isn't a shortcut to amnesia. One can hope there will be a reduction of the painful emotions attached to the event. Finally, if the young adult does not believe they have done anything wrong, you may need to forgive them, but sharing this with them may not be well received.

HOW TO FORGIVE OUR YOUNG ADULT

At a conference I attended several years ago, I met and talked with a woman from a company in Silicon Valley. I asked if she had a partner, and she said she didn't and felt no need for one. She said the love of her life was her two dogs, who gave her the love and affection she needed. She proposed a situation where I locked my dog and my wife in the car's trunk and, after an hour, opened the trunk. She asked me, "Who do you think would be happy to see you?"

Our furry, four-legged friends can teach us something about how to be unconditionally loving and forgiving. If you desire to forgive, there are steps to follow that help ensure you are doing it in the right spirit. Much research has been undertaken about forgiveness in the last twenty-five years. One model supported by research is the REACH model developed by Everett Worthington at Virginia Commonwealth University. The REACH model has been researched and tested with more than twenty-five randomized controlled trials in various settings.[14] I've applied this model to parental forgiveness, using points from other authors, researchers, and my experience to provide a simple, actionable process. I want to share that model with you now.

R = Recall the hurt. Enright calls this uncovering your anger. It is essential to face your anger and hurt, admitting that you have these feelings toward another person or their actions. Ask yourself if you have been obsessing about your young adult and their actions; you can't seem to shake these thoughts and emotions. There's a popular but credible belief that anger is a secondary emotion and that underlying the anger is hurt. This concept is particularly true in close relationships.

E = Empathize with the other. Empathy is the willingness to express compassion for the young adult. From Latin, it means *to suffer with, to feel* compassion and sympathy for another's misfortunes, along with a strong desire to alleviate the suffering. We need to see with eyes of compassion and understand that our young adult is struggling and hurting about the distance in our relationship. I ask the parent to return as far as possible to recapture positive images, memories, and emotions about their young adult. If, as you complete this step, you need help, look through old picture albums and focus on the feelings you experience as you see the pictures. Reconnect with the love you once had but may have lost due to the strain on your relationship.

Empathy is also the ability to put yourself in the shoes of your young adult. They may not be taking the same path you did as a young adult, but they are nevertheless working on their developmental tasks. Remembering when you were a young adult and your struggles with this life stage (including with parents) can help you identify and connect to your young adult's emotions. When our kids are inappropriate, offensive, or abusive, it doesn't mean they don't care or don't feel bad about their actions.

When I directed a drug treatment center for adolescent substance abusers facing juvenile justice sentences, I had them write letters to their parents as if they would never see them again. I anticipated letters that would blame and indict the parents for how they were abused or neglected. Instead, one after another described feelings of regret for how they treated their parents, indicating they were sorry and asking for forgiveness. I would argue that these fifteen-to-nineteen-year-old kids are no different from other young adults. They suffer if alienated from their parents and, at some level, realize they need forgiveness. Just because they don't show this sentiment doesn't mean it doesn't exist.

A = Altruistic gifts of forgiveness must be offered without condition. Forgiveness is one of the most valuable gifts we can give to ourselves and others. Can you recollect when you were forgiven by someone, perhaps your parents, for something you had done, and the parent never brought up the offense again? The forgiver doesn't necessarily forget but needs to commit not to revisit the offense. There must be a letting go. If we slip and bring up the offense, we must apologize, or forgiveness will be a hollow act.

C = Commit to forgiveness. Once you have let go of the anger, connected to your empathy, and understand that forgiveness is a gift we all deserve, you are ready to forgive. An important question to ask yourself is if the forgiveness would be meaningful and received as a gift by your young adult. Ask yourself, "Have I earned the right to forgive them by acknowledging and apologizing for actions I have taken over the years that have been hurtful?" If you are unwilling to acknowledge your need for forgiveness and apologize for ways you have failed as a parent, it may be a stretch to think that your young adult would welcome your forgiveness.

If your young adult is not speaking with you and is unwilling to accept any communication, the message cannot get through to them. Likewise, if they have died, you cannot physically communicate with them, but expressing your thoughts and feelings may still be important to help you let go. Since forgiveness is recognized primarily as a gift to oneself, you should not hold back from forgiving. Sometimes, you cannot share the gift of forgiveness with your young adult. Unlike the anger ritual described previously, where you shred the anger and hurt you have been harboring, in this case, write a letter or record your forgiveness message and hang on to it. You can read it occasionally to reconnect to empathy and compassion and to the experience of letting go of the past. If your adult child has died and you have unresolved anger toward them, write out a letter of forgiveness, read it at their grave, and let go of your anger.

Suppose a young adult is willing to admit to creating problems for you in the past or present and may have even apologized for that behavior. In that case, you can forgive and open a path toward reconciliation. Such a reconciliation doesn't have to be a formal process. It could arise out of a heartfelt conversation with them. You apologize for specific mistakes you have made and invite the opportunity for them to step up and acknowledge some of their own. After this happens—I believe these conversations frequently occur as young adults move toward mature independence—it can be a meaningful time of peace-making. I recommend that a parent undertake a more formal apology and forgiveness exercise through formal verbal or written communication. One caution is getting your hopes up for a positive reception; we need to do these things without expectations of "payoffs" by the young adult. The primary yield is the gift you give yourself. Nothing can diminish that fact.

H = Hold onto forgiveness. Sustaining a commitment to forgiving is critical. It is essential to have a strategy for blocking or challenging your past mindset to take you back to resentment, anger, and revenge. I recommend a ritual of purging yourself of the anger and hurt caused by an offense that your young adult committed. In an earlier publication on depression, *Illumination: Shedding Light on Depression*, I described that feelings are like the caboose of a train. They are the last to come across the track after thoughts and behavior change.[15] You may work hard to change how you think and act and still feel the pain of hurt or betrayal. Feelings take a while to catch up to your thinking and actions. Give it time. If the feelings come back, review your actions of purging and shredding the anger, retrace your steps of forgiveness, and tell yourself you are not returning to a state of resentment.

Commit to refusing to be a bearer of resentment. It's a poison that eats at one's psyche, damages the soul, and undermines well-being. Several years ago, I committed to living a life without resentment. I have done my best to follow a protocol of letting go of anger, apologizing for my part in a problem, and forgiving others, even if I believe I am justified in my anger. Too many families have members who hold resentment and refuse to attend or invite family members to their celebrations. Life is too short, and we don't want to waste time by being mad, indignant, and self-righteous at the expense of a significant relationship. I'm amazed at how many couples I see for whom the need to be right is more important than sustaining the relationship. As parents, we must step up, be the bigger person, forgive the young adult, and re-engage that person in the family.

HOW TO COMMUNICATE FORGIVENESS TO YOUR YOUNG ADULT

The following specific guidelines are critical once you want to express your desire to forgive. You can apply these measures whether you speak directly with your young adult. The communication can be in letters, voicemails, recordings, or in person if the young adult is available. Remember: this is a gift you give both to them and yourself.

APPROACH THE COMMUNICATION WITHOUT BLAME OR CRITICISM

1. Connect to your love for them and their good qualities.
2. Connect to the compassion you have for their failing or struggle.
3. Tell them the specific actions that have upset you without blaming them. Don't say, "You made me so mad" or "You hurt me so much," but instead, "I was hurt and angry when ..." You own your feelings.
4. Explain that holding on to this hurt and anger damages you, them, and the relationship, and you want to let go of this memory and its accompanying feelings.
5. Offer your forgiveness because you want to and believe it is the right thing to do.
6. Indicate that you will let go of the past and start a new chapter in your relationship with them.
7. Offer forgiveness without conditions, explanations, buts, and so on.
8. Offer your forgiveness freely without expecting the young adult to respond in any way or that your actions will bring about some reconciliation or restoration of the relationship.

An Example of Forgiveness Communication

A twenty-three-year-old young adult was struggling with a tragic addiction problem. He was an outstanding, sensitive, and considerate individual when he was sober. He would start a job and be reliable in showing up and performing the work, usually at a restaurant, but when he got his first paycheck, he would buy several bottles of vodka and go on a two- to three-day binge. Usually, he would take the bottles to his room in the basement of his parent's house and drink until he passed out. When he did not show up for work, he would be fired. This pattern occurred repeatedly. The previous summer, the parents had kicked him out of the house. He then lived in different places, including sleeping in a park. Should the parent kick this twenty-four-year-old out of the house?

When I met with the parents, the temperature outside was well below freezing, and such a strict, so-called tough love approach of booting him out again would likely have led to the son's freezing to death. He had been through treatment twice without success. Each time, he promised to stay sober and dutifully go back to AA meetings. In my meetings with the parents, we discussed ways they could continue loving and supporting their son while holding him accountable, but the pattern continued. The parents were distraught and felt helpless. They were filled with many emotions: fear, hurt, anger, resentment, frustration, and helplessness. The following is a letter I envisioned these parents could have composed for their son. It is important to note that sending or reading it to him while drunk would not be helpful to either the parents or the young adult. Most importantly, the message must be that we love you, forgive you, and won't give up on you.

Dear Son,

We love you very much and constantly worry about your health and well-being. It's tough for us to watch this pattern of binge drinking followed by a short period of sobriety and a new job, but then after the first paycheck watch, you go into a three-day drinking binge and lose this job. We have supported treatment for you that you have pursued without success. Whenever you sober up, you are very apologetic and contrite and promise this time to stay straight. We get our hopes up, as I suspect you do, thinking this is when you really will stay straight. But then the cycle repeats. We know you feel guilty about not following through on your commitment to sobriety.

THE PARENT'S LAUNCH CODE

We believe you are responsible for battling this addiction and finding a way to sustain your sobriety. We can see how overpowering this addiction is for you, and we appreciate your efforts to quit and try to stay straight. We know it's a difficult time in your life when friends are all moving on in their lives with jobs and families. We know you are being left behind or held back by your addiction. We want you to know that we forgive you for failing to stay sober and failing to succeed after your treatments. We also forgive you for times you have stolen from us or taken the money we gave you for a legitimate purpose and spent it on alcohol. Your dishonesty has been hard on us, but we love you dearly, and nothing you can do, or any failure will ever stop us from loving you. We will continue to forgive and search for ways to work with you and community professionals to develop a sustainable path to sobriety. We will do whatever it takes to help you in this regard and never give up on you. Please keep trying, and don't give up on yourself. We will never give up on you. We know that one of these days, through AA, treatment programs, and your despair, you will find the courage to make the "one day at a time" commitment to sobriety. We will be there when that day comes and cheer you on to get your life back on track to pursue school, career, family, or other goals we know you have.

Love,
Mom and Dad

Hopefully, most of you are not facing this type of situation. However, many parents can identify with these parents' emotions—fear, anger, hurt, resentment, frustration, and helplessness. You may ask: "If I do this, will it fix the problem and change the young adult?" I must remind you to go back to one of the core assumptions at the beginning of this book: we cannot control (or fix) our young adults. They are responsible for their actions, decisions, and consequences. Instead, we want to say that we love them, apologize for our failures, and forgive them. These actions are under our control and will bring peace in knowing we have shown love and forgiveness and, ultimately, did what was right.

TO SEND OR SHRED?

If you have followed the guidelines and crafted a letter of forgiveness, you should feel relief and a release from the anger, hurt, and resentment you have harbored. There is some value in giving your young adult a handwritten letter because it's more personal, but of course, they need to be able to read it! The next step is to determine what to do with the letter. Suppose your young adult has admitted to specific actions you wish to forgive and is contrite, maybe even apologetic. In that case, communicating this forgiveness is vital for both of you and can become a shared gift. Ask your young adult to meet somewhere neutral outside the home over coffee or a meal. Indicate you have been struggling with resentment because of their behavior and want to let go of these feelings. Tell them the goal of this letter and that sharing it with them is threefold.

First, you want to let go of any hurt, anger, or resentment toward your young adult that you realize has been unhealthy and damaging. Second, you want to be free from any guilt or shame you may have related to any actions that have been hurtful or destructive to you or the relationship. Third, you want to let go of the past and establish a better relationship with them. Read your letter to your young adult and give it to them if they want to reread it later. Indicate that you promise to let go of your memories of the actions that have been destructive and will do your very best not to bring these up in the future. Also, indicate you are open to being reminded of this promise should you slip. Invite them to accept your forgiveness.

You may be in a situation where you have carefully crafted a letter you would like to read to your young adult, but they don't believe they have done anything deserving of forgiveness. In that case, it is unlikely that your thoughts on the matter would be well received. If the relationship is contentious, you could trigger defensiveness and add to the tension. You can't share a gift that is not wanted, but it remains a gift to you. It doesn't mean your forgiveness effort is in vain, or you shouldn't proceed with expressing its content. What can you do with the letter? Consider sharing it with your spouse or a close friend. You would still be releasing your anger, hurt, and resentment and setting yourself free from these emotions' hold on you. In addition, it will change the way you relate to your young adult. You have softened your heart and forgiven regardless of its acceptance or lack thereof. In subsequent interactions with your young adult, you will be less likely to overreact or respond inappropriately because of harboring bitterness toward them. I recommend hanging on to the letter and rereading it occasionally. At some point, when you have truly let go of these feelings and thoughts, you may want to shred or burn the letter to celebrate that you have finally let go. In either case, you should begin to experience the benefits of forgiveness.

The value of forgiveness is not diminished by your young adult's receptivity or lack thereof.

HOW DO I KNOW I HAVE FORGIVEN MY YOUNG ADULT?

You will know that you have forgiven your young adult if you have expressed forgiveness without qualifications or expectations. In addition, you will remember the offense without accompanying feelings of hurt, anger, or resentment. Finally, you will feel a burden lifted, and your relationship with your young adult will change.

FORGIVENESS OF A THIRD PARTY

There are circumstances where a third party has had a damaging impact on your child. These include but are not limited to actions of your spouse, an ex-spouse, neighbors, strangers, friends of your young adult, pedophiles, teachers, or other authority figures. In Minnesota, there was the kidnapping and murder of an eleven-year-old boy named Jacob Wetterling in 1989. This case remained unsolved for nearly twenty-seven years until the murderer was captured and confessed. Undoubtedly, some good came from Patty Wetterling and her husband's tireless efforts to publicize their son's abduction and try to prevent the kidnapping of other children. Yet the final chapter of the murderer's confession and the discovery of Jacob's remains had to be heart-wrenching for them. So, how does one move to forgiveness in a horrible situation like this one?

In such cases, I don't claim to have all the answers or know if or how one could be forgiving. Forgiveness remains a choice. In these situations, our biggest challenge is overcoming the belief that we were neglectful and didn't protect our children. Although this is rarely the case, as parents, we have this hardwired belief that we are responsible for safeguarding our children's wellbeing no matter what. We must admit that bad things can happen even though we do our best to protect our children. We could add this to the list of assumptions stated at the outset of this book.

I recently read Sue Klebold's book *A Mother's Reckoning*. She is the mother of Dylan Klebold, one of the two mass murderers who killed students and one teacher at Columbine High School. She and her husband raised Dylan in a loving home with good values, but something went wrong. Dylan's secret planning of an assault on the high school, murdering other children, and taking his own life meant she had to do a lot of forgiving. Sue and her husband realized after the fact that there were clues to Dylan's depression, but he did a good job of covering them up. There was also evidence that his co-conspirator significantly influenced Dylan's participation in the shooting. Sue held Dylan responsible for his acts, but something broke down, and in the end, she concluded, "the hardest truth for a parent to bear, but it is one that no person on earth knows better than I do, and it is this: love is not enough."[16]

Many loving parents are burying their young adults due to an opioid overdose and wonder what went wrong and if they could have done something to prevent this. Admitting the powerlessness that we feel as parents can be difficult. *We all assume that everything will be well if we love enough and do the right things as parents.* However, doing so denies the truth that adolescents and young adults can act independently of us and our wishes. Ultimately, they alone are responsible for their behavior; sometimes, we can't protect them from themselves.

Obviously, Patty Wetterling's and Sue Klebold's circumstances were radically different, but both lost a child. Other instances exist when third parties do something hurtful and harm a child physically or emotionally. They could include a spouse being overly harsh in discipline or abusing a child physically or sexually. Though you may not have been complicit or even aware of the abuse, you may suffer tremendous guilt.

Arguments for the importance of forgiveness still apply to these types of cases. Forgiveness is always a choice and may be the only way to let go of such experiences.

We can't take responsibility for the actions of a third party who hurt our son or daughter, but we can apologize for failing to protect the child and pursue a path of forgiveness of the abuser. If, as a parent, you did not intervene when your spouse was abusive to your child, you need to find a way to apologize to your child and forgive yourself, whether you have stayed with this spouse or not. The emotions of guilt and shame you've absorbed for your lack of action and the anger toward the spouse poison your family relationships. You may need to apologize for not protecting your child. Here are some steps to follow:

1. **Recall and recognize the events and actions** that have damaged your child or young adult. At this stage, through writing or talking it out, you want to get out all the specifics—your thoughts and feelings—in an unedited fashion. This dump or vent stage is essential.
2. **Identify if there was any part you had in enabling or fostering the situation** that led to the offense by the third party. Be graceful and tolerant of what you did or didn't do and ask if you think other parents would have done the same. If you believe that you had some collateral or indirect responsibility for the actions of the third party, you may need to apologize. Be specific. Don't take on the blame for how the other party acted. You are not responsible for their behavior. When apologizing to your child, follow the guidelines in the apology chapter. If you continue to blame yourself for not being there and protecting your young adult, you may need to work through the section on self-forgiveness.
3. **Holding the third party accountable and forgiving them are not mutually exclusive.** It's important to address what happened, whether you had or didn't have a part. If there is a legal action, this is something that you should consider even if you decide to pursue forgiveness. Whether you pursue legal action or not, it may be time to let go of the thoughts and feelings related to the event. If the third party

is contrite and you wish to forgive them, then you should do this. But in the case where the third party isn't contrite or available, continue to write out a letter of forgiveness, but consider **a process of shredding or burning your writings about the event**. As you carry this out and say goodbye to these thoughts, promise not to try to "dig up the ashes" or "put the shreds together" and replay the event.

4. **Seek professional help to obtain further support and guidance on how to let go.** Parents who have experienced some traumatic event involving their children, whether at the hands of a third party or because of their actions, can suffer from post-traumatic stress syndrome. The result is ongoing emotional difficulties such as depression and anxiety. Professional help is an appropriate resource.

Although more is available on forgiveness through the writers referenced above, this chapter provides a primer for parents. I hope you recognize some of the challenges in your life but also embrace the opportunity to practice forgiveness. Most of us parents need to revisit the subject of forgiveness occasionally to be sure we have let go of the past and have become free to embrace the future with our young adults. Resentment is a poison to the psyche and a source of destruction to our relationships. Left unattended, it increases in intensity and is destructive to self and others. Whether the hurt, anger, or resentment is justified, forgiveness remains the one gift we can always choose for ourselves and our kids.

KEEPERS

At the end of these chapters, I have identified some "keepers" for consideration. Highlight any that I have suggested below or add your keepers. Decide on a plan to apply one or more of these keepers and share these with your spouse or close friend.

THE PARENT'S LAUNCH CODE

1. Forgiveness and apology are the two practices that can heal a broken parent-young adult relationship.
2. Forgiveness assumes our young adults are responsible for their actions and decisions but deserve forgiveness.
3. If you harbor anger, hurt, resentment, regret, guilt, blame, and a sense of failure toward your young adult, apology and forgiveness are the answers.
4. Forgiveness is a choice that requires a change of mind, heart, and behavior toward the young adult.
5. Forgiveness sets the forgiver free from being a victim, leading to many positive health and relational benefits.
6. Self-forgiveness for parents who suffer guilt from their actions or responsibility for their young adults is often the most challenging but most important practice to embrace.
7. _____
8. _____
9. _____
10. _____

CHAPTER FIVE

SHOW BACKBONE

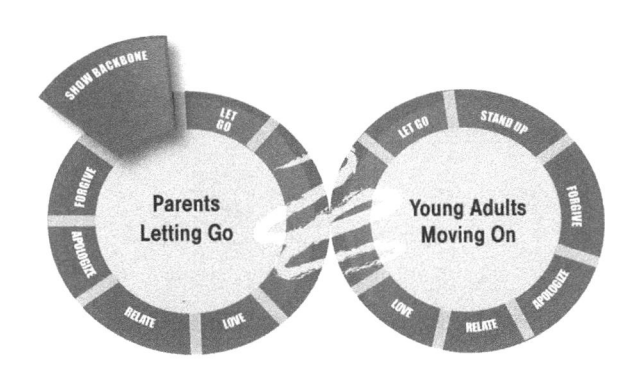

*If we always excuse and prop up our young adults,
How will they ever stand on their own?*

WHAT WOULD YOU DO?

Rhonda and Paul are parents of a twenty-year-old son, Adam, who started his first year at a school in another state, did poorly in the first semester, and was put on academic probation. He decided to withdraw early in the second semester and return home. Adam never explained what happened, but isolation and remote classes from his dorm room during COVID likely played a role. When he returned home, he became isolated and depressed. Efforts to encourage him to take a course at a local community college or get a job fell on deaf ears. He went to therapy at his parent's encouragement but dropped out after three sessions without telling his parents. They worried that pressuring him too much to get help, a job, or a return to school might make his depression worse. He refused to go to therapy, get a job, or take classes at a community school. This scenario, described later in chapter seven, describes a "Stalled" failure to launch, which is not uncommon, and parents struggle to balance nurturance (love) with firm expectations (backbone).

You may have concerns about your young adult, like in the situation described above, and want me to cut to the chase and tell you what you should do. You are mistaken if you think that just getting tough is the silver bullet to launch a young adult. In this chapter, I will offer principles and approaches needed to exert love and backbone in the launch process. The next chapter will dive into specific situations and applications of love and backbone. But before this, check to see if you have laid the groundwork for exerting a backbone.

Rate the extent to which you have completed or made progress on the four codes of practice below.

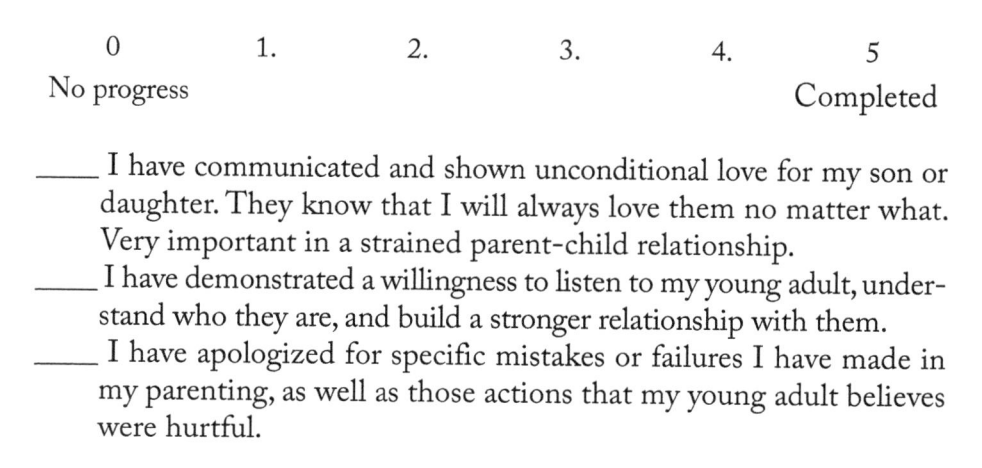

0	1.	2.	3.	4.	5
No progress					Completed

____ I have communicated and shown unconditional love for my son or daughter. They know that I will always love them no matter what. Very important in a strained parent-child relationship.

____ I have demonstrated a willingness to listen to my young adult, understand who they are, and build a stronger relationship with them.

____ I have apologized for specific mistakes or failures I have made in my parenting, as well as those actions that my young adult believes were hurtful.

____ I have forgiven myself for my mistakes and failures, and I have forgiven my young adult for actions that have been hurtful to me.

How did you do? If you didn't score at least a 4 or 5, you should return for a refresher to that code or practice and take further action. Understanding is not enough. Execution and the extent to which your young adult believes you have carried these out are the keys.

WHAT IS PARENTAL BACKBONE?

Another word for backbone is integrity. *Integrity is the clear and demonstrated principles, values, and ethics that govern life and relationships.* I will use backbone and integrity interchangeably and supportive integrity as the combination of love and backbone. Parents must display honesty, fairness, clear and strong moral and ethical qualities, words, and actions that match principles. We must take a stand on principles and prepare to face the consequences. Ethicist Michael Josephson, in his various writings, describes integrity as having the courage to maintain consistency between what we believe, say, and do and what we are morally obligated to do.[1]

Parents' commitment to consistently applying their values and principles is essential to teaching young or old children how to approach life and relationships effectively. We can't expect the schools, churches, or courts to take on this parental role. It's our job and doesn't end at eighteen or twenty-one. We may be unable to impose values on young adults, but we should not back away from modeling and communicating these. We need to be sure we "walk the talk." We can only expect our young adults to follow our values if we are consistent in our words and actions. If a parent is abusing alcohol, for example, criticizing a young adult for smoking pot may be viewed as hypocritical.

I have worked with families where the adolescent is out of control, and their illegal actions result in the courts taking over. If we can teach cause and effect and consequences for actions during childhood, young adults are less likely to experience this kind of correction from the justice system. That said, I have worked with very loving and firm parents whose young adults have chosen a path of self-destruction. In such cases, we must remind ourselves of two assumptions: We can't control our young adults and aren't responsible for their actions.

Young adults need a solid foundation to define and differentiate themselves. Imagine you are trying to launch your young adult out of a vat of Jell-O created by your inappropriate disabling and caretaking. How can they push off and get out of the Jell-O? If we continue to cover for them, excuse them, and cave in when they are demanding or inappropriate, how will they ever stand on their own? To help you fully grasp this point, imagine the following situation. What if you were to lean back and your young adult leaned on you to hold them up? If you stepped away, they would fall. That's not a loving action. However, many parents disable young adults by propping them up. Why would the young person move from their comfortable leaning post? What would force them to stand on their own? The answer? If we stood up straight. Here are a couple of examples from my practice of parents having difficulty with a backbone:

> *A mother and father of a thirty-two-year-old had his apartment but continued to "squat" at the parents' house most nights of the week. The parents wanted him to stay at his apartment. The son complained that his parents bugged him about going back to finish his degree all the time. Still, he couldn't remedy the situation and stop their comments because he needed access to their WIFI while waiting for this at his apartment. He had almost a full-time job and could afford all of these expenses, but the parents and the son couldn't seem to initiate the launch. We agreed to a date after which he will not be continuously staying at the parents' home. Two weeks later, we met to see how it was going. Though he was staying at his apartment, the parents continued to call him to check in and bug him about school. Also, his mom stopped from work to peek in the apartment window to see if he was there. Whose problem was this failure to launch?*

> *Parents of a twenty-seven-year-old who worked and lived in an expensive West Coast city asked for help in weaning him off their subsidy. For several years, they had been paying his rent and other expenses. The parents told him he needed to take over his expenses.*

Although he agreed, nothing changed. Why should he do anything if the check keeps coming from the parents? He spent money on gas for his commute and a costly apartment and ate out frequently. We devised a plan to "wean" him off the subsidy.

These young men needed to become self-sufficient. When parents, albeit well-intended, continue to surveil as in the first instance or underwrite their young adult's expenses as in the second, they disable the young adult. It can be uncomfortable to back off and let go. It may be scary to cut off the ATM because you don't know if they can make it, but how will you ever know unless you exert your backbone in love?

Incidentally, love is not the opposite of backbone. I am using love to describe the soft or nurturing side of parenting. Showing backbone may be the most loving action a parent can take. Showing love in a nurturing way is not the opposite of showing backbone. They are not mutually exclusive. In fact, my argument is that effective parenting at any stage involves demonstrating nurturance and backbone. It's imperative at the launch stage of the family life cycle.

PRINCIPLES FOR DEMONSTRATING BACKBONE

THE PRINCIPLE OF THE RIGHT MINDSET

As discussed in chapter 1, consider the following assumptions when approaching your young adult to facilitate the launch process. We cannot control our young adults and are not responsible for their decisions, actions, and feelings. We will not use the past as an excuse for our or their actions. We can only be accountable for our choices, actions, and emotions; we believe that change starts with us. Furthermore, we must balance love (support) and emancipation (letting go).

THE THREE QUESTIONS TO ASK

Our love for our kids is our most powerful leverage or influence. We need to ask ourselves three questions to determine if we are making the right decision or taking the right action.

1. **Are we acting out of love and not fear, anxiety, frustration, guilt, and the like?** We need to approach our young adults through our hearts.
2. **Are our actions aligned with our values and principles?** If we believe in honesty, dependability, self-sufficiency, responsibility, and persistence, are we exhibiting these in our words and deeds?
3. **Will our communications, decisions, and actions support their independence and self-sufficiency or contribute to greater dependence?** *Are we helping or holding them back?*

Beyond adhering to these three guidelines, it is essential to acknowledge and elevate actions that show our kids are moving toward responsible independence. Most parents with whom I work spend their time and emotional energy focused on a current problem or why the young adult isn't moving forward. This behavior results in much criticism, efforts to persuade the young adult to do something, and contentious interactions. At a minimum, we need to balance negative feedback with observations of what they are doing right, admirable qualities they have, and encouragement and praise for efforts toward responsible independence. There's a common belief that we should give at least three positive comments to every negative one. Ask yourself how you are doing on this ratio. But it's not just about the ratio; it's about reinforcing indications of responsible independence. Young adults are naturally inclined to move in this direction, and we need to find a way to align our comments and actions to reinforce this. In chapter seven, we will discuss a specific strategy for joining and partnering with your young adult's efforts toward independence and self-sufficiency.

TOUGH LOVE

A school of thought supports a "tough love" approach by parents to their adolescents and young adults. What does this mean, and how did this way of thinking start? The idea of tough love comes from a book written by a colleague of mine when I was doing youth work in an organization called Young Life. The book is *Tough Love,* and it was written by Bill Milliken in 1968.[2] The book describes his experience as a youth worker in the tough Lower East Side of Manhattan in the late sixties. This concept, as developed by Milliken, has a spiritual origin. He attributes his ability to combine love with toughness to his faith in a loving God. Essentially, Bill learned that you need to love, in this case, gang members, despite their behavior, and confront them when they make poor decisions and take wrong actions.

Over time, tough love has become associated with the addiction movement and the actions people must take to prevent or intervene in drug usage situations. Tough love is the opposite of enabling, another term used in the addiction field. Resisting enabling behavior is tough love in action. Holding a young adult accountable for moving toward independence in an encouraging and supportive way is tough love in action. Maintaining a loving connection with your young adult is crucial even though you may tell them they can't live at home or refuse to give them more money. Why? Because we as parents are wired to love our children and never lose that desire, even though it may get buried under hurt and anger. The anger often masks the more profound emotion of rejection or hurt on the part of both parents and kids.

Our young adults need to know that, no matter what, they are loved. There has been considerable research on tough love approaches to treating addicts, and there is evidence that harsh treatment within such programs for teens can be detrimental. These programs often exhibited a harshness to their approach, which was not grounded in love. The matrix below illustrates these two dimensions of tough love—holding a young adult responsible and loving the young adult. Appropriate parental tough love is the sweet spot of integrity and unconditional love. The goal is to be in the upper right quadrant, demonstrating high integrity and love.

TRUE TOUGH LOVE

Harsh Rigidity	**Tough Love**
Uninvolved	**Disabling**

INTEGRITY (vertical axis)

UNCONDITIONAL LOVE

Our kids need to know that the door of our heart is always open to them, even though the door to our house may not be.

PERSONAL QUALITIES ESSENTIAL TO SHOW BACKBONE

Show fortitude. It is courage in the face of pain or adversity. Being a parent is challenging. We don't get an operating manual when we have children. And being a parent isn't a popularity contest. Although these statements may sound trite, we can't sacrifice our integrity to ensure our children like us. We must sometimes make the hard decisions that involve saying no, expressing disapproval, or standing behind consequences that we or others have set. You owe it to your young adult not to be a wimp or a doormat. Be someone they know has a bottom line, a limit, and clear values that are solid and unmovable. Again, remember the foundational assumptions: You are not responsible for their actions—you are responsible for yours. Also, taking a stand is something parents must do, and children expect it.

SHOW BACKBONE

We need to show backbone! Say what we mean and mean (and do) what we say.

Model values and principles. Young adults are quick to spot inconsistency and will call parents on it. It's important to ask yourself: How consistent am I with my young adult, the young adult's siblings, or people outside the family? Honesty is foundational to any relationship. It is as important as love. Without honesty, there is no trust, and love won't survive. Saying one thing and then doing another or the opposite is dishonest and leads your kid not to trust your word. Swearing in front of our kids but requiring them to refrain from the same seems inconsistent to me, even though I know some parents excuse it as adult talk.

> *One mom I worked with tried to get her twenty-one-year-old son to step up and become more responsible. She said he had to pay for his food to live at home. In a subsequent call, she told me she had gone to the grocery store with him and paid for his food since she knew he was getting low on money. This inconsistency in word and action says Mom won't hold her ground. Most likely, he wouldn't starve, and she took away his chance to learn that he needed to get a job if he wanted to eat. Our young adults need to realize they are unconditionally loved by us but not by the world.*

There is no free lunch in life.

Be transparent. Allow your young adults to see that you don't have all the answers and that you are trying to figure out how to be a parent of a young adult as much as they are trying to figure out how to be a young adult. Sharing your own young adult experience, particularly if it was difficult, can affirm your young adult's experience. It's important to acknowledge that we make mistakes and try to do the right thing as parents but still be open to learn. Be real, be honest, and be open to change. No one, including parents, has a lock on the truth.

Being vulnerable and transparent invites the same from our kids.

Be flexible. Although we need to stand our ground when we take a position with our kids, we also need to be open and flexible and not believe our way is always right. This may seem like a contradiction, but there are some areas where parents need to hold the line, such as no illicit drugs or no threats or acts of violence in the house. There are other areas where flexibility is important. We may need to be flexible on whether our kids attend church each week, eat dinner with the family every night, or get a piercing. It's important to recognize that our young adult's values may differ. Be willing to negotiate and compromise in seeking a more collegial relationship versus one where the parent is always right and in charge.

Rigidity often triggers resistance in young adults. This period of parenting is one of moving from control and being right to one of shared power, decision-making, and identifying solutions. In the research and literature on effective parenting, it's clear that an approach that is firm but flexible, sometimes referred to as the "authoritative" approach, is most effective. Parents need to avoid both extremes of authoritarian or lax or, worse, an unpredictable swing between these extremes. One final ineffective parenting approach is that of "uninvolved or detached." Some parents think they should step back and not say or do anything at the launch stage, which can lead to confusion and feelings of abandonment by the young adult.

In times of change and transition, flexibility is critical.

Demonstrate empathy and compassion. These qualities represent the soft side of showing backbone. Empathy involves connecting to their feelings and not just their thoughts. Compassion is an ability to identify with the suffering and a desire to help them eliminate it. Being firm and being compassionate aren't mutually exclusive. You can do both.

Genuine empathy involves a heartfelt connection to your young adult's needs and desires.

SHOW BACKBONE

DO YOU HAVE A BACKBONE?

The following self-assessment will help you identify actions that suggest you have trouble exhibiting backbone. Ask yourself: to what extent do I exhibit these behaviors?

Use the following scale and write your number in front of each statement.

```
0     1     2     3     4     5     6     7     8     9     10
Not at all                                              Completely
```

____ Avoid bringing up an issue or concern because you fear your young adult's reaction.

____ Do things for your young adult that they could do for themselves.

____ Support, excuse (they are stressed, depressed, forgot), or allow irresponsible behavior.

____ Give in on a request you know is wrong according to your values.

____ Intervene with people and institutions (school, work, doctor) on behalf of your young adult.

____ Do things for your young adult to make you feel better or less guilty.

____ Tolerate verbal or physically abusive behavior.

____ Blame others for the failures of the young adult and promote a victim mindset.

____ Excuse behavior due to a condition or disability that does not prevent the young adult from performing the task

____ Ignore your needs and self-care and overextend yourself on behalf of your young adult.

How did you score? Take note that, like golf, a lower score is better. Can you identify some actions that you need to change? Which two of your actions scored the highest? Check them on the list. Decide to address one or more of these. There are many resources on "disabling" the type of behavior illustrated above; they are listed in the bibliography. Find one or more that interests you in understanding and changing this behavior.

WHY PARENTS FAIL TO SHOW BACKBONE

We end up enabling irresponsible behavior and not taking the necessary stand for many reasons. We may consciously or unconsciously try to compensate for what happened to us as children. Although we should strive to be better parents than ours, we need to guard against overdoing it. For some parents, if unresolved guilt exists, we cave into inappropriate demands and excuse irresponsible behavior because we want our children to be happy and like us. We undermine their confidence and competence when we overprotect our children by intervening, not letting them take risks, and make mistakes. I think it's fair to say that some of our young people and many of those I see with failure to launch difficulties lack a certain resilience or "grit." We have to help our kids develop this capacity.

Some of the parents I have worked with describe themselves as enablers. Others acknowledge that they are pleasers, fixers, or doormats and know this robs the young adult of a solid foundation to launch. Quite a few parents are conflict avoiders and would rather ignore or deny a problem behavior of their young adult than confront it and risk an argument. Some bend over backward to be fair with each child, as if their personalities and circumstances are the same. If we do this to a fault, they will have a rude awakening in the real world outside the home.

Parents in two-parent families must agree on guidelines and expectations. If not, they send mixed messages to their young adults and, at worst, allow them to take advantage of the parents' disagreements and end up playing one against the other or just doing what they want. Often, one parent is too harsh, and one is too soft, and they end up canceling each other. Playing good cop, bad cop is a bad idea (See blog on parentslettinggo.com website with this title). Divorced parents who disagree on money, resources, and expectations create a challenge for adult children who feel caught in the middle.

SHOW BACKBONE

BACKBONE READINESS

Are you ready to step up and take a stand? Are you prepared to be supportive and loving but firm on what you will accept or not accept from your young adult? Rate your readiness to become a parent with a backbone. Use the following scale and write your number in front of each statement.

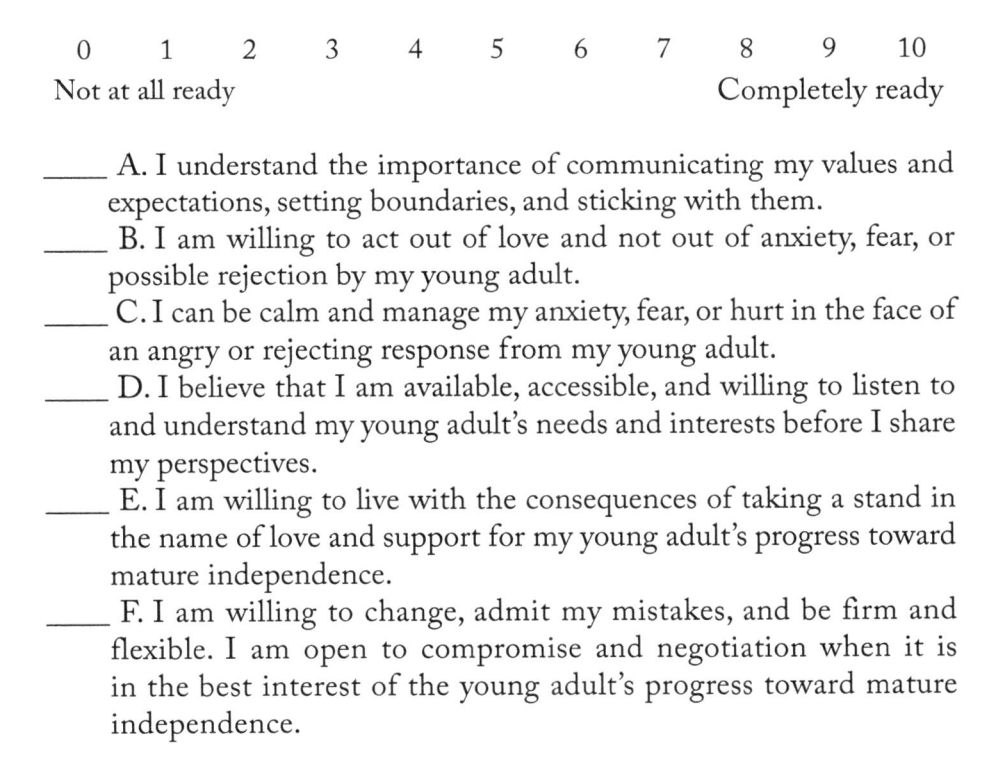

```
    0     1     2     3     4     5     6     7     8     9     10
Not at all ready                                      Completely ready
```

_____ A. I understand the importance of communicating my values and expectations, setting boundaries, and sticking with them.

_____ B. I am willing to act out of love and not out of anxiety, fear, or possible rejection by my young adult.

_____ C. I can be calm and manage my anxiety, fear, or hurt in the face of an angry or rejecting response from my young adult.

_____ D. I believe that I am available, accessible, and willing to listen to and understand my young adult's needs and interests before I share my perspectives.

_____ E. I am willing to live with the consequences of taking a stand in the name of love and support for my young adult's progress toward mature independence.

_____ F. I am willing to change, admit my mistakes, and be firm and flexible. I am open to compromise and negotiation when it is in the best interest of the young adult's progress toward mature independence.

How did you score? Here, a higher score is better. Identify your two lowest scores and find the tips below for strengthening that score.

TIPS TO STRENGTHEN BACKBONE READINESS

A low A score will mean developing a deep *understanding of the importance of communicating expectations and setting boundaries*. The best thing to raise this score is to review earlier parts of this book. Take some time and write down why you need to exhibit the backbone for yourself and your young adult's progress toward mature independence. Please review this list and discuss it with supportive people so you have it well embedded in your thinking.

Regarding B, avoiding *acting out of fear or anxiety* **is essential**. It's imperative to know that the right thing to do is to let go and let your young adult take responsibility for their life. Hard as it is to let go when you are afraid or anxious about their decisions or actions, it is what needs to happen developmentally. Understand that you don't want to be controlled by fear and anxiety; even if this does exist, you can still let go and let them be responsible. You might say as a parent, "I'm worried about you, but I know I have to back off and let go, let you make your own decisions, and I will do my best to do this."

C is about doing the best you can *to stay calm*. Remaining calm is critical. We know from research that we lose our ability to reason once our pulse rate gets over 100. Practice staying calm, and if arguments escalate, ask for a time out so each can calm down, but offer a time to come back and talk again. See managing conflict guidelines later in this book.

D refers to *being available, accessible, and able to listen*. Parents need to reach out and respond to their young adults sincerely to understand their point of view. Doing this gives you the right to be heard and share your perspective. Being present is not just connecting through different mediums; it is saying in a heartfelt way, "I see you and am here for you." This generation lives in a digital world, and if we want to connect, we will need to meet them in their world.

The E statement concerns being *willing to live with the consequences of taking a stand*. If you act out of love and integrity and believe your stance toward your young adult helps them become more independent, you are on the right track. You need to have a higher and long-term view versus being liked or accepted by your young adult in the short term. Ask yourself: Did I act out of love? Did I do what

I thought was right? You may tell your angry young adult, "I'm sorry you are unhappy about my expectations and decisions, but I have to do what I think is best for you, even if you are angry at me. I'm acting out of love and supporting your desire to become more independent."

Finally, F requires demonstrating a *willingness to change, admit mistakes, and compromise*. Being firm is not being rigid and never changing or compromising. Being willing to listen to your young adult, empathize, consider their point of view, and seek common ground may be a more important lesson than one that says: "I never change as a parent." It's helpful to acknowledge that you are as new to parenting young adults as they are to being young adults.

What approach should you take when you believe you are ready to act with love and backbone? A good starting point is to engage your young adult through an interview process to understand them better. If you have a relatively comfortable and open relationship, they may respond favorably to such an idea where they can share their perspectives. However, facing a crisis, contentious situation, or estrangement may be more challenging.

ASK YOUR YOUNG ADULT

As in earlier chapters, I have given you a chance to check your perceptions against your young adult's perceptions through an interview and questionnaire process. Here, I'll do the same concerning backbone. There are two options. The first option is to ask your young adult how you could show more backbone, referred to as feedforward, a concept introduced in chapter three. Ask your young adult for two or three ways to demonstrate more backbone as a parent. Don't ask if you should or shouldn't show more backbone. Hopefully, you will get one or two ideas; as such, you have received permission from your young adult to exhibit backbone in these ways. When you adopt one or more of these suggestions, you can remind the young adult that these were their suggestions. Most young adults know when parents are being too lax or allowing inappropriate behavior to continue and likely would not tolerate this if they were parents.

A second option, particularly if they have trouble coming up with suggestions, is to ask if you could interview them to gather their thoughts about showing backbone as a parent. See interview questions related to supportive integrity under chapter 5 in appendix A. An interview assumes that you have a solid relationship with your young adult and have communicated your love for them, apologized as necessary, and forgiven them and yourself for past mistakes and failures. If you don't have this solid relationship, you may need to work to reestablish your credibility. When done with a sincere goal of stepping back and listening for understanding, the interview process invites the young adult to move toward you. This process can support the desire of most young adults and parents to have a more friendly and satisfying relationship with each other. One parent said, "The workshop exercises enabled me to begin a dialogue with my young adult daughter."

I'll offer some reminders regarding interviewing your young adult. Listen nonjudgmentally to understand their experience and point of view, and do not engage in a debate. Don't listen with a bias of what they should be experiencing or what you experienced in your young adulthood. Check for understanding if their response needs clarification; it's fair to ask for examples but don't contradict them, or they may shut down. Use your best listening and reflecting skills. After each answer, check for understanding or ask for clarification if needed. As I suggested earlier, consider getting out of the house for the interview. If they are unwilling to meet face-to-face, offer an option of reading and recording their answers to the questions by email or text. The goal is to get the information to help you understand them rather than control how you get it. Welcome these questions to foster dialogue and transparency. To keep the flow of gathering their thoughts, offer to answer their questions at the end of your interview. Also, be prepared and offer to answer any questions they may have of you with the same option to pass if you want to avoid answering them. Please make a note and come back to them.

Interview your young adult to listen and learn.

One discovery you may make when answering the interview questions is that your young adults support your attempts to show more backbone. Most young adults know when they can manipulate or persuade you to do something they want but believe you should resist. You can use their feedback to support showing more backbone. For instance, your young adult may say you are inconsistent. In the future, when you need to say no to something you know you can't support, you can say you are trying to be more consistent, as suggested.

SHOW MY YOUNG ADULT I HAVE BACKBONE

Although each situation or challenge parents face is unique and personal, some general guidelines can be helpful.

Be clear about your values and principles and be willing to share these with your young adult. Consider making a list of what you believe are your fundamental values. Google the words values, integrity, and character. Reflect upon the values you want to embrace. Make another list of factors essential to family relationships and society: truth, transparency, respect, honesty, caring, loyalty, responsibility, independence, and cooperation. You may ask your young adult to do the same and compare your lists. Your responses may be close.

Don't measure the success of your advice to your young adult based solely on their response and actions. This warning is particularly true in the short term. Many adolescents and young adults try to establish independence in thought and action and may resist your guidance. How do we evaluate our efforts? Look in the mirror at the end of the day and ask yourself: Was I loving? Was I faithful to my values? Did I do what I thought was right to help my young adult move toward mature independence? This is about your report card. Consider the long-term value of taking a stand versus your young adult's short-term reaction.

Adopt a different parenting style to accommodate the developmental needs of young adults. As children age, they need more freedom and responsibility, which requires the parent to move back from a more directive or authoritarian role. Parents must move from providers and protectors to partners with their young adults. In this regard, new skills need to be learned and adopted. There may still be a place for being directive and implementing specific rules and consequences if the young adult is at home. However, the natural developmental process would argue for less. It is vital to engage your young adult as a young adult with the freedom and responsibility they deserve to make their own decisions.

Risk the discomfort and have the courage to ask the tough questions. Our time with our young adults is short. Don't waste this time sitting on some concern or fear that holds you back from approaching your young adult. These undisclosed questions or concerns and subsequent assumptions will undermine your relationship with them. Approach your young adult with honesty—perhaps even telling them that you're trying to be more candid—and a willingness to acknowledge that you have difficulty raising a concern. They will appreciate your vulnerability.

> *One mother of a twenty-three-year-old young adult confided in me that she thought her daughter was suffering from gender dysphoria. In case you aren't familiar with this term, it is the feeling that one's emotional and psychological identity as male or female is the opposite of one's biological sex. The mother worried about her daughter because of some of the daughter's comments in high school. She observed her daughter's commitment to fitness and becoming a personal trainer, which added to this concern. She finally approached her daughter, who told her mother that she viewed her gender as female and heterosexual. The point is not to suggest a critical approach to someone with gender dysphoria but that the mother had worried because she was unwilling to broach the subject with her daughter.*

Pick your battles and be willing to seek common ground, compromises, and solutions. Often, a hot button for parents is when young adults challenge our authority or expertise. Some of this comes from old school thinking when we were growing up when we heard the age-old explanation for why we should behave: "Because I said so." Even though we hated that phrase from our parents, we often absorbed that voice and were shocked to hear our mother or father's voice coming out of our mouths. Some of us have a harder time giving up authority and being right, which can create problems in our relationships with our young adults. Incidentally, as much as we should have credibility and authority simply because we are the parents, it doesn't work that way with today's youth. As kids, we never liked our parent's refrain, "Because we said so." Today's youth like it even less. We must rely on something other than our position of power over our kids, especially in the adolescent and young adult stages.

> *A former marine dad believed the service concept "chain of command" applied at home. He became verbally and physically abusive when his adolescent son pushed back on his authority. He realized he needed to back off and take more of a coaching and consulting approach than command and control.*

When deciding, first determine who and how to make the decision. Is the decision up to the young adult, or do you need to come to some mutually agreed upon outcome? If it is the young adult's choice, use consulting and coaching skills—see chapter 6. But ultimately, they decide and are fully responsible for the consequences. On the other hand, if parents are paying for college, they may want some say in selecting schools and the costs associated, and the final decision may need to be mutual. A good bit of confusion and conflict can be avoided if we establish who decides and how you will make a choice.

No is not a four-letter word. No is not a bad word, and it is necessary to say to let go and let the young adult grow to mature independence. It takes backbone to say no, but it can be the most caring and empowering word you can speak to your young adult. It can demonstrate a belief that they are capable of doing something on their own. *No* does not mean you don't care or reject them. Grit or resiliency is often in short supply for many young adults because we have been too quick to excuse their behavior or step in. By stepping back, they can accept the responsibility and consequences for their actions.

> *While in college, my youngest daughter called me one night sobbing about how her roommates had ditched her and went out to eat. She felt terribly rejected and asked me to come and pick her up. I told her that I wouldn't go and get her, that she had excellent interpersonal skills, and that she could work this out with her roommates. She said, "So you are not coming to pick me up?" My response was, "Correct!" She called the next night, and I asked*

how things were going with her roommates. "Oh, fine," she said, "I talked to them, and we're good."

When considering saying no, apply the three-question criteria. It may help if you reflect upon a time when your parents took an unpopular stand with you as a teen or young adult and now see the benefit of that decision.

When my son was a junior in high school, we happened to discover a bunch of beer cans, some empty, behind his room in a utility space. We confronted him on this discovery and told him he was grounded and couldn't hang out with his friends for one month. When his friends drove by, my wife waved them on. Today, he is thankful we did this and believes it was critical to his changing his friendship group. Ultimately, he thinks it helped him become captain of the football team. We didn't always do the right thing, but we think we did in this case.

Agreements. Some parents write up very "legalistic" contracts. One parent with whom I worked wrote out three pages of expectations, which seemed excessive and was not well received by her daughter. I prefer the more organic process of sitting down with a pad of paper, writing out the guidelines with the young adult, and then having both the parent and young adult sign it. Agree to an interval of time for routine check-ins on the contract idea. One page of expectations is a good target. Grabbing a template from the internet written by an attorney can come off as less personal than generating the agreement on a blank sheet of paper. It's good to have it in writing, but doing this is not the magic answer. Following the agreements is much more about the spirit than the law. There is more likelihood of success through mutual understanding and respect for the process of letting go and supporting mature independence than nailing down every possible rule and potential infraction. I would also choose "agreement" over "contract" for the language. In chapter 6, I discuss common expectations parents might have of young adults and give examples of these by parents from my practice. In appendix A, under chapter 5, there is a template for a contract that you may wish to use.

BEWARE OF THE DEFAULT APPROACH

We learn specific values, words, and behaviors and store these in our long-term memory. You may recognize this as the inner voice that sounds uncomfortably like your mother or father. We sometimes default to this inner voice of experience, particularly if we are not making conscious decisions. When things get tense, we will revert to long-term, autopilot memory. If our parents did a good job, that might not be so bad. Sometimes, we listen, and act based on our experience of young adulthood, which may not be helpful. We lived in a different time and were raised differently, so the past generation's approach to parenting and our experience may not fit.

When I work with couples, I focus on helping them build a conscious marriage driven by clear values and thoughts, not one run by subconscious past experiences or learnings. Likewise, in working with parents, they need to process what they may have learned through the filters of love, support for independence, and their values. This book surfaces principles, qualities, and approaches that you might consider as an alternative to "the way our parents dealt with us in our twenties." I'm not advocating ignoring what you learned from your parents but instead stepping back and asking yourself: Is this the best approach to what I have learned through my experience and reading this book?

TEACH GRIT

Young adults today may show some signs of entitlement, as discussed earlier. This entitlement may show up in their approach to work. They expect considerations for their work-life balance orientation, sometimes expecting parents to fund various endeavors or fun activities that may not lead to successful careers. Providing free room and board without expectations sends an unintended message. First, it says that, as parents, we believe young adults need help to make it. Second, it says that we don't require them to step up and contribute to the costs and responsibilities of living at home. In the messages that young adults receive, like those that lead to entitlement, we do not challenge them to step up.

I am concerned for the so-called trust fund babies who get distributions from the trust fund without expectations that they need to step up, get a job, and become financially independent. If our kids have not developed a certain toughness or "grit," as some say, aren't we, as parents, partly to blame? I don't say this to add to the guilt you already feel but to challenge you to make some bold changes in your approach in the future that will enable your young adult to become more self-sufficient and independent.

When I worked at 3M as an executive coach, I had a chance to work with and observe the best leaders and their qualities. I concluded that the best leaders had two essential qualities. First, they demonstrated a personal interest and concern for their direct reports as persons and not just employees. Second, they challenged their employees. In this regard, these leaders challenged or stretched their direct reports to do more than they thought was possible. They raised the performance bar and believed in their direct report's capacity to meet it. One leader, in particular, was Rosa Miller, who was Vice President of the Latin America Region when I was assigned to work with her. It was a time of significant growth in many Latin American countries, but Rosa pushed for even more—double-digit growth. Many of her managing directors of these countries told her she was crazy to think they could attain double-digit growth.

Rosa told them she had their backs with senior management and worked with them when she visited their countries. She showed a "hands-in" or partnering approach versus a "hands-on" or controlling approach. These leaders developed "grit" built upon a belief in themselves and their capacity to stretch. Their belief started with Rosa's belief in them. I found evidence of my observations about effective leaders like Rosa in a book by Michael Murphy.[3] His research of over 17,000 business leaders found that the most successful leaders demonstrated connection, or an "emotional bond," with their employees while "challenging" them to perform at a higher level.

Parents are leaders and mentors, whether we accept that label or not, and we can learn from my experience at 3M and the work of Mark Murphy. If we want our kids to step up, we must connect to them with love, believe in their capacity to take responsibility for their lives, and challenge them to stretch. Below is the "2 x 2 matrix" from Mark

Murphy's work. He labels the leaders in the four quadrants that reflect their leadership style and calls the 100 percent leaders the ones who combine high connectedness with high challenge. You will notice the similarity to the model related to "tough love." Considering the collective information from these two graphs, can you identify your parenting and leadership style?

MURPHY'S LEADERSHIP MATRIX

CHALLENGE	Intimidator	100% Leader
	Avoider	Appeaser

CONNECTION

A son was struggling with the one course he had left to fulfill his requirements to graduate from college. This young man had a history of depression and suicidal thinking and had been hospitalized on several occasions. The mother questioned whether he would cross this last hurdle without relapsing into depression and potential hospitalization. She decided he was capable of completing this course and offered concern and love for him while expressing a belief in his ability to meet this last challenge. She became involved just enough to help him across the finish line. What a gift she gave him because he did this with her love, support, and belief that he could stretch himself to finish his course. Yes, this mother was enabling, but in the best sense of the word.

THE MAJOR TYPES OF FAILURE TO LAUNCH (FTL)

In my practice, I have identified four types of failure-to-launch outcomes: stalled, disabled, derailed, and estranged. These categories are not discreet and may overlap. Within these overall descriptive categories, you may have young adults who are emotionally unlaunched, as described in the opening chapter. In other words, you may have a "stalled young adult," as described below, who is positively enmeshed, negatively enmeshed, or disconnected.

STALLED

These young adults are primarily stuck at home but may be back and forth to housing or out of the house in accommodations provided by their parents. Still, they can't get traction on life's developmental challenges of identity, independence, and intimacy. The common characteristic of this FTL group is inertia, or in other words, a tendency to do nothing. These young adults are often depressed, anxious, withdrawn, have low self-esteem, are irritable, noncommunicative, contentious, sedentary, passive, and may suffer from ADHD or other issues. Do they have a clinical condition such as depression? They may have, but both parents and the young adult have fallen back on this perception as a way of explaining, if not excusing, the lack of progress on life goals. Is it depression/anxiety or failure to launch?

In my experience, at a minimum, the failure to progress on developmental goals significantly contributes to young adults' mental health problems. Furthermore, many parents have been fearful that too much pressure to get a job, go to school, or get out of the house or apartment may cause depression to become worse. If there is a history of depression or anxiety traced back to high school or earlier, one could argue that the mental health challenge preceded the failure to launch. In such cases, answering the chicken and egg question isn't helpful. The fact is that depression and anxiety are both a result of and the source of failure to launch. Each feeds on the other.

Martin Seligman coined the phrase *learned helplessness* to describe a condition that occurs after someone reacts to a stressful situation (think COVID isolation) by succumbing to these stressors and repeatedly failing to meet certain challenges.[4] These stalled young adults reach a point where they no longer believe they can change or succeed. Many of these young people have become comfortable with the insulated experience of being at home, playing video games, and eschewing any challenge to break out of their cocoons. Even with medication, many think that their depression or anxiety prevents them from getting a job, going to school, or in the worst cases, even leaving the house. I have discovered that nudging them to get out, work, volunteer, or attend a class to move them forward often reduces depression. I believe that the problem is depression and failure to launch, so only addressing the former will not solve the problem. In a recent conference, a speaker referenced the "protective" value of work, and I would say the same about getting out and doing volunteer work. Such actions contradict young adults' view that they are helpless victims of depression or anxiety. More about this in chapter 6. Here are two examples of a stalled failure to launch where taking some steps to move forward made a difference in the depression.

> One young man, we'll call him Jay, went to college but failed to attend class and keep up with his work. He eventually gave up after the first quarter and withdrew from school. At the time, he lived with college friends but could no longer afford to pay rent, so he moved back home to live with his single-parent mother. Jay was ashamed of his failure, described himself as a loser, sometimes threatened suicide, and had a pessimistic view of life and his future. His mother tried to get him to see a therapist, but he refused. He avoided hanging out with his friends because he would have to admit that he was living with his mother and was not enrolled in school or had a job. Jay withdrew from needed friendships and social support because he was embarrassed to admit they lived with his mother. Then, I met with Jay and helped him develop a five-year independence plan. Sadly, his vision of the future was unclear and pessimistic. Sometime later, his mother got him a part-time job in a local office. He began learning about the business and eventually started taking classes as a paralegal. To Jay's surprise, he began to do well. Although he continues to refuse mental health services, his story is far from over. To this day, Jay continues to do

well in his studies, and as he does, he is beginning to believe that he isn't a total loser but a young man with worth and value. In fact, as of the time of this writing, Jay has obtained a full-time job in the legal field. Mom's persistence and not buying into the I'm-a-loser, victim mentality Jay espoused, was instrumental in his progress.

There was another young adult we'll call Mike, who also believed he was a loser. He had depression and anxiety and a history of academic performance problems. He returned home after an unsuccessful attempt to attend college. His parents tried to get him to see a therapist, but he refused, like the example above. Mike decided to turn things around after living at home for a while. He began to dig himself out of his perceived hole of failure by taking one class in a subject he found interesting at a community college. He did well and started to get his confidence back. He has been able to add more classes and get a part-time job. In working with his parents, our goal was to help him get a win that could create positive momentum and rebuild his self-esteem. Like Jay, the story continues, but the signs are that this dropout, living at home while friends went to college, was beginning to regain his footing.

What happened, and what changed in these two examples? Both young males had experienced failure, were depressed and ashamed, and believed they could not succeed. Before experiencing some success, both young men were stuck in a negative feedback loop, saying, "I'm depressed or anxious, a loser, and so I don't try, and that proves I'm a loser." In both cases, the parents lowered their initial expectations of the young adult and worked to find a win. To the surprise of these young adults, they succeeded academically and at their jobs. They regained some confidence, and the parents reinforced their success and abilities.

Has it been on the scale that the parents wanted? No, achieving success and shifting the momentum in a positive direction is more important than the parent's desired ultimate measure of success. The young adults and the parents have something on which to build. You may resist lowering the expectations of young adults, but it may be necessary to start small and build on any success.

Many of these stalled FTL situations began to resolve once the young adult got a job, began to succeed in a class or two at a local college, or began to build more friends. When I interview young adults like Jay and Mike to hear their five-year plan, I ask how happy and satisfied they are with their current situation on a scale of 0–10 (0 = not satisfied at all and 10 = completely satisfied). Most of the time, the answer is 2–5.

Then I ask them to rate how happy they would be in five years if they met all their goals of obtaining a job, moving into an apartment, financial independence, and finding a significant other. My experience is that they rate their happiness and satisfaction in life in the 7–9 range. I didn't ask them if they would feel less depressed or anxious in five years but what their satisfaction with life would be. This change in score validates the argument that the failure to progress toward independence and other developmental goals is a factor in their current depression or anxiety. I'm not proposing a job or a class instead of getting help from a professional for their mental health challenges. Ideally, there would be value in pursuing both, but if they refuse therapy, don't just let them sit around and reinforce a loser mentality. If these young adults are in therapy or willing to pursue professional help, I encourage them to take their five-year plan to the therapist and ask for help with this plan and not simply work to reduce their symptoms. We'll cover the five-year plan approach in the next chapter.

Some parents believe that antidepressant medication is the silver bullet to help their young adults get back on track. Many parents are disappointed when the anticipated medication miracle doesn't occur. I describe antidepressant/anti-anxiety medication as an aid in leveling emotions. A splint on one's arm doesn't heal the arm but holds it in place while healing occurs. Antidepressants provide a hold on the nervous system that can help rein in extreme mood states. But meds don't solve the problem of school, job, relationships, and gaining traction on life's tasks. These challenges are all still there at the end of the day. Medication is one of the tools, along with psychotherapy, that can help address the inhibiting moods that trip up many young adults. What can parents expect from this failure to launch an adult child?

1. Expect them to work or go to school full time or combine the two or show by actions that they are moving in one or

the other of these directions. They may start with one class and a part-time job. If they don't want to go and are anxious about getting a job, give them work around the house without pay or require them to volunteer in the community. Getting out of the house is essential. Depression and anxiety moods can partly be explained as a condition perpetuated by a closed feedback loop from the brain to the emotions. The more one focuses on one's feelings or mood, the more depressed or anxious one becomes. Distraction through work, volunteering, and helping others can break up the negative thinking that keeps feeding the depression. It gets harder to continue to reinforce negative thoughts of helplessness and hopelessness if you are doing something constructive.

2. Require them to exercise at least three times a week, which could, among other activities, involve gym membership and attendance, walking, or taking the family dog out daily. A lot of research supports exercise as a significant antidepressant. It counters feelings of helplessness and increases positive energy.

3. If an assessment by a medical professional indicates they could benefit from medication, encourage them to take this as one tool to address their mood state and not the single solution. If they complain that the medication isn't doing any good or don't like the side effects, have them talk to their prescriber rather than immediately quit. Many who take antidepressants, especially young people, don't give these meds enough time to realize the benefits. One study found that the first antidepressant medication isn't often effective, and a higher dosage or a different medication needs to be considered.[5]

4. Expect them to participate in family life, such as family gatherings, meals together, cooking a meal a week, doing their laundry, or helping with chores. Please don't treat them as incapacitated and reinforce their self-perception as such. Their improvement can start with your belief that they can overcome their struggle with mood and dependence. It may require the application of some backbone to take specific actions on your part. If they complain and indicate that the

depression or anxiety is holding them back, ask them to get outside help, or if they are in therapy already, discuss this with their therapist. However, don't let this be an excuse for failing to step up in one or more of the ways mentioned above. It counteracts their helplessness as they start to do things, get out of the house, and connect to others. You can reinforce their positive actions and even argue that though the stretch you require is challenging, they can do it. Incidentally, use the idea of stretch to challenge not just this FTL type to move forward but the next two.

DISABLED

"Wyatt" is a twenty-four-year-old male diagnosed with Asperger's, ADHD, learning disabilities, and depression. He was living with his parents when I began to work with him. The parents wondered if he would ever be able to be independent. It was clear Wyatt would need to get his driver's license if he were to seek more meaningful and higher-paying employment. With the help of some disability services, he obtained a job at a local grocery store within walking distance from home. He maintained this working arrangement for over a year and earned his driver's permit. Wyatt began to practice with his parents. The parents were quite anxious about being in the car with him behind the wheel, and Wyatt sensed their anxiety, so he then turned down their offer to take him out to practice driving. Eventually, after hearing about Wyatt's dilemma, a local adult friend from church offered to teach Wyatt how to drive. Wyatt also got help from a local disability service, which helped him get to the front line for his driving test. Wyatt passed his driver's test the first time. After getting his driver's license, he moved to an apartment close to his parent's home and secured a more permanent job in a manufacturing company. He continues to progress in being self-sufficient and independent, much to the delight of his parents.

Disabled FTL young adults like Wyatt have specific physical, mental, and learning disabilities or other conditions that interfere with the progress of leaving home and gaining traction toward developmental goals. These are not situational conditions, as is the case of stalled young adults. With any of these more severe disabilities, having a young adult receptive to help is the primary factor in successful progress. Many older adolescents and young adults resist acknowledging that they have one or the other of these problems due to shame, denial, or a belief they can handle it on their own. It's essential to help them understand that they can better manage their condition and make a difference through self-care actions and utilizing resources in the community. The more they feel empowered and understand that identifying and accessing supportive resources is not a sign of weakness but strength, the more progress they will make. I also recommend not setting limits on progress with work, school, or career progress to allow them to find their upper limits.

It's important to acknowledge that we do have some responsibility for providing help and resources to these young adults with special needs. I recognize this is a change in my assumptions about parents of young adults, but the disabling conditions of these adult children warrant it. We can't and won't just walk away and say we are no longer their parents or have any duty to take care of or help these children reach their potential. We don't have to do this alone because there are services and resources to support these young adults and parents. The challenge with this type of FTL is determining realistic outcomes. It's important to remember that these young adults want to be more independent and self-sufficient regardless of their condition. What can you do to help them in this regard? Use persuasion, influence, and love to address any independence-inhibiting factors. If you sense they are depressed or suffering from mental health problems, partner with the young adult to find the right providers and treatment professionals. Seek various forms of assistance for those with special needs like state disability services and state and national associations—Google services for young adults with autism, learning disabilities, and physical disabilities. For parents with young adults on the autism spectrum, a helpful publication by the Agency for Healthcare Research and Quality entitled "Interventions for Adolescents and Young Adults with Autism Spectrum Disorders" is available online at www.ahrq.gov.

Parents should partner with young adults to identify appropriate and valuable resources at local and national levels. Get them to work with you to search for and evaluate resources as much as possible. The more they have a say in choosing appropriate resources, the more they invest. If they want to and can take on this task of finding the right resources, give them that latitude—the more they can do on their own, the better. If they live at home, treat them as capable of meeting the responsibilities described above under the stalled FTL example. They can do more than you might think. My experience is that the parents' anxiety can lead both the young adult and the parent to avoid challenges and find ways to stretch the actions of the young adult. Parents fear pressuring the young adult may make things worse or elicit more resistance, which can happen. Again, I prefer to use the term "stretch" versus pressure. We all must stretch at one time or another. Believing in their ability to move forward says they are capable and responsible. You must be realistic, but my experience is that parents often expect too little, do too much, and don't provide enough "stretch." But there is no black-and-white answer for this, and parents must trust their heads, hearts, and the support of various services and professionals to calibrate the right level of stretch.

If you question their ability to continue to live at home or on their own, you may seek professional advice. The situation may be contentious or unmanageable for both the young adult and the parents, or the parents can't provide the necessary services or safety. Sometimes, these young adults may function better in a group home with others with a similar disability. Considering placement out of the house is difficult and should be done in love and in the best interest of the young adult. Furthermore, the assessment of whether placement outside the home should consider the ability of the parent to provide the necessary care for this young person.

DERAILED

Bill and Sharon contacted me because they were trying to find a way to help Tom, their twenty-eight-year-old son. He had been in college but experienced a significant mental illness breakdown in his junior year and was hospitalized. He then didn't return to college and could not live at home because of his aggressive and antagonistic behavior. Tom failed to obtain employment or lost jobs shortly after starting them because of his angry, reactive behavior. His parents got him an apartment and helped him obtain social security disability so he could have some income. Over time, Tom threatened the parents and demanded money to the point where he was not allowed to visit them at home. Tom refuses therapy but has been willing to go for a monthly antidepressant injection. His father takes him for this injection and delivers a bag of groceries every Saturday as a message that the parents still see and love him.

This third type of failure to launch may be one of the most challenging and heartbreaking failures for parents. These young adults have become seriously derailed because of the impact of a severe and persistent mental health or substance abuse problem. They are unlikely to make progress on developmental goals or a successful launch until they address the mental illness or substance abuse problem. Continued failure in the developmental goals is the trademark for this FTL type. In the case of substance abuse, if the problem started when they were fourteen or fifteen, there is evidence that they stopped their development at that point. You now have a twenty-something-year-old drug addict who thinks and acts like a fifteen-year-old. Whether there is an actual delay in their executive function—the prefrontal cortex—or just a failure to learn specific skills over time, these kids have difficulty gaining traction on the tasks of young adulthood.

With severe mental illness, there may be a long history of hospitalization and treatment starting in adolescence and continuing into their young adult years. Some, however, have done well up to their young adult period, when a significant mental illness surfaced, such as in the example above. This emergence of mental illness is particularly true with schizophrenia, which may not show up until the late teen years or early twenties. These troubled and seriously ill individuals are often homeless or in shelters with public assistance. It's heartbreaking for parents to see this happen, especially when these individuals refuse help. The above situation reminds me of a family I worked with over thirty years ago, where a disturbed 29-year-old son held a gun to his father's head and threatened to kill him. The son was removed from the home, but the parents continued to show they were not abandoning him by regularly buying and delivering groceries like the father in the example above. They wanted him to know they still loved and cared about his welfare but that living together could not happen.

> *Jake was an eighteen-year-old who brandished a knife one night in anger at his father. The father had to call the police, press charges, and obtain a restraining order. These actions were painful for the father, and the time of no contact with the father was difficult for Jake. Through Jake's lawyer, the son indicated that he wanted to reconnect with the father if not live with him again. Jake moved back in when the father withdrew the restraining order, and the threatening behavior ceased. Sometimes, when the young adult is out of control, control needs to be addressed by the courts to send a signal to the young adult that not only the parent, but society won't tolerate such behavior.*

Over the last six months, I have worked with several parents with seriously mentally ill young adults living at home or in the community. The young adults are struggling, as are the parents. Here's an example:

> *Mary and Bill's daughter had been physically abusive to the mother, and he was no longer allowed to live at home. The parents had tried many approaches to help this twenty-five-year-old with both mental health and substance abuse problems but to no avail. She moved out of the home and picked up some part-time work but became suicidal and was hospitalized. Residential treatment followed but was not successful. Due to her condition, the mother told me she feared that the next time she would see her daughter would be in a body bag. Every time the phone rang, she experienced a jolt*

of adrenalin. Parents struggle with the sense of helplessness and despair that often mirrors the young adult's experience.

A couple with whom I worked had a thirty-two-year-old son living alone and unemployed. The parents, especially the mother, would get calls from him where he would become verbally abusive and threaten to kill himself. I coached this mother to tell the son that she would hang up if he became belligerent or threatened suicide; otherwise, she would be glad to talk to him. Initially, he fell back into old behavior, and the parent had to say she was hanging up, and when he calmed down, he could call back, and she would talk to him. It didn't take long before his behavior changed in the phone calls. This situation would not qualify as estranged since the young adult was persisting in contacting the parent, but, in this case, the parent had to restrict physical contact and control the nature of the phone calls.

What can a parent do? There are no easy answers because parents can't force help or, for that matter, even learn if the person is getting help due to HIPPA privacy requirements.

1. Acknowledge that you are not responsible for this young adult's condition or behavior.
2. Acknowledge that the young adult has not asked for help with this problem but still has a responsibility to seek and accept help from community services.
3. Recognize that these individuals with serious mental health or substance abuse problems need professional help and a range of services beyond what a parent can provide.
4. Concerning substance abuse problems, relapse is common. It often results in negative consequences such as losing a job, a marriage, or a DWI that can provide some impetus for getting help. How often should a young adult repeat treatment in an inpatient or outpatient facility? My answer is as often as it takes them to embrace sobriety. I have had clients with up to seven inpatient treatments before they experienced "the moment of truth." This is a phrase in the AA community that refers to the point where something clicks in the addict's

mind, and they realize once and for all, they cannot ever use it again, or they will die.

5. If a young adult cannot work due to mental illness, an application for Social Security Disability is warranted. Understand this is not easy to get but may be necessary so the young adult has some income to pay for housing and other expenses.

6. There is also the option of applying for state or county disability services if the young adult is on medical assistance and has a diagnosed condition that limits their ability to be self-sufficient.

7. Parents take advantage of organizations such as NAMI (National Association for Mental Illness) and join one of the support groups for parents. NAMI and its support groups are excellent sources of emotional support and resources.

8. For parents, being unable to help directly doesn't mean you should stop looking for resources to offer to the young adult and continue to express love and concern. Mental illness and the scourge of substance abuse are devastating problems for young adults and the parents who love them. I have lost two extended family members to an opioid overdose. Young adults are the highest risk group for opioid use and overdose. A recent report found that opioid overdose, often due to fentanyl, has become the number one cause of death of ages 18–49. Mental illness among young adults has continued to grow, and the pandemic has been an accelerator. You may be a parent of an adolescent/young adult suffering from mental health issues or substance abuse. In that case, I recommend you consult the book *When Your Child Breaks Your Heart: Coping with Mental Illness, Substance Abuse, and the Problems that Tear Families Apart* by Joel L. Young and Christine Adamic *in my bibliography.*

ESTRANGED

> *Two adult children from a divorced home told their father that they no longer wanted to have any contact with him. This occurred several years after the divorce and after spending time with the father and his new wife. The two children indicated that they never felt like they fit in with their father and stepmother. Efforts on my part to reach out to these two young adults and ask if there was anything their father could do to restore the relationship were futile. They wanted no communication.*

More often today, the cutoff comes from young adults, not parents. These cutoffs will be less likely as parents strengthen the practices outlined in this book. The causes of these cutoffs are varied. First, if a contentious divorce exists between parents and the child or young adult favors one parent, the young adult may end contact with the other parent out of loyalty to the parent with whom they are aligned. This is the example above. This cutoff may be particularly true if the other parent is seen as the cause of the divorce. In Josh Coleman's study of 1,600 estranged parents, seventy-five percent became estranged after their divorce.[6] Second, adult children may have been hurt by the parent physically or mentally and have been unable or unwilling to forgive the parent and reconcile. In such cases, whether we like it or not, we cannot control our adult children. The following story illustrates this cause of estrangement.

> *One young man cut off all communications with his father, who constantly criticized and found fault with his son. The son's anger masked a deep hurt since he believed he had done everything he could to please his father but always fell short. He decided to end the relationship with his father for fear of being wounded again. His father offered a somewhat insincere apology but continued expressing self-righteous anger toward him. The father said, "I have done everything I could to reconcile this relationship, and I just can't understand why my son doesn't respond." This father has been told why his son won't talk to him, but it hasn't diminished the father's anger or efforts to connect to the son. In this case, it's not a matter of understanding but acceptance.*

A third example involves in-laws who pressure sons or daughters, causing them to distance themselves from their parents, if not cut off the relationship. The son-in-law or daughter-in-law may feel unaccepted by their in-laws, resent them for some reason, or have conflicts they wish to avoid by eliminating the contact. Other factors that can lead to a cutoff or estrangement by either party include mental illness and personality disorders, substance abuse, gender identity, sexual preference, religion, and politics. In my experience, I have seen differences in political and religious views lead to empty chairs in family gatherings on Holidays. It's unfortunate, and parents need to be the bigger person in the room and reach across this divide to celebrate these important occasions and invite their children to these events. Maybe you have to stay clear of divisive political or religious conversations, but there are plenty of positive memories to share.

When it comes to helping parents with estrangement from their young adults and other manifestations of a failure to launch, I think of my work as upstream from my colleague Josh Coleman. If you are experiencing alienation from an adult child, consider connecting with Dr. Coleman through his website and buying his excellent work on estrangement titled *Rules of Estrangement: Why Adult Children Cut Ties and How to Heal the Conflict.*

Some may take issue with my inclusion of an estranged or alienated young adult who is self-sufficient and independent as a failure to launch. My argument for including this situation when discussing FTL is that the relationship is broken, and there is no positive emotional connection. The independence and self-sufficiency aspects may exist, but the amicable relationship between the parent and the adult child is not. It fits my definition of failure to launch. In certain situations where the relationship with the parent is too toxic to be tolerated, cutting off may be necessary to survive. Even in such situations, parents should still reach out to say they love their kid, even if this is only a card on special occasions. We need to do this as parents because we still love our son or daughter even though contact is not possible. Such cutoffs are a breakdown of the relationship between parents and their kids and undermine the normal transition from adolescence to adulthood, regardless of whether one or both parties are the cause. Furthermore, a wound will persist for both parties because each knows this is not how it should be.

SUMMARY OF PRINCIPLES FOR SHOWING BACKBONE

We have discussed the importance of the fundamental practices or codes of unconditional love, relationship, apology, and forgiveness, which are prerequisites for demonstrating an effective backbone. Here is a summary of the principles and strategies for showing backbone.

1. Model essential values and principles and stick to them. Walk the talk.
2. Act out of love and what is right, not fear, anxiety, anger, or resentment.
3. Ask your young adult for feedback on backbone and suggestions and follow through on one or more of their suggestions.
4. Understand the different types of failure to launch and adjust your approach accordingly.
5. Do your report card relative to your actions and not your young adult's response.
6. Never cut them off, no matter how much they may reject you. When it comes to our need to love our child and for our child to love us, such a cutoff wounds both parties.

BACKBONE REQUIRES SELF-CARE

We can't be much help to our kids if we are depressed, anxious, fearful, discouraged, frustrated, and not addressing these emotions. As illustrated in the disabled example above, our anxiety, depression, or fears are experienced by our kids. They trigger reactions of anger or anxiety in our kids, or they may feel added pressure to do better to relieve the parent's negative emotions. We also need to send a message to our kids that it's important to acknowledge and find ways to cope with emotions that can drag us down. We need to be models of self-care.

YOU ARE NOT ALONE

In my experience, parents dealing with teens and young adults who are out of control or pursuing self-destructive ends are the most stressed and emotionally distraught people I know. The element that makes this particularly disturbing and frightening is the loss of control over our adult child's actions. The good news is that we are not alone. As I have pursued developing materials for parents struggling with the launching process, I am amazed at how many folks have said, "Wow, we need this help." And when I have held workshops on this subject, one of the highest-rated components is sharing with other parents that they are not the only ones struggling to launch a young adult. Dealing with the challenge of successfully launching a young adult is not for the faint of heart. It takes courage, stamina, and resilience. We must take care of ourselves.

HOW PARENTS CAN TAKE CARE OF THEMSELVES

- Strengthen practices that enable you to let go and give the young adult the best chance to launch without unresolved family attachments and expectations.
- Embrace the assumptions stated at the outset of this book. We need to practice living out these assumptions; we cannot control our young adults and are not responsible for their actions. Remember to do your own report card, as discussed in an earlier chapter.
- Strive to be on the same page with your partner if you are in a two-parent family. By this, I mean committing to working out differences in house rules, setting limits, and showing love and support. You must present a united front, or the outcome can be disastrous for parents and their young adults. A specific action you can take is committing to being a team to find win-win compromises in different approaches.
- Take care of yourself first. There's a reason why the airlines instruct adult passengers, in the event of an emergency, to put on their oxygen masks first and then the children. Can you imagine trying to put the mask on your child without

your mask on and the child resisting, pushing it away, and refusing your help? You may ask yourself, in stressful situations, am I trying to put the mask on my young adult and not getting enough oxygen myself? Eventually, you both will pass out. Find ways to detach and de-stress from your problems with your young adult. Don't churn about things 24-7. Set up a time to discuss with your spouse or a friend and save ideas or concerns for those discussions. In other words, segment your talk time on the issues with your young adult. Don't let these issues dominate your thinking or communication 24-7.

- Increase your physical exercise. Exercise is an excellent antidepressant for both you and your young adult. It increases your serotonin and endorphins and gives you more strength, emotionally and physically. Walking side by side with your partner or even with a struggling young adult can benefit both.
- Plan a getaway, go out with friends, or take up a hobby that gives you pleasure and a temporary escape from obsessing about your young adult. Some parents, especially those not working or retired, make the young adult their new project. This potential overinvestment can be a burden for both parties. Both you and your young adult deserve a separate life.
- Build a support network, including a spouse, other family members, or friends, to encourage you when you try to backbone with your young adult. Social support is a huge factor in managing depression and anxiety. There's a saying by Augustin Burroughs, "Your mind is an unsafe neighborhood; don't go there alone." It's good advice for all of us parents. We need other parents and supportive people in our lives to keep us grounded and able to stand up for our values and beliefs with our young adults. It's great to have a partner to discuss how to approach your young adult and apply the principles in this book. If you are a single parent, find other parents or friends with whom you can obtain feedback on your thinking and plans for handling your young adult. Consider joining Ala-Non either in person or online to learn how to let go.

- Seek professional help if you can't get on top of your anxiety or worries about your young adult. It's not an admission of defeat but a show of openness and strength. You may have suggested and encouraged your young adult to seek counseling to support their efforts. Why shouldn't we practice what we preach? In many instances, the parents are more distraught than the young adult and may have a greater need for professional help.

The next chapter will dive into more specific failures to launch challenges and tactics to address these issues. But be sure you have absorbed this chapter's principles and strategies because your unique situation may not be addressed. As such, you will have to translate the concepts and methods of this chapter to your young adult's circumstances.

KEEPERS

As usual, below you will find my starter list of possible keepers. Feel free to add ones that you found most valuable and wish to embrace and apply. Decide on an action, practice, and share with a partner or friend.

1. Don't overlook the four practices leading up to "Show Backbone, "especially foundational ones of showing unconditional love and building a closer relationship.
2. Demonstrate integrity that your young adult can count on keeping promises, being clear about expectations, and following through.
3. Be patient. They will not always be the way they are today. This, too, shall pass.
4. Show tough love that is truly nurturing and firm.
5. Model and act as a leader who is both loving and challenging—requires stretch of the young adult.

THE PARENT'S LAUNCH CODE

6. _____

7. _____

8. _____

9. _____

10. _____

CHAPTER SIX

LOVE AND BACKBONE IN ACTION

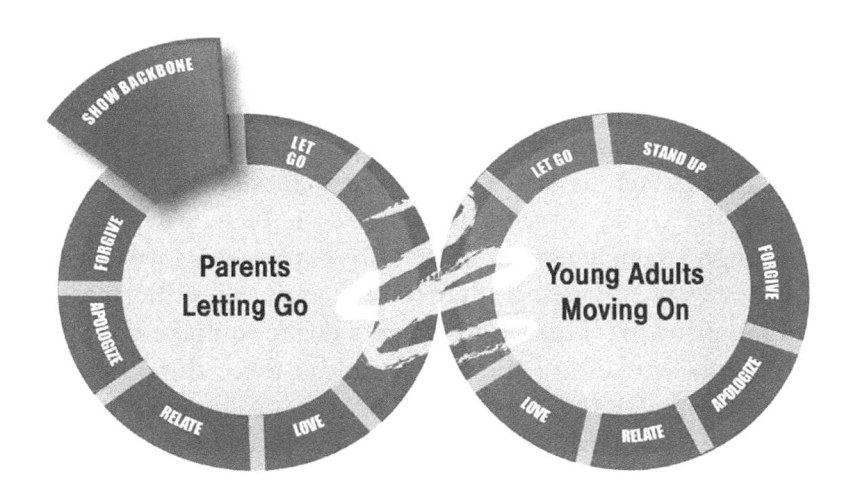

Jeff was a twenty-one-year-old male on probation at his college for falling below the acceptance threshold to remain enrolled. He lived with friends, smoked pot, and had little motivation to succeed. Part of the problem was that Jeff chose a specialized major that was not likely to lead to a job upon graduation. He switched to a Business Management degree but was still unsure whether this was the right major and had lost some confidence in his academic success. I met with the parents and followed up with Jeff to help him envision a future with a five-year horizon. Jeff and his parents explored options, and the decision was mutual for him to

live at home, reduce pot smoking, and focus on doing well in the fall semester. He had a plan, a path forward, and the support of his parents, giving him the best chance for a successful transition into adulthood.

PARTNERING ON THE FUTURE AND INFLUENCE STRATEGIES

This chapter will discuss specific strategies a parent can use to launch their young adult and influence their developmental trajectory. None of these strategies and accompanying techniques are foolproof. We can't make young adults follow a specific path, including the one we think they should follow. Their resistance to our influence and desired direction may be their way of asserting their independence. Initially, we'll cover a partnering approach to engage your young adult to support their future plans. After that, I describe specific techniques you can use to foster this alliance with your young adult on a successful launch. The partnering approach is based upon three fundamental assumptions underlying my work, described in chapter 1. First, parents love their kids; although you may have doubts at times, your kids love you. Second, both parties want the young adult to be happy, self-sufficient, successful, and independent. Third, both share a desire to make the process of letting go and launching amicable. Based on these three assumptions, parents and young adults can partner on a future that the young adult envisions. This partnership orientation shifts the dynamics in the family from the day-to-day challenges (i.e. don't leave dirty dishes in your bedroom) to an emphasis on creating and implementing a future.

GETTING ON THE SAME PAGE: THEIR PAGE

When I work with parents and their adult kids, I foster a partnership around the future aspirations of the young adult. It takes time and patience. Remember: today's 18–29-year-olds have a more elongated development process than past generations. My experience and research confirm that most young adults seek to attain similar goals as those we have had—career, marriage, family, and so on. Contrary to our worst fears, they don't strive to get a van, head to Big Sur, or find a box and live under a bridge. However getting them to talk about their long-range aspirations can be challenging.

The starting point of engaging your young adult in a future orientation is to ask them if they would be willing to answer some questions about their future plans and what support they want from you to achieve these. If you invite input from your son or daughter regarding their plans, here's what I would say to them. "We want to learn more about your future plans, especially for the next five years, and how we can be helpful to you." Some of my parents have said they tried to pry out plans from their young adults, but their kids said they didn't have any or didn't want to discuss it. Often, this question is raised by parents with a critical tone and is met with resistance. I've never found that they had no plans, even with the youngest kids, a sixteen-year-old I worked with. Here's some language I recommend using to ask them for an opportunity to learn about their future plans and needs.

> *We (or I if single parents) want to understand and support you as you plan your future. To help us, we'd like you to answer some questions related to your future. We promise to listen and not judge or challenge your answers. If you would answer these questions either in person or return your answers to us online, then we will meet with you to discuss how we plan to help you.*

Note: It is always advisable to give choices (meet in person or complete online) that will increase the young adult's sense of agency.

Find the best time and vehicle to communicate your request and suggest if they are willing to meet in person to go for breakfast or lunch—your treat. Indicate you would like to learn about their plans for the next five years and how you can help them. Getting out of the house is always a good idea because it creates a more adult-to-adult experience. By asking sincerely and more formally in a text, how you can understand them and be helpful can increase receptivity. If your young adult balks at a meeting, ask if they would respond to the questions by email or text. The following is a set of questions you can ask your young adult. These questions constitute what I call the young adult's five-year plan. Because young adults think in more short-term timeframes, five years out is about all one can expect of them. There isn't anything magical about a five-year horizon, but the exercise gives parents and young adults a chance to work together. Some of these questions are similar to those in chapter 2 related to understanding your young adult; however, these are more focused on identifying a specific plan and action steps to begin to achieve this.

Questions for the Young Adult
In five years:

1. Where will you be living? Part of the country? An apartment or house?
2. Would you be living alone? With a roommate? Or a significant other?
3. What will you be doing to earn a living?
4. What will you be doing for fun?
5. What skills, natural talents, or qualities will help you succeed?*
6. What has been one of the most successful accomplishments in your life?
7. What skills or personal strengths did you use in this accomplishment?
8. How could you apply these skills to support your five-year plan?
9. What roadblocks or difficulties might you face in achieving your five-year plan?
10. How will you overcome these?
11. What one or two actions can you take in the next six months to help you move toward your five-year plan?
12. What can you do in the next month to begin moving toward your five-year plan?
13. What can you do in the next two weeks to begin moving toward your five-year plan?
14. What one or two actions can we take to help you with your five-year plan?
15. Regarding your five-year plan, what are some ways we are being helpful now?

16. What are one or two ways we are not helpful toward your five-year plan?
17. What one or two things do you want us to understand about you?
18. What will your relationship be like with us in five years?
19. If you live at home, what expectations should we have of you?

* This is the only time I invite you to add your observations since many young adults undervalue their abilities. Beyond this, only ask clarifying questions and listen—chapter 2.

At the end of your information gathering, you can indicate that you will get back to them with ways you will be helpful. Practice non-judgmental listening, and don't challenge your young adult's answers or aspirations. If the plans seem unrealistic, hold off on your opinion and appreciate that they have a plan. You can be sure they will discover if their plans are unrealistic. Once you receive their vision of the future, you are ready to respond with what you will do for them, what you won't do, and your expectations if they live with you. You are putting your page together with theirs.

GETTING ON THE SAME PAGE: OUR PAGE

Begin a written response to their five-year plan with a message of how much you love them, want them to be happy and successful in life, and desire to be a part of helping them reach their dreams and ambitions. Here are some examples of how some parents introduced their response to their child's five-year plan.

> *You are my son, and my love for you is unconditional. I will always love you no matter what the future brings. I want you to succeed in reaching your dreams, and I will support you throughout that journey.*
>
> *I'm so proud of who you are—your humor, intelligence, and caring shine through in your relationships with your father and siblings. I love you unconditionally and want what's best for you, including supporting your five-year plan to gain independence,*

finding a meaningful relationship with a partner, and finding work you can love—but at a minimum, helping you financially. I believe in your potential and know you will succeed in your chosen path in life.

You are responsible for responding with or without their information. If you get their description of what support they need from you, address this in your response. Your first comments should be about your love for your young adult and your desire for their happiness and success. Second, state what you will do to support your young adult's five-year plan and use their requested practical actions if possible. Third, describe what you will "not" do to support their five-year plan and desire for independence because you believe they need to step up and do these things themselves. Finally, if the young adult lives at home, list expectations for them. Here are two examples of how the parents phrased the initial responses relative to what they would and would not do.

Will Do

Here is the type of assistance that we can provide for you as you prepare for the next chapter of your adult life:

- shelter
- food
- access to Wi-Fi for school
- cell phone and charger
- health and dental insurance
- car insurance
- financial assistance for education
- initial help with the purchase of transportation
- a sounding board for you to formulate your ideas
- wisdom
- encouragement and empathy

Some parents have broken out the costs of maintaining a home and itemized the portion the young adult receives, such as gas, electricity, water and sewer, and garbage collection. At a minimum, I encourage parents to offer support for health insurance and car insurance because of the catastrophic vulnerability and risk to their young adults and parents. Beyond these modes of assistance, consider the other offerings noted above to help them move forward. For instance, you could pay for a cell phone and data plan to aid them if they seek employment or further education. Also, offer to pay for psychiatrist or therapist visits if mental health concerns exist. If they have the means, many parents will pay for all or some part of a young adult's further training or education. In the last two offerings, the parents have the right to verify that the young adult utilizes counseling and confirm passing grades in school. On the latter point, parents should, with permission of the young adult, assess whether their young adult is receiving passing grades before the end of the semester. A common experience for new college students is to get behind in their studies and give up but wait to tell their parents until it's too late to withdraw and obtain a refund on the tuition. If you are paying for school, you have a right to verify their performance during the semester or quarter. This is essentially a return-on-investment verification.

Won't Do

Here are some suggested actions parents won't do to support a young adult's five-year plan. One parent would not do the following for their twenty-eight-year-old son living at home.

- Pay for personal items, entertainment, etc.
- Pay for car repairs or replacement
- Lend money
- Cosign for lease on an apartment or any loans
- Allow moving back home after other living arrangements occur.

THE PARENT'S LAUNCH CODE

EXPECTATIONS FOR LIVING AT HOME

NEGOTIABLES AND NONNEGOTIABLES

It is essential to consider guidelines or expectations for young adults who live at home. The following are some common expectations, but these are open for negotiation. Outline expectations of the living arrangements and responsibilities of both parents and (*young adult's name*) that will ensure both can have a positive experience living together. This arrangement temporarily provides an opportunity to transition to the young adult living outside the home. Indicate that the negotiable expectations, as outlined below, will be reviewed every two weeks to monthly by parents and (*young adult's name*), at which times adjustments in the terms can be considered. With agreement by both parties, the check-in on the plan and the parent's response can be moved to monthly.

One of the young adults I worked with was a twenty-five-year-old male who did editing and copywriting part-time from home. Though he could not fully support himself, nor was he going to school, he and his parents had worked out conditions for living at home while he moved toward these goals. He agreed to take the dog for walks, shop for food, prepare a meal once a week, or get takeout.

Consider requiring rent for young adults working and living at home and not attending school. This rent should be calibrated to the young adult's income and not the market rate, but it will get them used to paying for housing. I advise parents to bank the rent money and give that to them when they move out to pay a security deposit, first month's rent, and so on. You can make an exception if the young adult is attending school, or you can cover some school costs and expect them to work part-time and cover some of their expenses.

Establish a separate living space where they can come and go comfortably if possible. It could be a basement area or someplace where they can watch a TV or play video games, but not in the family room. The common stereotype is the basement dweller with a TV, comfortable furniture, microwave, and bedroom. Although I know that there is a risk in such an arrangement in that it becomes too comfortable, this setup can allow a smooth transition to living apart from the family. I recognize that not all parents have the luxury of a "bachelor or bachelorette pad," but allowing as much separate space as possible is helpful. Some experts argue for making the home as uncomfortable as possible, such as having the young adult sleep in a small room or closet so they will want to move out. One parent recently described making their son sleep on an air mattress outside his bedroom. I know the thought may have crossed your mind, but I am a proponent of creating an environment at home that most closely relates to living with a roommate or partner, so the transition is relatively easy. One young adult said, "I'm paying rent, making meals, cleaning, and doing my laundry, I might as well move out where I am not nagged about my actions." Often, the trigger for moving out is a girlfriend or boyfriend who isn't too happy about their partner living with Mommy and Daddy.

Outline specific ways the young adult will need to take care of their areas of responsibility. Explain that you want to treat them as an adult and help them to be able to live on their own. For example, they could clean their room, do their laundry, buy essential items like toiletries, pay their cell phone bill, pay gas for the car, and pay for auto insurance. The more they can take responsibility for their lifestyle choices, the easier the transition to living independently. Establish guidelines for common areas. Some guidelines might be keeping clothes, food, or other items out of common areas. Also, it is necessary to identify specific household responsibilities and indicate that the young adult must take on X number of these tasks per week. These chores include cleaning the house, making meals, doing outdoor maintenance, and shopping for and contributing food. Give some choice of their contributions to keeping the home but retain the right to set the number of duties. In addition, there should be some guidelines for having friends over and whether parents need to be home when guests are there. Other guidelines may include being quiet if they come home late since the parents likely need to get up for work in the morning. You can frame these expectations as helping them prepare to live independently with friends or a partner.

Offer consultation on money management, budgeting, finding jobs, finding places to live, car maintenance, and so on. It is surprising how many young adults today have never changed a tire. I must admit that it is something none of my three young adults have done. And

THE PARENT'S LAUNCH CODE

what about changing the oil? They may need help finding the dipstick! These types of services are readily available, so our young people have yet to find a need to learn these things, but they should know how to get help when needed. Most young adults seem more comfortable finding YouTube instructions than asking their parents. YouTube has saved me from a disastrous repair job more than once. Be willing to ask for help from your young adult, which elevates their role.

The second bucket of expectations is those which, if not adhered to, would mean the young adult needs to live elsewhere. These nonnegotiables are deal breakers. They are nonnegotiable and usually line up with the expectations of society at large. Parents who allow these behaviors without consequences do the young adult no favor. If the young adult does not learn to adhere to these rules at home, the results of such violations in society are much more severe. If young adults cannot meet certain nonnegotiables, they indicate that they want to live elsewhere with different rules and expectations. In this regard, you are not "kicking them out." They can choose to live elsewhere either by their words or their actions. They will find that, wherever they live, there will be requirements, especially as relates to the nonnegotiables.

One twenty-five-year-old with a substance abuse problem returned home to live with his mother after being evicted from an apartment for drug dealing. At home, he is no longer dealing, but he is not respecting his mother's requirements about no drugs or alcohol in the house. He knows he's not meeting her expectations and taunts her, "Just kick me out." She's started to go to Al-Anon and learn more about tough love. If you have a situation like this, get to Al-Non either online or in-person meetings.

Here's a list of possible nonnegotiables warranting their move out of the family home.

1. No violence or threats of violence
2. No stealing
3. No verbal attacks, abuse, or name-calling
4. No destruction of property
5. No use of or possession of illicit drugs in the house (or alcohol if underage)

6. No driving under the influence
7. No engagement in illegal activities.
8. School or a job or some combination of the two.

Young adults may still be waiting for the perfect job that fits their degree or major, but in the meantime, they need to work. If they are still looking for a job or enrolling in an academic or training program, indicate that they should work on projects around the house or volunteer outside the home instead of paying rent. Sitting and doing nothing is not an option. One young man came home from college after one semester because of problems in school that led to depression and anxiety. The parents wisely allowed him to have some time to recover from the school problems and get some counseling and medication before raising the expectations of work. You want to look for some effort or actions, even if small—take one class—that show a desire to move forward. Small accomplishments are a step in building momentum.

Any failure to comply with the nonnegotiable expectations, particularly 1-8 on the list above, would be interpreted as the young adult's desire to live elsewhere. The truth is that the real world outside the home is not very forgiving. Young adults can indicate they don't want to live at home in two ways. They can say they prefer to live elsewhere, and their parents can help them move out. Second, they can show by violating these nonnegotiables that they want to live elsewhere. They may claim you are kicking them out, but it's their choice. You would do them no favor to allow them to violate rules that society would not tolerate. You love them enough to hold firm on your principles and offer to help them find another place to live, which gives them a chance to start moving toward independence. If they have no place to live, they may need to avail themselves of county shelters. I'll repeat a situation that I described earlier, where a father had to drop his son off at a shelter.

A nineteen-year-old male living at home continued to defy and disrespect his parents by smoking pot, bringing drugs into the house, and stealing money. He had also run afoul of the law and faced legal charges. The parents had exhausted all efforts to provide counseling and offer the use of the car if he met expectations at home, but nothing changed. Finally, after another incident of bringing drugs into the house, the father reluctantly told him to pack his bags. The father then dropped his son off at a shelter for juveniles and young adults. As the father drove him to the shelter, I can imagine tears in the parent's eyes. No parent wants to do this, but to continue to allow his illegal behavior would be failing to prepare him for the real world.

There are alternatives to shelters and leaving indefinitely. You may ask the young adult to leave for a week, and if they decide they want to come back and abide by the house rules, welcome them back. Suppose they need to be away for a more extended period. In that case, consider relatives or grandparents if they are primarily struggling with their dependency issues with you as parents. This respite for you and them may work if they have a positive relationship with the relative. However, it is not advised if they have violated certain nonnegotiables, such as stealing, destroying property, using illicit drugs, or driving under the influence. Sometimes, young adults may move in with a friend and their family. If this other family agrees, and the arrangement continues for some time, the young adult should contribute to household expenses and chores with this new home. In all of these cases, acknowledge that they were signaling by their actions that it was time to leave and check with them if they have specific needs such as clothes, phone, or help with work or school options. In other words, don't take a rejecting or punishing approach. It may be time for them to launch.

Leaving home should be approached and supported by the parents as a normal transition into adulthood, regardless of the circumstances. Parents can provide the young adult with furniture, food, or other supportive actions or words. Parents should offer such provisions whether they move out by their decision or actions. Recognize it may be time for them to be on their own. It doesn't have to be, as some ill-advised tough love advocates recommend, dumping their stuff in the front yard and changing the locks on the door. Even though this thought may occur, please don't do it. Take the high road and treat them with respect and a desire to assist them in getting started in life outside the home. This approach aligns with my definition of a successful launch—independence with an amicable relationship with the parents.

DISCUSSING THE FIVE-YEAR PLAN AND PARENT'S RESPONSE

Once the young adult has created a five-year plan, the parents indicate what they will and will not do and their expectations. Establish an initial meeting to review the five-year plan, the parents' do's and don'ts, and expectations. To approach this initial sharing of the five-year plan and the parent's response and the check-ins, utilize concepts covered in chapters three and four—listening, inquiry, feedback, and feedforward, and do your report card. The tone should be positive, reinforcing any small action (any win), and collaborative as to how parents can help the young adult advance on **their** plan.

The young adult should begin by reviewing their plan, where they want to be in five years, and how they will get there by actions in the next six months, one month, and two weeks. The emphasis for the young adult is on beginning the process of moving forward toward self-sufficiency and independence. Parents should listen and ask clarifying questions rather than critique the plan. My experience is that these plans change over time as the young adult finds a different interest or determines that a direction isn't realistic. Let them find this out. It's best if they discover this versus us telling them it's unrealistic or a pipe dream. It's about them taking responsibility for future plans and actions and doing their report card. I suspect Bill Gates and Steve Jobs' parents were critical of these two for dropping out of school to pursue some entrepreneurial pipe dream.

The parents should share what they will do and won't do to support the young adult's five-year plan and answer any clarifying questions the young adult asks. Once this sharing is completed, the parents can share their expectations of the young adult, especially if they live at home. But even if not living at home, there may be expectations such as when they can come back home for a visit, access to resources in the house, and requirements parents might have if the young adult is in school or living in an apartment they are subsidizing. Once you exchange this information, decide on the next meeting two weeks out to begin to build some momentum. The goal is to get some action or movement from both parties within the first two weeks. Getting one thing done that is part of the plan and the parents coming through on one or more of their supportive actions generates momentum.

Check-In

As noted above, the first check-in should be in two weeks with the expectation that the young adult can take at least one action to start moving forward-call on two or three possible jobs, call on volunteering options, contact the school to learn about programs and resource, exercise two to three times a week, and so on. The goal is to stimulate some forward action and movement. Each party starts with a review of their plan with a reflection on what has been accomplished or gone well (feedback)and what one or two actions each party wants to take to do better in the next time frame (feedforward). While the young person starts assessing their progress, parents listen without critiquing. Clarifying questions are appropriate, as well as asking if there are one or two additional actions by the parents that could be helpful to the young adult in the next time frame (before the next check-in). Parents will need to decide whether they can meet a request by the young adult by considering if the action would be done in love, consistent with the parent's principles, and likely to contribute to greater independence than dependence.

Parents review what they have and have not done and how they can improve before the next meeting. Any actions that either party agrees to are noted on each party's one-page documents for review at the next meeting. The final discussion should be around parents' expectations for young adults living at home or away from home. The young adult should first reflect upon what they have done to meet these expectations and what one or two actions they will take before the next check-in to improve on these. The parents can give positive feedback on any expectations the young adult has met and feedforward suggestions for improvement before the next meeting. Parents need to look for any evidence of progress and reinforce this with a belief that this is the start of forward momentum. Progress may be slow on these expectations, but we should try to build on any evidence of efforts to meet these.

Note: *A one-page description of the process for check-ins is available in appendix A under chapter 6. You can print this out and put it on the table as a reference guide for the meeting. Also, keep in mind that revisions to these protocols may be made from time to time and posted on my website*—parentslettinggo.com.

LOVE AND BACKBONE IN ACTION

MAKING LIVING TOGETHER WORK

While you and the young adult share your home, there are ways to foster a healthy relationship. The following is a list of suggestions to discuss with your young adult to achieve that goal.

1. Discuss with them the concept of becoming more of an adult and *roommate* in the home and identifying a time they believe would be good to move out. Reframing the experience of living as roommates prepares them for the future. They will likely face this experience when they move out. If they have been to college and lived in a dorm or house with other students, they should be able to identify with this type of living arrangement. See the blog on parentslettinggo.com regarding the roommate concept.
2. Explain how the relationship will need to change with the new adult roommate arrangement. What does the young adult expect in changes from the parents with the new role? How do they think the parent should change in treating them like a roommate? What do the parents expect from the young adult in this new role? Understand that they want to be treated as an adult, even if it sometimes doesn't seem that way. Apply the assumption that relationships are reciprocal—treat them like adults, and they will act more adult like.
3. Identify and reduce actions that treat the young adult as fifteen." Did you eat dinner? What time did you get up? When did you come home last night?" It is more difficult to change than you might believe because parents and young adults regress into old parent-child patterns naturally or unconsciously. Here is an example of a common discussion between a parent and a young adult falling into old roles: Parent: "Why are you playing video games until three in the morning? How are you going to be successful sitting around playing games?" Young adult: "Why are you always nagging me about playing video games? I play with my friends. What's the big deal?"
4. Make an adult connection with them outside of the home. This connection can be a monthly breakfast time to catch up

with a rule that you set aside all conflict issues. Such a new type of social connection sets up a bridge experience to the one you want to have with them when they leave home. Beyond this, road trips are great for spontaneous conversations where you don't have to be parenting them. I fondly remember road trips with all three of my adult children. It is a casual, less threatening opportunity to sit side by side in a car and engage in conversation that will deepen the relationship. Some of the questions related to the interview in chapter 2 could be discussed on such trips. These adventures extend beyond when your kids live at home, as my son and I found while sailing together a few years ago.

MANAGING TENSIONS AND CONFLICT

Tension and conflict are inevitable in families and can be very challenging with young adults. The approach a parent takes to disputes with their adult children is critical. There are many opportunities for disagreements between parents and their adult children. The goal should not be to avoid or ignore conflicts but to manage them effectively. Regarding the launch process, parents and young adults may differ on when and how to leave. Choices the young adult makes for his life or his life partner, work, and career decisions, what parents should pay for, and what the young adult should take on are some of the possible differences. Parents need to pick their battles and be willing to seek common ground, compromises, and solutions. Leaving dirty dishes in their room doesn't deserve the same response from parents as lying to the parents or stealing.

When the parent-child relationship is strained, everything becomes a source of contention. A hot button for parents is when their authority or expertise is challenged, and they know or believe they are right. Some of this comes from old-school training when we were growing up, when we heard the refrain "because I said so," referenced in the last chapter. Some of us have a hard time giving up authority and being right, which can create a problem in our relationships with our young adults. Our ability to build credibility and influence with our young adults depends on how we address differences and conflicts.

When deciding where there are disagreements, first determine how the decision will be made, including who will make it. Is it totally up to the young adult, or do you need to come to some mutually agreed upon outcome? If the choice is the young adult's sole responsibility, use consulting and coaching skills—see later in this chapter. They must face the consequences of their decision themselves. On the other hand, if parents are paying for college, they may want some say in choosing schools and the costs associated. In such cases, choices may need to be mutual. Confusion and conflict can be avoided by deciding how and who will make the final choice. Work with your young adult to come up with guidelines for handling conflict.

GUIDELINES

Here are some **suggested guidelines** for when you face conflict: stick with them even if your young adult violates them.

- No violence or threats of violence
- No swearing or personal attacks
- Listen without interrupting, state what you heard the other person say, and allow clarification before communicating your position.
- Avoid starting with "you." Start with "I" and express your feelings, observations, and perceptions. Don't say, "I think you are lazy." That's a dirty "I" statement. Say, "I am upset and concerned that you are watching TV when you could be out looking for a job."
- Make every effort to stay calm and not get hooked into violating these guidelines. Slow down your breathing and keep your voice calm even if your young adult raises their voice.
- If you are stuck in an argument with no resolution, or the tone escalates, and you feel uncomfortable, ask for a timeout. Allow the young adult to call a timeout as well. Calling a timeout indicates that you believe that the argument is escalating,

becoming destructive, or derailing, and you want to stop this pattern because you care about the relationship. Too many people in conflict walk away, and issues never get addressed. **But whoever calls time out must state a "time back in" before ending the discussion.** This time back in should be within twenty-four hours at the outer limit. Stating a time back indicates that you value the relationship, think the issue is important, and want to come back to it when you both have calmed down. Don't use this time to bolster your argument. Instead, use the time prior to reconvening to brainstorm solutions you could propose that would satisfy both parties when you time back in.

- Each parent must incorporate clear values and expectations into their practices and actively show love and backbone. If you tend to gravitate to one or the other side of these two actions, you must increase your efforts to balance your approach. A common approach I observe is that one parent tends to be more lenient and permissive, and the other is more controlling and firmer. If this method exists with parents, it's a good cop and a bad cop. I have had parents change roles for a week or two and then debrief. If Dad is the tough guy, he becomes the accepting, nurturing parent, and Mom takes on the tough role. Each parent needs to exhibit both nurturance and backbone. Young adults need consistency in their parent's approach to them and know that each parent must be firm and loving. If you disagree on an issue, then have a sidebar conversation without the young adult where you arrive at a decision between you and your spouse, which enables you to present a united front. Avoid inconsistency both between parents and as individual parents.
- Seek repair after a difficult argument where either you or your young adult may have violated the rules or said something they regret. Offer an apology for your part relative to the issue or how you argued about it. You don't have to take all of the responsibility—"It takes two to tango." Warning: don't apologize and then say "but" or "however" and then point out a failure on the young adult's part (chapter 3). You will reignite the argument.

WHY WON'T THEY LEAVE?

There are some common reasons young adults don't move out of the house. These are not specific to any parent or young adult demographic. Understanding the source of resistance to moving out can help devise a solution and plan. Here are some reasons young adults don't want to move out. Just a reminder, these discussions about moving out are meant for situations where the parents or the young adult believe that moving out needs to happen. The following does not apply to those situations where the young adult is a responsibly independent and collaborative member of the family.

- Believe the parent has the means and the responsibility to provide room and board.
- Comfort, familiarity, predictability, safety, and low-stress qualities of being at home.
- Fear of the unknown or unfamiliar—school, work, social settings.
- Fear of failure—"I'm a loser!"
- Desire to save money that can become protracted.
- Depression and anxiety or other mental illness problems.
- A belief that the parents want or need the young adult to live at home.
- A relationship, job, or school failure can land the young adult back home.
- Can't afford to move out due to the cost of an apartment and a low-paying job.
- Don't believe due to physical or mental disability that, they could make it on their own.
- There is no reason to leave because they have no life plan—purpose, career, education.
- Negative enmeshment between parents and young adults can be binding. They don't get along but don't want to separate.
- Positive enmeshment is where the young adult would view leaving as a rejection of the parent.

Some factors from the parent's side impact the normal transition of the young adult toward responsible independence. Sometimes, parents don't believe their young adult is mature enough or capable of being on their own. Such a perception may reinforce their young adult's underlying doubts about their abilities. Often, parents describe their young adults as one of their best friends. Enjoying the company of the young adult or considering them a best friend are positive qualities unless they undermine the young adult's ability to become self-sufficient and independent. Many cultures support two and three generations living together. We're not typically one of those cultures, but if the young adult and parents get along and the young adult fully contributes to the household, is this a problem?

YOUNG ADULT LIVING AT HOME OR BOUNCING BACK AND FORTH

It's essential to understand and accept that moving out is a natural development stage in the family life cycle in American culture. Both parents and young adults are programmed to let go and separate. At the same time, living at home does not necessarily constitute a failure of this stage of development. *Moving out should not be the primary focus for engaging your young adult, but rather supporting young adults' actions toward mature independence.*

I am not in the camp that says there is a specific date the young adult needs to be out of the home. That's not to say you may not have to force the issue in some cases. There are young adults living at home who have achieved mature independence, and some living outside the house have not. There is also a risk that a primary, if not exclusive, focus on when the young adult moves out can create a sense of insecurity and rejection and trigger resistance. Another factor, as stated earlier, is that many parents enjoy (over 60 percent) having their adult children at home.[1]

The decision to move out is not just the young adults alone. Parents often encourage young adults to move out in my work because interactions between the two parties are contentious. Invariably, the relationship between the young adult and the parents improves when they move out, especially if the parents help with the move. One caveat is that there are special circumstances of physical or mental health reasons a young adult may not be able to move out of the home and make it on their own. Disabled or derailed young adults may not be able to move out unless a level of progress is made on their disability.

REASONS TO MOVE OUT

The reasons for moving out can arise from the young adult's desire for more freedom, independence, and, in some cases, privacy. Privacy can become essential if a young adult enters a relationship with a significant other. Sometimes, the young adult may be unhappy at home with different expectations, pressures, or rules and decides it's time to leave. Or the impetus for moving out may be with the parents. They may agree that the atmosphere at home has become so contentious and toxic that it would be best for the long-term health of their relationship if the young adult moved out. The impetus for the young adult's exit from the home may originate with the parents.

- Violation of the nonnegotiables described above.
- A desire to enjoy the empty nest period of their lives. Parents may want to travel and not be concerned about their young adults at home.
- Facing retirement and needing to conserve funds.
- They may want to downsize because they don't need such a large house. One couple in a very contentious relationship with their thirty-two-year-old son hesitated to push for his leaving but decided to downsize, indicating they did not have room for him in their smaller home.
- The parents believe that young adults have become so comfortable that they are not growing or pursuing an independent lifestyle. If you have a couch potato playing video games late at night and sleeping in your basement, it may be time to develop an exit plan.

Obviously, the best case is one in which there is a mutual agreement related to moving out. Many parents and young adults achieve this outcome. No matter how the transition out of the home takes place, parents should help the young adult get started with whatever is reasonable and affordable. This aid could come in the form of contributing funds towards a security deposit for an apartment, critical costs such as health or car insurance, or some furniture to set up their new living arrangement. Manipulative efforts, such as saying you will buy them furniture or help them buy a car if they leave, are not a good idea. These kinds of bribes can backfire, and you might find not only your young adult back home, but now you have a car loan and a bunch of extra furniture.

LIVING OUTSIDE THE HOME

What are the guidelines that should apply in this situation? The arrangement comes with the critical assumption that you cannot control your young adult. You don't even know what they are doing, especially if they are discrete and resistant to discussing their personal lives. When they were living at home, you had leverage, a say-so, because they were trading their freedom for the benefits of a roof over their heads, food, safety, and other comforts. You could observe them and even communicate with them at times. Now, you don't have that same type of leverage or the ability to observe them. The latter may be a blessing. Out of sight, out of mind.

In some cases, young adults move out, but the parents still fund many of their expenses, such as the cost of an apartment, school, insurance, car, and so on. You have leverage if you are doing all these things, but applying this without triggering anger and resentment is tricky. Start with an understanding of your young adult's goals and aspirations. If you have not done the exercise regarding learning about the young adult's five-year plan, this would be an excellent time to complete it. Begin a conversation with, "Now that you are living on your own, I can no longer tell you what you can and can't do, but I'd like to hear more about your plans and interests."

Another discussion is about how you would like the new relationship between you and them to be. Ask them how they would like to stay in touch and support or help them as they venture forth independently. It's also a time to clarify any support they would like to have from you and what things you are willing to do and not do. Sometimes, parents can impede the natural evolution of an adult-to-adult relationship by trying to stay too involved.

If you are in a two-parent home, work as a team to determine what funding you will make available, if any, and for what reasons before meeting with the young adult. Discuss how the financial assistance will help them with their goals and path to mature independence. It's appropriate to elicit information about your young adult's needs and desires, but don't negotiate with your partner in front of them. Present a united front. Parents should not give a blank check but may consider funding some of the young adult's expenses. Now, I can hear some parents reading this saying, "No way, I didn't get any help with school or my expenses, so why should I do that for my young adult?" Times have changed, and schools, rent, and living expenses are higher today than thirty or forty years ago. According to a recent PEW study, seven out of ten Americans think that young people today have a harder time with financial challenges such as saving, paying for college, and buying a home.

Don't do for them what they can do for themselves or, at a minimum, meet them halfway. Offer "matching grants." Take on or subsidize critical costs such as a car or health insurance. Without such insurance, you and the young adult may be at considerable risk of a catastrophic event. Propose a gradual decrease in financial support to incentivize them to increase their skin in the game. For instance, you may use a decreasing contribution to help them get into an apartment.

Don't compromise your values or principles regarding how they treat you or their relationship in the house. Disrespect (swearing and verbal abuse) is unacceptable, and there are rules regarding reentering the home and what they can haul out. They must learn to ask permission to take stuff and call ahead if they drop by. Please make every effort to treat them in a more adult fashion. Have them over for dinner, go out to eat, let them pay the bill, split it, or have them cover the tip. Praise and reinforce their actions consistent with moving toward greater independence and responsibility. Be graceful and forgiving when they screw up, as they will, and remember your miscues at this stage. Discuss or follow their lead relative to frequency and form of communication. Most young adults prefer to text, but that's fine if they prefer phone calls or emails. There is much more communication between parents and young adults now than in any past generation.

THE YOUNG ADULT'S OPENNESS TO CHANGE

The saying: "timing is everything" is true in trying to manage the dynamic of the letting go process with young adults. Knowing when to move in with love and support and when to back off is challenging. This dance is about joining, synchronizing moves, and timing. Regarding how much to let go and support autonomy, parents may have a different understanding of the timing compared to when they were young adults. Some young adults pull away too soon and may bounce back home. Others have a hard time moving out. So, it's important to use language that can match the young adult's stage of moving toward independence.

James Prochaska developed a model of change in 1974[2], and he and his colleagues have researched and applied this model to several different change opportunities, beginning with smoking cessation. He proposes a model that identifies six stages people undergo to change, whether breaking an old habit or starting something new. Let's look at the application of this model to the process of helping adult children transition to responsible independence.

Stage I: Precontemplation. At this stage, the young adult gives little thought to moving out. They may be enjoying their current status and feel no need to contemplate a change. These young adults don't feel any particular need to plan or take any action toward being responsibly independent. If you start discussing dates to move out, the young adult will ignore or resist such discussion. It's just too early to start talking about such a transition. At the same time, you can challenge them to step up and be more responsible in the home—do chores, laundry, cook meals, and clean—which increases their experience of being a responsible adult and lays the groundwork for a launch.

Jim and Lisa contacted me regarding their nineteen-year-old son, who barely finished high school and has been at home for the last year, pursuing his passion for playing video games with his friends into the night. He has expressed no interest in getting his license, finding work, or moving on with his life. Their son Eddie was at stage 1 in the change process with no plans or desire to move out. Although we set up a time to meet to discuss future plans, the focus with Eddie needed to be on increasing his adult-type behavior and responsibilities—getting his driver's license, getting a part-time job, doing household chores, laundry, and other life skills to help him move to a second stage where living outside the home becomes more realistic.

Stage II: Contemplation. There is a recognition that the young adult may need to make some changes in the future. At this stage, the young adult recognizes that their current status is not sustainable and may need to consider making a change someday. The young adult and the parents realize that the young adult's peers are moving on with their lives by moving out of the home and pursuing school, work, marriage, and so on. It's a stage where parents can begin to explore with the young adult where they want to be in five years—the five-year interview described above. The young adult may find discussions about the advantages of living outside the home compelling. Parents may offer an additional reason to start thinking about moving out, such as their plans for retirement and downsizing.

Stage III: Preparation. At this stage, the young adult intends to take actions that would enable them to move to a different place—independence, new identity, and intimate relations. They likely have a job to support their living elsewhere, possibly friends with whom they could live, and maybe even a significant other. There is also a recognition that the current status is unsustainable. They can't continue to deliver pizzas as a career. They can't live at home for the rest of my life. At this point, parents and young adults can lay out the transition plan, launch date, and the respective responsibilities of both parents and young adults in preparation for the move.

A twenty-one-year-old still living at home and delivering pizzas was challenged by his parents to identify a career and move toward self-sufficiency and independence. He had tried to go to a local community school but didn't follow through and dropped out. Finally, he landed a career in the trades and began a program. Although his parents didn't say he had to leave, he knew they expected him to move forward. His parents' encouragement, the decision on a trade school option, and support from his girlfriend enabled him to set a date to start school and move out.

Stage IV: Action. In this stage, the young adult begins to progress in addressing the tasks of this developmental stage—moves out, gets a job, and possibly finds a significant other. So, there is a clear lift-off from the launch pad. Parents need to continue to invest in the relationship with a welcome change to a more adult-to-adult connection—invitations to come over for dinner or go out to dinner, plans for holidays together, and so on. Two-way phone calls or, more likely, text messages on how things are going become the new norm for staying connected. It's a time when parents can announce that their young adult needs to make it on his own, and although the parents will always be available, the house will not.

Stage V: Maintenance. At this stage, young adults persist, progress on their committed changes, and overcome obstacles that might interfere. They resist moving back home or asking for help from their parents. My advice, with rare exceptions, is that a move out of the home should be a one-way ticket. Stage five becomes the new normal that involves regular contact between parents and young adults. Young women do a better job staying in touch with parents, especially moms, partly because they are more relational. Dads and sons may need to plan times together often around activities—golf, attending a sporting event, shopping, going out to eat, and so on.

Stage VI: Termination. The young adult has achieved a state of mature independence and has faced and overcome obstacles that may have interfered with this accomplishment. This achievement may occur at eighteen or thirty-five; some adults may struggle with this for the rest of their lives. Oops! I shouldn't have said that because I can imagine some of you who are reading this have thought—they may never move out. There is a very small chance you will have a border for life, barring certain debilitating physical or mental conditions. Termination does not mean the end of the relationship but the end of dependency. Chapter 7 addresses this stage in the letting go process.

How is this model helpful to parents of young adults? The model highlights that movement or "change" to mature adulthood is dynamic and not something that happens one day. It helps to identify where the young adult is in the stages of the change continuum. For our kids to change, they must have a growing awareness of the benefits and confidence they can change. They must also formulate ideas about how to navigate the path forward. Parents can be great coaches and consultants in this process, and recognizing timing is essential in matching our words and actions to the young adult's stage of change.

WAYS TO INFLUENCE YOUR YOUNG ADULT

> *A single-parent mother of a twenty-eight-year-old was ready to boot her son out of the house. He was noncommutative at times, and when he did talk, he was disrespectful. He continued violating house rules regarding coming home drunk, smoking in the house, and dragging his feet about finding employment. This mother indicated that if he can't abide by the house rules, he needs to leave. He then said," Boot me out if you want." She didn't but kept reaching out to him in love and concern. She offered help with his finances and asked him to prepare at least one meal weekly. Over time, there has been progress, but it has been very slow. He now willingly helps at the house, makes more than one meal a week, has not come in drunk for months, and has not smoked in the house. Given this progress, she continues to allow him to stay at home. They have developed a more collaborative relationship where she will offer suggestions, or he will bring up ideas related to work opportunities to discuss with her. Although he is underemployed and not out of the house, he is showing incremental progress. This. Mother has had great patience, and there are signs this is paying off, but the path ahead is still somewhat daunting.*

Although, as stated at the outset of this book in the introduction, parents can't ultimately control young adults, this doesn't mean that they can't influence them. There is no way to influence if, as parents, we haven't done the foundational work of showing unconditional love and understanding. Likewise, our influence may be reduced if there is unaddressed guilt or resentment. The following are concepts and strategies that can be helpful in influencing the trajectory of our kids' path to responsible independence.

1. GO LONG

The example above is of a young adult who defies the mother's expectations for living at home and fails to follow through on expectations she has stated and promises he has made. It is common for young adults to resist pressures from parents to get a job, stop smoking pot, clean up their room, and so on. As noted in an earlier chapter, young adults are wired developmentally to establish an identity, attain independence, and establish intimate connections. Conflict can arise when parents have different ideas about how the young adult should achieve these goals. As parents, we have told our kids as they are growing up to think independently and not just follow the crowd. Unfortunately, when they enter late adolescence and young adulthood, apply this lesson, and adopt different ideas from ours, we may feel a sense of betrayal or rejection. When this happens, and there are conflicts on values or lifestyle of goals, we have some choices. We can ignore the differences, but they won't go away. We can challenge these differences, and the young adult may become more resistant, or, finally, we can find a way to work with the differences.

One of the ways I do this is to shift from a day-to-day focus on what's working and what isn't to a long-range focus on the young adult's goals related to independence and self-sufficiency. Both parties share the independence and self-sufficiency goals and become a way to partner with them. Rarely have I done this five-year plan exercise, and the parent isn't relieved to find the young adult has any goals at all. Think of ways to partner with your young adult. The goal is not to get them to do what you want, which will undermine their sense of independence, but to find ways to join them in aspects of their journey that reflect a desire for responsible autonomy.

The focus that you want to use to engage them is their future direction. The questions outlined earlier will allow you to learn about this future direction and identify ways to help and work with them. When you discuss their five-year plan, use open-ended questions to elicit more information that will give you and your young adult more clarity regarding their future and your opportunities to partner with them. Be sure to draw out their ideas and plans because they will be more invested in these than your ideas. Try to listen to their *passion*. Joseph Campbell popularized the expression "follow your bliss." If your son or daughter wants to be a tattoo artist and you find this career objectionable, try to broaden the discussion of how they may use their artistic skills but not object directly to this interest. If you say, "That's a terrible career choice, and you'll never make a living," you can unintentionally strengthen their resolve in this career pursuit to prove their independence.

2. AFFIRM

> *Judy, aged twenty-two, lived at home with a history of learning disabilities and attention deficit disorder. She liked to draw and was quite good. Judy also wanted to write, but her parents feared she couldn't make a living with these skills and would have to continue to live at home and be supported by them. Judy did understand that it would be difficult to live off her writing or art and was resigned to working at other jobs while she developed her craft. The parents had a choice. They could ignore her interests, try to convince her of another direction, or support the development of Judy's interests and her willingness to earn a living through other avenues.*

Judy's story is about negotiating what parents see as *realistic* for the future and what their young adult *desires* for her future. How can you undergo this kind of healthy negotiation while fostering a healthy relationship between both parties? Consider the following. It's essential to affirm actions that indicate taking responsibility for their lives and recognize and "lift" their underlying strengths and personal qualities. Our young adults need to know we "see them" and validate their strengths and positive character traits. Sometimes, our belief in our young adults and their potential carries them forward when they struggle to believe in themselves. Affirm both who they are, as well as what they do. These affirmations represent a much better way to encourage positive change than criticizing their actions or calling attention to how they fall short. Parents also need to set their observational radar for what is working both in their efforts and actions as well as outcomes. When something is working, recognize and amplify these positive actions. If it works, do more of it. If it doesn't work, try something else.

Many young adults who are stuck and depressed or anxious can't see anything positive about themselves or their lives. "I'm a loser, and I'm never going to be successful" is not an uncommon sentiment. We can argue with them about this or find exceptions to these statements. Just saying you are not a loser, or I love and believe in you isn't enough. One young adult pointed out to his mom, saying, "You're my mother; you have to love me." Finding exceptions can create a dissonance between what a person says to themselves and their behavior. These exceptions can be current or past. For instance, telling them they are a good cook who can prepare delicious meals contradicts that they have nothing going for them. Maybe they want to be something other than a chef, but they have talent.

Reviewing their accomplishments of the past can also contradict their "loser" view. I had parents of two Eagle Scouts who struggled as young adults. Describing or asking them to describe what strengths they used to attain such a rigorous distinction, highlight strengths. It also challenges their loser self-concept by reminding them of qualities they can use to deal with their current difficulties. At a minimum, when they succeeded in a task, they set out for themselves in the past, they had to demonstrate resilience and persistence. Indicate that they still have these qualities and how to use them to deal with their current challenges. I wouldn't get into a considerable debate about these exceptions because you may get pushback in negative thinking with a "yes, but...I suck at this today" or other types of arguments.

One mother of a so-called loser described earlier resisted getting pulled into the debate of whether or not her son was a loser. He did a lot of whining and complaining about being a loser while he attained A grades in a post-high school paralegal course. I reminded her to focus on the actions and not the words.

3. FIND THE WIN

The twenty-five-year-old unemployed young woman referenced earlier, who was overweight and used food stamps to buy junk food, unemployed and living in an apartment provided by her mother, seemed hopelessly stuck. The mother's efforts at persuasion, threats, and offers to help with needed self-care actions were ignored. Finally, after avoiding it for years, this young woman got her hair cut. Shortly after this, she made an appointment and went to the dentist. These were early wins that the mother seized upon to affirm her daughter's progress and encourage more forward movement. She then began to see a psychiatrist and a therapist for ADHD and her obsessive-compulsive disorder and went back to work full-time. The mother described the change which took over a year, as remarkable and something she would never have anticipated. Early wins can jump-start forward momentum.

The partnership with our young adults occurs when we build the relationship, elicit a focus or direction they desire in life, and establish a long-range (five-year) plan. We can tap into their motivation and support forward movement by getting them to focus on the next five years. Beyond this, we can look for opportunities to recognize efforts and accomplishments toward the five-year plan to show we are with them and see their commitment. It's essential to look for small actions that you can take to reinforce their efforts to move forward. They also need early wins, even if you must do a lot to ensure these accomplishments. You can take them for a job interview, come up with job opportunities for them, or invite them to join you in a volunteer activity. A couple of parents I worked with have been able to pry their young adults out of the house to volunteer, which has led to meeting other people and feeling some sense of worth. With actions like these, we are trying to establish positive forward momentum. Some parents become dug in and are unwilling to help, saying it's "enabling" and that the young adult should take responsibility. You may have a long wait if you think they will wake up and change their behavior one day. Many young adults need a nudge or a jumpstart to move forward.

4. PULL THEM OUT—DON'T PUSH THEM OUT

One mother was concerned about her son's isolation in his room after returning from a failed semester in college. She got him to do some gardening and work around the house, but he immediately returned to his bedroom. She invited him to accompany her when she delivered Meals on Wheels to older adults. He reluctantly joined her and began to provide a service to these elderly shut-ins, start conversations, and get to know him. My advice to this mother was to come up with an excuse as to why she couldn't do this one day and state that her son needed to. When he does this on his own, it increases his confidence and social skills, and he receives a warm welcome from the seniors who get meals.

I fondly like to describe this as the "Bill Smith" tactic in honor of my mentor when I was a resident at Wilder Child Guidance Clinic in St. Paul. As part of my training, I sat in with Bill as he led a group of divorced and widowed adults in a program called, We Care. After sitting in two or three times, Bill approached me in his typical nervous fashion and said he had a last-minute conflict and I needed to lead the group that evening. I protested and said I wasn't prepared to do this and didn't feel confident about my skills to do a good job. He reassured me that I would do fine and rushed off before I could talk him out of this handoff. I led the group, and it went well, and I gained confidence in my skills that I would not have anticipated. Pretty soon, I was leading the group, and Bill was off to another project. Think about how you can pull your young adult out of the house by doing something with them—volunteering, going to a health club, taking a class together, and so on. The goals are getting the young adult out and exposed to others to build friendships and build confidence in their ability to move forward on the continuum of responsible independence.

Just a reminder. You can't pull your young adult out of the house if you are still there. If you want to get them out, you have to go together to the gym, do volunteer activities, take a road trip, go fishing, and so on. You trade off time nagging at them about what they aren't doing and should be doing by getting out and doing something together. One father and his son went to "Magic" board games in the neighborhood because the son liked to play the game, which could lead to meeting other people. Who knows, maybe a job will come out of these excursions out of the home. On my website, parentslettinggo.com, under resources and young adult resources, are lists of many different domestic and international volunteer opportunities for young adults. I like the idea of a skip year but not for playing video games.

5. COACH

Coaching is a term that businesses have borrowed from the sports world but has a different application. As applied in industry and parenting, coaching starts with the person, the young adult. Rather than the parent offering ideas and suggestions, the parent seeks to elicit and understand the young adult's ideas and thoughts. In this regard, the coaching parent needs to adopt certain practices. First, it begins with believing that young adults can develop good ideas or solutions. Second, the parent must practice nonjudgmental listening, as Chapter Two describes. Third, using open-ended questions helps surface the thought processes and ideas the young adult might have. Reflecting on what you heard and asking clarifying questions engages the young adult in exploring solutions to their problems or goals. Listen for ideas that reflect an effort to move toward self-sufficiency and independence and affirm them. "Can you tell me more about this idea?" or "Can you give me an example?" invite dialogue and exploration. Fourth, reassure the young adults that they have to make the decision but encourage them to consider the pros and cons of different choices. Coaching is a way of saying you believe in them and their ability to come up with solutions to their problems and challenges. Nonjudgmental listening and open-ended inquiry are the tools to be an effective parent coach—see chapter 2. From my experience, asking for "feedforward" suggestions as to how the parent can help the young adult become more self-sufficient and independent is also an effective coaching technique?"

6. CONSULT

Consulting is often associated with business. A consultant is an expert in an area that provides companies with recommendations and suggestions on how a company can be more successful. The company's leadership team listens to the advice and then decides to follow, modify, or reject the recommendations. There is no obligation on the company's part to follow the direction, and the consultant accepts the company's response. When parents offer consultation to a young adult, the same principles apply. The young adult is free to accept, modify, or reject the advice. When consulting with your adult child, here's an approach that will increase their receptivity.

- Ask permission to offer some suggestions. Assure them it is their decision.
- Offer your suggestions with supporting points or pros and cons.
- Reassure them that it is their decision, and you won't be mad if they do not follow your advice.

On one occasion, I hesitated to advise my son about an internship choice he was considering after he had completed medical school. He said, "Dad, tell me what you would do. I will still make my own decision." So, I did, and he made his decision. He felt like he got my advice and could make a decision that was aligned with my recommendation without giving up his freedom to choose other options. I would not have been upset or tried to talk him out of a different internship than I recommended. It's best to start with a coaching approach and then with permission to offer your consultation. There are often opportunities to share one's experience and advice in areas where the young adult is uninformed. Such areas include insurance, purchasing cars, investments, taxes, home maintenance, cooking, career decisions, business, and so on. Remember to ask permission and indicate it's their decision. By the way, with the knowledge young people have today about the digital world and social media, they may reciprocate by offering their consultation or advice to us. Welcome this. As a digital immigrant, I need all the help I can get from my three adult children.

7. PARTNER ON SOLUTIONS

This approach involves partnering with your young adult to identify solutions, decisions, or actions that support their progress toward self-sufficiency and responsible independence. The ideas below come from two schools of thought. One is solutions-oriented therapy, and the other is motivational interviewing. *Collaborate* with your young adult to find ways to work together, areas to compromise, and win-wins. Avoid fostering a situation that suggests it is a parent's way or the highway. This approach can trigger resistance as the young adult may need to demonstrate independence by choosing a different path.

Often, arguments occur around money, parental style, young adult relationships, lifestyle choices, careers, and jobs. The arguments often emerge from past problems, behavior, blame, and defensiveness. One way to break this pattern is to take *a solutions approach* versus a problem approach. This concept grew out of the brief therapy movement and has been applied in business settings and, to a limited extent, in parent-child relationships. In this approach, picture sitting around the kitchen table with your young adult, discussing their challenges and generating possible solutions together. Be sure to keep the responsibility on your young adult to devise options to meet those challenges and ultimately choose which one they will carry out. You are a collaborator working with your young adult to generate solutions. The goal is to establish a process and accompanying steps to attain mature independence.

This approach assumes that the developmental tasks of identity, independence, intimacy, and a need to find happiness drive decisions and actions. As strange or controversial as the young adult's actions or decisions might be, they are in the service of trying to accomplish these developmental goals and happiness. Solutions to problems are also critical for this technique to be effective. This viewpoint looks to avoid revisiting issues in the past and blaming. Instead, solving challenges is achieved by looking to the future. One cannot change the past. Focusing on solutions reduces resistance, engages the young adult more effectively, and fosters more of a partnering approach to issues. Assume solutions exist in your young adult's mind. The young adult has the resources and strengths to apply strategies for resolving challenges. As described above, coaching enables you to listen, ask questions, and elicit these ideas and solutions. Consulting allows you to offer your nonbinding suggestions. The goal is to uncover or elicit solutions that the young adult will embrace and the parents can support.

A SOLUTIONS-ORIENTED EXAMPLE

> Joe was a twenty-eight-year-old male living with his parents after attending college briefly but did not complete a degree. He obtained a service job that involved working with customers, and although he was earning a good salary, the job was stressful. Life at home had been contentious, and Joe needed to meet his mom and dad's expectations of caring for his room and helping around the house. In addition, he was holding onto resentment of his parents for not being more helpful when he was teased in school. The parents both apologized for not recognizing how much he was suffering and wished they had done more. Such actions by the parents relieved their guilt and reduced the extent to which Joe could continue to hold a grudge. The main problem was that Joe needed to be in his own place, so the goal that he and his parents agreed upon was that Joe would move out. But "when" was the challenge. He hesitated because of the cost of renting an apartment and threatened his parents. Joe was angry at the parents for pressuring him to move and said he wouldn't talk to them again if they kicked him out.
>
> I met with Joe to help him develop a five-year plan. Knowing his parents wanted him to move out within the next three months and not five years from now, we started discussing how this could be possible. Both Joe and his parents identified ways that he could move out closer to the parent's timeline, and the parents offered multiple ways that they would help him with the move. They saved money that he paid them for living at home and would give it to him for a security deposit and ongoing rent at his new apartment. They offered to help him find an apartment and

suggested he could work with a local nonprofit group that helped people manage their income and expenses. Because of some signs of depression and the stress with the job, the parents offered to support him in seeing a therapist. Joe found a couple of roommates to share the apartment cost and made plans to move out. Joe and his parents worked together to agree on a path forward.

First, these parents have used effective listening to communicate understanding and empathy. Repeating what they heard the young adult say helped them reevaluate their statements. Knowing that their parents are listening and trying to understand their needs and concerns invites the young adult into a collaborative process. The second step in the approach to Joe was shifting the focus from how contentious life at home was to a vision of the future where Joe would be independent and the relationship between Joe, and his parents would be much more amiable. This exercise aimed to find a goal to which both parents and Joe could agree. Joe would become more independent by moving out. The goal with parents is to find common ground in supporting the young adult's future.

The third step involved working with these parents to use open-ended questions to learn Joe's intentions and plans. In my interview with him, I asked several open-ended questions about his five-year plan and what his parents could do to help him. These inquiries require more than a yes-no response to draw out the young adult's thinking and solutions. Here are some examples: What ideas do you have about how you will make a living five years from now? What ideas do you have about how you could afford to move out? What one or two actions could your parents take to support your plan to move out? For a review of this type of inquiry, go back to chapter 3. Joe was at a pre-contemplation stage but moving toward a preparation stage. The parents' giving Joe a time frame to begin to explore options for moving out helped him move to the preparation stage.

A fourth step involved these parents openly addressing Joe's hurt feelings and resentment about their lack of support for the teasing he got during elementary school. They each talked to Joe, told him how much they loved him, and apologized without excuses for not being supportive when he was feeling rejected in school. I think this decreased some of Joe's anger and resistance to their influence.

A fifth step involved both parents and the young adult searching for solutions. Joe and his parents explored different ideas about how he could move out more in line with the parents' timeline. Joe came up with the idea of finding friends to share an apartment with. Joe and his parents searched for and brought forward ideas to consider facilitating the transition to independent living. Most adults are familiar with brainstorming, a collaborative problem-solving method. One technique I use, but not in this situation, is to have both parties develop three or more solutions to address a problem or attain a goal, put these on 3 x 5 cards, and then turn them over and read them to find the best idea. You may be pleasantly surprised that the young adult may come up with the same idea you described, or there may be a way to blend some ideas. When young adults come up with solutions or are part of the process of finding them, they are much more likely to invest in them than if a parent imposes a solution.

Sixth, the parents identified strengths and personal qualities that Joe had that would contribute to their success. When I interview young adults to talk about their five-year plan, I always ask about their strengths, special skills, or personal qualities that will enable them to progress toward this plan. I ask the parents to offer their observations regarding strengths, which show support and belief in their ability to succeed. His parent's confidence in his ability to function independently helped Joe see that he had the skills, strengths, and capability—a good-paying job—to move forward. Overall, his parents did an excellent job of expressing love, saying they were sorry but showing backbone relative to the timeline for Joe moving out.

TEACHING A CHILD TO RIDE A BICYCLE

Teaching our children how to ride a bicycle may contain some lessons for how we should help our adult children transition into adulthood. Do you remember how you taught your child how to ride? Typically, the parent helps the child onto the bike and steadies the bike. Next, the parent tells the child to begin to pedal as soon as the parent pushes the bike forward. The parent reassures the child that they will stay next to the child in case of trouble. Finally, the parent gives the child a push, yells "pedal, "and runs alongside for twenty or thirty feet as the child begins to ride on their own. Learning how to ride a bicycle can be a metaphor for launching the young adult. Launching our child into adulthood is another letting-go experience.

- We ready them for the journey by reassuring them that they can do this on their own.
- We provide encouragement and guidance to our young adults.
- We stand behind them and help them begin peddling.
- We tell them we will be walking with them on their journey.
- We partner with them to provide the initial push (backbone) and challenge them to pedal on.

At the risk of stretching this metaphor too far, we recognize that some stalled young adults have their feet on the ground and resist getting up on the bike to pedal. Some impaired young adults may try to pedal, but they wobble and fall and must ask us to help them return to the bike. Some derailed adults have ignored our guidance, peddled off the pavement, crashed, and need help healing before returning to the bike. And, finally, some estranged young adults, sadly, may ride off, never to be seen again.

Parents need to move from a directive to a facilitative approach to the process of a successful launch. In this regard, parents can work with and partner with the young adult to support their plan and aspirations to become self-sufficient and independent. You are not powerless and don't need to be inactive or uninvolved, but the type of involvement you choose, timing and your persistence to implement your influence efforts can be critical.

SELF-ASSESSMENT

Which of the different influence strategies could you strengthen? Rate the extent to which you have an interest in adopting one or more of the following influence strategies.

0	2	3	4
No Interest	Some	Interested	Very Interested

_____Go long
_____Affirm
_____Find a win
_____Pull—don't push
_____Coach
_____Consult
_____Partner to find solutions

CHANGE ONE THING

Marshall Goldsmith speaks of the need to change one thing about our behavior as leaders and parents and try not to overachieve. This is good advice. Adopt and implement one of the strategies above, including trying to be more of a coach or consultant to your adult child, then ensure that you follow through on this. Try to make the change you want to undertake with your young adult a habit, not just a one-and-off. It's clear from the field of neuroscience that developing a habit requires three actions. First, focus on the change you want to make as a parent. Second, practice, practice, practice the change. By doing so, you are demonstrating integrity and reliability. Finally, communicate your success in making the change by writing these down, telling a friend or spouse, or, as described in chapter two, asking for feedback from your adult child on how you are doing. This enriches and strengthens the neuropathway underlying a new habit. There are different views on how long it takes for a habit to develop, but focus and persistence are required. Remember: you want a sustainable positive relationship with your son or daughter, so have patience and "go long."

KEEPERS

As in previous chapters, I have identified some keepers or takeaways for your consideration. You may have your own list of reminders to add. That's great!

1. Take a "go long" approach to connecting with and supporting your young adult by engaging them in creating a five-year plan and finding ways to support this. Practice patience.
2. Shift the focus of the relationship from a directive or critical parent to a collaborative partner, coach, and consultant for their future.
3. Work around their resistance through listening, empathy, eliciting their ideas and finding ways to support one or more aspects of their plan that lead to responsible independence.
4. What is my successful launch strategy? What influence strategies will I implement?

5. _____

6. _____

7. _____

8. _____

9. _____

10. _____

CHAPTER SEVEN

LET GO

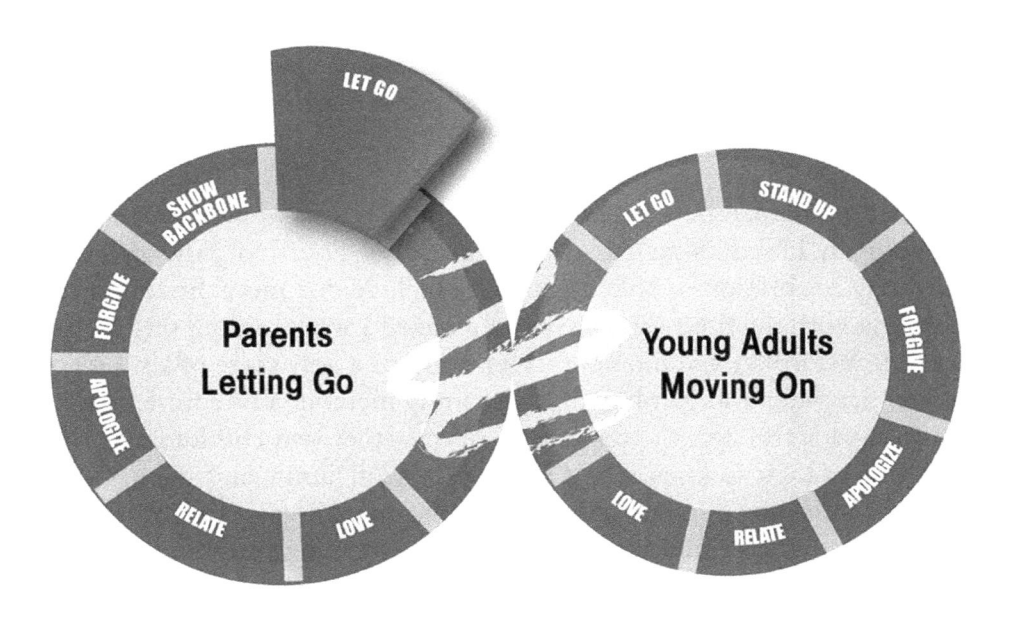

Parenthood is a never-ending journey down a wide river of worry and love. You get in the boat with your kids, and you never get out. They get out—they build their own boats and row into their destinies—but you stay in the original boat, always a parent, forever caring.

—Elizabeth Lesser, *Broken Open*

THE PARENT'S LAUNCH CODE

My wife forewarned me that our future son-in-law would stop by about seven o'clock to talk to me about marrying my oldest daughter. I noted this, but as we finished dinner, I made my way to my home office and opened my laptop, only to find it wasn't working. Fortunately, the company I worked for had IT people on twenty-four hours a day, so I called for help. What I had anticipated would take five or ten minutes was now more than thirty minutes, and it was past seven o'clock. My wife came upstairs with a perturbed look and said our future son-in-law was downstairs patiently waiting for his audience with me. I said, "Yes, I know; it will only be a few more minutes." Somewhat closer to seven-thirty, I finally had to end the call with the IT tech. As I walked into the room, all eyes glared at me, and my future son-in-law popped the question—asking for my daughter's hand in marriage. I thought about my father-in-law's line when I asked him for my wife's hand in marriage: "You can have her if you can afford her." But I played it straight and said, 'Yes.'

At that moment, it became clear that our family unit would never be the same again. Holidays such as Christmas, Easter, Fourth of July, and even birthday celebrations would most likely include one more. Stalling in a meeting with my future son-in-law, I realized I was avoiding this inevitable transformational moment. It represented a new stage of letting go of my daughter and gaining another family member. Over time, I have had to work through the departures of my other two children and the addition of their spouses as part of our expanded family unit. Then there was the addition of grandchildren—eleven as of the last count, but who's counting anymore? Initially, I resisted the plan to have the grandkids call me grandpa and suggested "Uncle Jack," but that didn't fly—more resistance to change on my part. We all outwardly celebrate these changes in the family composition but inwardly experience a twinge of sadness or grief, as we know the family we created and our unique relationship with our children will never be the same.

LETTING GO: THE FINAL STAGE OF THE LAUNCH PROCESS

It's important for us to recognize that letting go starts a long time before we launch our kids. From the day our baby arrives until our last days on earth, we are engaged in a dynamic of holding and letting go. We can't let go of something if we don't first hold on. We do this by holding on physically when they are infants, but we hold them in our love throughout our lifetime. We are given many opportunities to hold and let go. Here are a few:

- When our child is born.
- When the child starts to toddle away from mom or dad.
- We let our kids go with strangers on the first day of school.
- When our kids reach puberty.
- When they celebrate a milestone like confirmation, bar mitzvah, or bat mitzvah.
- When they start to drive and take off in a car.
- When they leave home for service, college, or work.
- When they commit to a partner in life.
- When they have children.

Each milestone is an opportunity to hold them in love, let them go, and say goodbye. These are great opportunities to send a message to our kids of our love for them and our hope for their next stage in life. A note in the lunchbox—oh, how embarrassing—or in a suitcase as they head to college are ways of honoring this transition in our relationship. If we have younger children, don't miss these opportunities to build a ritual that will become important in our adult relationship with our kids.

The dismemberment of the family when children leave represents both a loss and an opportunity for growth. It is no longer about growing as the original family but a new era of growing apart from the family. Parents must evolve in new ways without children, and young adults must mature in new ways without parents. How do parents let go in a way that enables growth and differentiation on the part of both parties without sacrificing the caring connection? I've used "differentiation" earlier, but let me revisit what I mean by it.

Healthy differentiation implies separate connectedness. In my research cited in Chapter One, I was able to document the relationship between a parent's love and support for autonomy (letting go) and healthy separation from parents.[1] This chapter concerns the ongoing "letting go" process parents face when young adults leave home, find a partner, and have children. As parents of adult children, letting go doesn't end as we wave goodbye to our kids. It becomes more complicated. Every engagement with our young adults, their partners, and grandkids is an opportunity to connect and let go. Mastering this balance is the key to having the relationship we want with our young adults and the significant others in their lives.

The graphic below illustrates a healthy, launched young adult in a relationship with a parent. Both are autonomous, but the white squiggly lines show that there continues to be a caring connection. What happens if one party has resolved old wounds and reached out to the other, but they have been rebuffed or shut out? This "estrangement" does occur in family relations. When this happens, and our young adult has shut us out, we must reconnect with our limitations to control or fix the young adult. If we have cut off our communication with the young adult, we must reevaluate this and take action to reach out so that both parties can attain this healthy separation. We must ensure that we use the healing practices and continue to make efforts to say we care and desire reconciliation. Even when the relationship with the young adult is toxic, and parents are relieved that they have left home, parents will experience some level of grief.

PARENTS LETTING GO MODEL

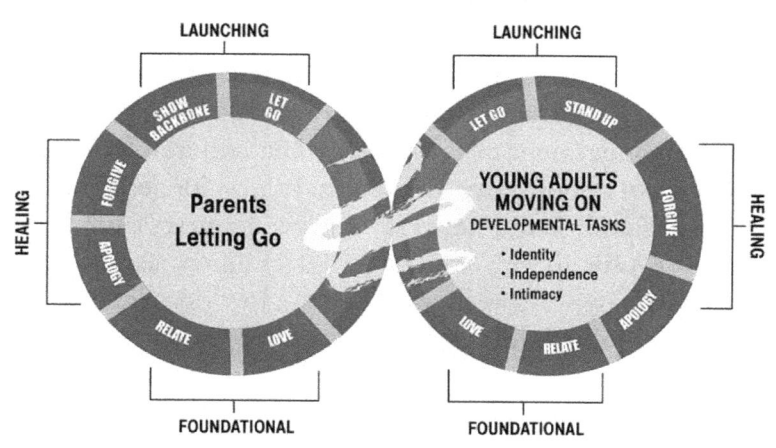

LAUNCHING — LAUNCHING

Parents Letting Go: SHOW BACKBONE, LET GO, FORGIVE, APOLOGY, RELATE, LOVE

Young Adults Moving On — Developmental Tasks:
- Identity
- Independence
- Intimacy

LET GO, STAND UP, FORGIVE, APOLOGY, RELATE, LOVE

HEALING — HEALING

FOUNDATIONAL — FOUNDATIONAL

LET GO

This last practice code centers around the necessary letting go and grieving that parents must do to launch their young adults. My bias is that most of us need help with this task, even under the best circumstances. Over sixty percent of parents provide some funding for their young adult children.[2] Sixty percent of parents of adult children living at home enjoy having them there.[3] I know some continue overstaying their welcome, and parents can't wait for them to take off. Even in contentious circumstances, parents need to prepare for the loss and grief accompanying the young adults' exit from the family. Without our letting go, our young adults can never attain the autonomy that enables them to have their unique identities and pursue their dreams. Below is a noninclusive list of what we need to let go:

- our vision of who we think they should be
- our idea of what we believe they should accomplish
- the way the relationship has been
- our usefulness and expertise regarding their matters
- our ability to control or even influence them
- our need to keep them the way they were when they were younger
- our regrets, resentments, guilt, or other emotions that keep us enmeshed
- our time and activities with them
- our prominence in their lives (we are no longer #1)
- our nuclear family
- our connection in beliefs (e.g., religion) and values (work ethic)
- living in the past or trying to retain the way things have always been
- the feeling of being needed by them
- our physical closeness if they move out of town
- family fun and vacations together

If you don't feel sad as you read this list, you are not in touch with the feelings of loss accompanying letting go. Maybe you are relieved they are gone, have finally found a job or sobriety, and are not ready to grieve. When my youngest daughter got married, we did the ceremonial father-and-daughter dance to the song "I Loved Her First" by Heartland. As I reflected on my daughter and her new husband in their first dance and heard the lyrics of the song my daughter chose for our dance, tears came to my eyes because I knew I would never again be the first man in her life.

> *Look at the two of you dancin' that way.*
> *Lost in the moment and each other's face.*
> *So much in love, you're alone in this place.*
> *Like there's nobody else in the world.*
> *I was enough for her not long ago.*
> *I was her number one; she told me so.*
> *And she still means the world to me, just so you know.*
> *So be careful when you hold my girl.*
> *Time changes everything; life must go on.*
> *And I'm not gonna stand in your way.*
> *But I loved her first; I held her first.*
> *And a place in my heart will always be hers*
> *From the first breath, she breathed.*
> *When she first smiled at me*
> *I knew the love of a father runs deep.*

Fathers who have given their daughters away to another man know the feelings expressed in this song, and for those of you who have this to look forward to, get ready to enjoy this bittersweet moment. And, mothers, this song is clearly for you as well as you dance with your son on the wedding day. Mothers and sons have a unique closeness that fathers and sons don't share. In fact, as a psychologist, it's disconcerting that my son is more willing to seek out my wife than me to share his deepest concerns and fears. That's okay because it is a heartfelt connection he has always had with her, and I hope they never lose. Before we discuss some of the losses that come with letting go, at the risk of repetition, I'll reground us one last time with assumptions necessary to let go and add a couple more.

As a parent, I:

1. Cannot control my young adult.
2. Am not responsible for their decisions or actions.

3. Am responsible for my decisions and actions.
4. Will not use the past to excuse their actions or mine.
5. Must balance love (support) and emancipation (letting go).
6. Believe that relationships are inherently reciprocal.
7. Must step up and change first.
8. Must accept the dismemberment of the family and the loss of our primary relationship with the child and face our sadness and grief. This is especially true when our adult son or daughter has a new number one.
9. Must move forward to find personal growth through new sources of meaning, happiness, and fulfillment beyond my adult children or grandchildren.

We will be well served if we approach the letting go stage of the family life cycle with these assumptions in mind. The grief we may feel over the end of the primary relationship with our young adult or the fact that they have moved on with their own lives sets the stage for a new adult friendship. Letting go doesn't mean we stop caring about our young adults or detach because we no longer want or need a relationship with them. As I have said, others, such as Daniel Seigel (*Mindsight*, 2011), have documented we are wired for relationships. This wiring is particularly true of family relationships.[4] We don't need to continue a relationship with one of our family members, be they young adults, siblings, or parents, but our lives will suffer.

Letting go is about opening our arms to allow a different relationship. Maybe you are familiar with Al-Anon, a support program for men and women in codependent relationships with another person. This other person may be a parent, spouse, child, or significant other who has become addicted to drugs or alcohol. I have sent parents to Al-Anon groups where they acknowledged being codependent or enablers in the negative sense of the word. The issue doesn't have to be substance abuse because the principles apply to letting go in any relationship. Please take a moment to read through this revised description of letting go of a relationship. You'll recognize some of the themes from my list above. Think about how this might apply to your relationship with your young adult.

Letting go does not mean to stop caring about someone; it means I can't do something *for* them.

Letting go is not to cut me off from someone; it's the realization that I can't control them.

Letting go is not to enable (disable) another but to allow them to learn the consequences of their actions.

Letting go is to admit powerlessness over their lives, which means outcomes are not in my hands.

Letting go is not to try to change or blame another; it's to make the most of myself.

Letting go is not to care for but to care about.

Letting go is not to fix someone's problems but to support them.

Letting go is not to judge them but to allow them to be their unique person.

Letting go is not to protect another; it's to permit them to face reality.

Letting go is not to deny someone but to accept them.

Letting go is not to regret the past but to grow and live for the future.

Letting go is to fear less and love more.

CHARACTERISTICS OF A PARENT WHO LETS GO

Letting go is necessary for a new relationship. It allows for new experiences for both the parents and the young adults. We've discussed earlier the characteristics of a differentiated or emotionally separated and connected young adult, but how can we describe an emotionally separated and connected parent? Take a minute to read through these and rate the extent to which these are true of you. I will briefly elaborate on the particular action or characteristic in each case. The more descriptive the item is of your thoughts, actions, and feelings, the higher the score. Here is the rating scale.

LET GO

0	1	2	3	4
Never	Rarely	Sometimes	Often	Always

____1. *I exhibit a degree of autonomy in my actions and decisions.* When this is present, you do not compromise your values or principles. I don't avoid decisions or actions because I believe my young adult would disapprove. An example might be the partner you choose after a divorce or the death of a spouse. I want their input but don't require their approval.

____2. *I continue to love, care, and connect with my young adult regardless of their response.* Unconditional love is just that—absolute, no matter what. I can disapprove of their decisions and actions but love them unconditionally.

____3. *I focus on what's most important and best for me as an adult.* For many parents, "children come first" has been the mantra that now needs to change. If you are married and have not put your marriage first, it's time. It is a season in your life to ask deeper questions about how to spend the rest of your life without having responsibilities for children.

____5. *I invest in developing an adult-to-adult relationship with my young adult.* Practice listening and talking less, become a mentor to your kids, coach, and provide consultation, but let them make the decisions even if they are not aligned with your thinking.

____6. *I welcome new family members—sons or daughters-in-law and grandchildren.* We will discuss this in the latter part of this book. It's difficult to let go of our young adults, but sometimes more difficult to embrace their choices, including choosing a life partner.

____7. *I face and resolve conflicts with my parents.* So many unresolved conflicts or contentious relationships with elderly parents can cause stress and rob us of time to enjoy our lives. These conflicts can become more pronounced or challenging when parents face illness or death. It's important to address these unresolved relationships with elderly parents to avoid jeopardizing the time and connection with your children.

____8. *I find new purposes, opportunities, and experiences to pursue without children.* Since raising children has been a dominant purpose in many parents' lives, think about the second half of your life. This time is also a stage of life where more time becomes available for adults and couples to explore or rediscover, things they enjoyed in the past but put aside during the child-rearing years. It's a time to pursue those ideas of what would be fun, meaningful, and challenging.

____9. *I expand adult and couple friendships.* Much of the positive psychology and happiness research points to the importance of social connections. It is a time to reach out to other couples, expand your activities, and build deeper friendships. These will help replace some of the emotional needs you have met through your kids.

____10. *I communicate with my young adult children in ways that respect their time,* boundaries, and preferences. For example, do not drop in on them unannounced. And if they prefer you not to call at certain times of night because this is their family time, honor that choice.

____11. *I demonstrate backbone in saying no to actions that would increase my young adult's dependency upon me.* Even though young adults are working toward increasing their independence, they may still approach you for time, help, or money. It would help to consider whether your response would be loving, aligned with your principles, and foster greater independence.

____12. *I can be a "special person" for my grandchildren.* Carve out a unique role and relationship with your grandkids. Be a mentor, an advocate, and a guarantor. It's important that parents move into this collegial role with their young adults and not try to relive their glory days and adopt the grandchildren. Grandparents are not surrogates for the parents. Some parents become overbearing with grandchildren because they miss this parent role or try to assuage their guilt over their past parental failures. It's important not just to be another parent but a special person in the grandchild's life.

____13. *I desire to leave a legacy—values, gifts, learnings, and the like.* It is a time when parents begin to think about what they can and want to leave to their children and grandchildren. Many parents of young adults set up a college fund or 529 for their grandchildren. Some begin giving various furniture or jewelry items to their young adults. It's also a time in my family when young adults call dibs on certain family items upon the parents' death. "I want your coffee table when you are gone," my youngest daughter exclaimed. It's a little disturbing to hear statements like this one. I checked my pulse and wondered if she knew something I didn't, and then I reminded her that I was not planning to "check out" anytime soon.

____14. *I detach from feeling responsible for the young adult and for fixing or rescuing them.* It's tempting to sweep in, offer to pay for something, or address a young adult or couple's pressing need. But one must weigh the value of the young couple's struggle to make ends meet and get through a tough time. My wife and I were tempted to help our oldest daughter with crushing childcare costs but decided they needed to struggle through this trial independently. In the end, they were able to experience the pride of perseverance and accomplishment.

____15. *I allow my adult children to define the relationship and communication they want with me.* Today, communication is becoming easier but more complicated. There are multiple ways to stay in touch with our grown children—cell phones, texting, and email, to name a few. For others, communication may include Facebook, Snapchat, or Instagram. As I've said, it's important to find your young adult's preferred communication method and be willing to connect that way. Some parents have stubbornly said they will not use email or texting, but they limit contact and information from their young adults. Should you come partway? Okay, maybe you could communicate your preferred mode to your kids, and they can do the same for you. It's about staying connected and less about whose model is correct.

How did you do? Are there lower scores that suggest an opportunity to expand your healthy separation from your young adult? Consider one or more of these areas and choose an action to help you become a healthier, more differentiated parent. Keep the areas you've selected in mind when we get to the "report card" section at the end of the book.

WHY LETTING GO CAN BE DIFFICULT

Typically, parents of young adults are in their midlife or later and often face challenges that may complicate the letting go process. This time of midlife and the emerging young adult is complicated for both. For the young adult facing the second period of individuation (differentiation), the first being in the toddler years, the challenges are monumental—from an identity, establishing independence, and building intimate, lasting relationships to finding purpose in life. Parents face a transformative time in their lives as well. Childrearing and related expenses and requirements start to drop off. We have to deal with changes in the physical environment, which include not only the young adults leaving but also considerations of downsizing, which can compound the sense of loss. As we discussed in chapter three, the developmental tasks of the parents and those of the young adults complicate the letting go process.

If our young adult becomes committed to a significant other, we must open the family circle to include this new person. This inclusion changes the dynamics of the interactions to accommodate the new addition. The extra effort we make early in the inclusion process will reap benefits over the long run. There will be a need to reconstitute or transform the marriage without kids. Parents who have lived with the value that "kids always come first "may be challenged to shift to "the marriage comes first."

One of the challenges for parents in midlife is to move forward on these tasks while doing the final work of letting go of the young adult. Midlife parents face new challenges that can interfere with the successful transition into this new stage. It's a time of loss but also of potential gain. See Carter and McGoldrick (2005) and Lachman (2003) in the bibliography for a fuller discussion of these family life cycle challenges. Successfully navigating these troubled waters of midlife will enable you to reach a more satisfying and meaningful life, with and without your young adults. We face the new reality of life without children, which contains loss and opportunity.

THE EXPERIENCE OF THE EMPTY NEST SYNDROME

> *In general, we prepare for marriage and parenting but don't prepare for an empty nest. That leaves us flailing and reactionary, and that is a bad combination that results in hello, who are you, and what do we do now?*

This comment was made to me by a parent in my May 2018 survey of parents of married young adults. It illustrates a common complicating midlife factor that affects a process known commonly as the "empty nest syndrome." What is the empty nest syndrome? It sounds like a disease, and in a way, it is, but it is not an illness but a feeling of "dis-ease." It is a time of discomfort due to the breakup of the family. Since I'm not inclined to label everyday life events and experiences as syndromes, let's use the phrase "empty nest experience" to describe the process. Parents experience "nest emptying" with many emotions, from joy and relief—"I thought they would never leave"—to profound sadness and loneliness. I want to affirm this wide range of emotions to normalize these emotions; you do not have to think you should feel a certain way.

Most parents will experience some loss when a child leaves the nest because life is changing in the family. In a national survey of over one thousand parents of young adults by Clark University in 2013, Jeffrey Arnett found that 84 percent of parents missed their kids once they moved out.[5] The change may be favorable for the family and the young adult. But if you have had a close and easy relationship with your young adult child and they move out, you may feel like you have lost a close friend. This loss may be particularly true if you could not effectively transition your relationship to more of an adult friendship while they were still living at home. But many parents consider their adult child to be their best friend.[6] Having a caring and close relationship with parents once kids have left home is the desired outcome, but seeking to be the best friend of your adult child suggests difficulty letting go.

The more comfortable and closer the relationship, the more likely a parent will feel normal sadness and loss. There are even parallels in this kind of loss to what we experience when a loved one with whom you have not had the best relationship dies. If the relationship with your young adult has been contentious, the emotions about their leaving home may be mixed, and the loss may be complicated. By complicated, I mean that you can't just feel the loss of a close friend but rather a loss confounded by the sadness of the relationship you didn't have. As described in chapter 1, my relationship with my father was distant and somewhat contentious in my growing-up years. When he died suddenly in my late thirties, I experienced sadness, knowing he would no longer be available to me. However, the more profound regret was related to losing the closeness we could have had over all those years of growing up. How can you tell whether the relationship was close or not if you are struggling with this empty nest experience? Here are some characteristics of the empty nest experience.

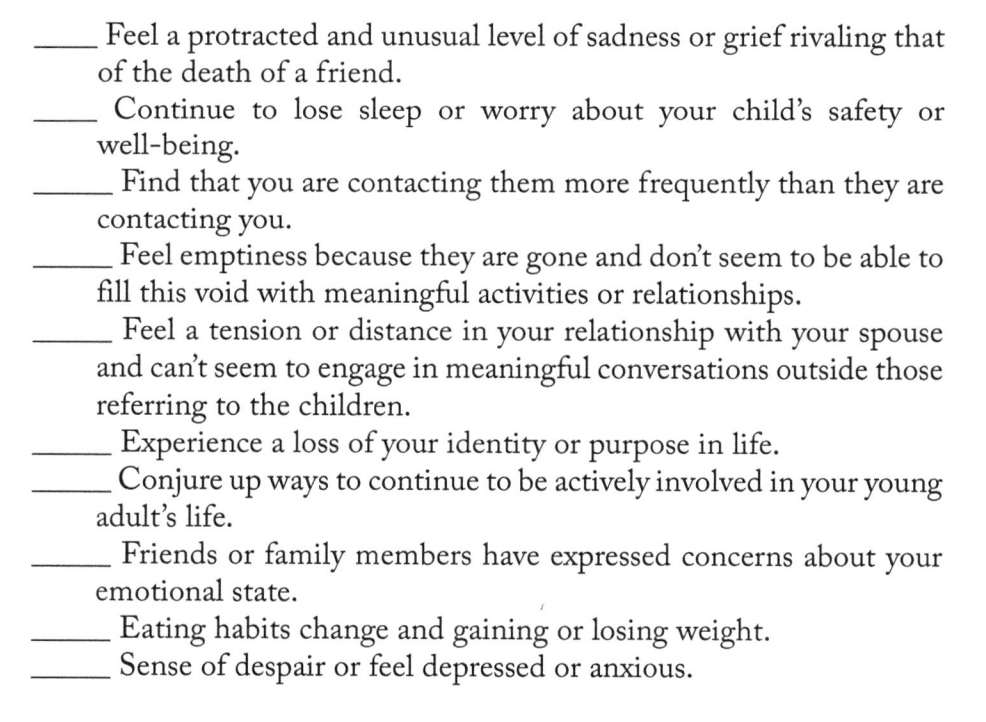

____ Feel a protracted and unusual level of sadness or grief rivaling that of the death of a friend.
____ Continue to lose sleep or worry about your child's safety or well-being.
____ Find that you are contacting them more frequently than they are contacting you.
____ Feel emptiness because they are gone and don't seem to be able to fill this void with meaningful activities or relationships.
____ Feel a tension or distance in your relationship with your spouse and can't seem to engage in meaningful conversations outside those referring to the children.
____ Experience a loss of your identity or purpose in life.
____ Conjure up ways to continue to be actively involved in your young adult's life.
____ Friends or family members have expressed concerns about your emotional state.
____ Eating habits change and gaining or losing weight.
____ Sense of despair or feel depressed or anxious.

If you experience one or more of these empty nest signs, the good news is that they will diminish over time. If these characteristics are protracted and talking with friends and family members doesn't help, you may consider speaking with a therapist. Resolving these empty nest emotions is essential to letting go and moving on with your life.

THE PRACTICE OF LETTING GO OF OUR YOUNG ADULT CHILDREN

There are multiple opportunities to practice supporting your independent young adult while simultaneously letting go. In general, there may be tendencies to fall back into old patterns that existed when the young adult lived at home. This falling back is most likely to occur when the young adult visits you in your home. Also, parents can get pulled back into caretaking rather than consulting and coaching if the young adult struggles with job, finances, marriage, and family challenges. Two areas that involve letting go while demonstrating concern and desire to help our independent young adults are finances and in-laws.

PARENTS AS THE 24-7 ATM

Financial support can become less of an issue when young adults marry, but there are still challenges. It's always a good practice to support the young adult couple's independence, including their financial independence. The more the young adult couple can "make it on their own," the stronger they become. Watching your young adult couple struggle to meet living expenses is worrisome. My wife and I remember when we barely made it to the end of the month or rushing off to deposit a paycheck before we over-drafted. But now we look back with pride on getting through that stage of our lives. There's something to say about getting through a tough time in life.

There may be times when parents should intervene or offer to help. Here are some things to consider as the opportunity to offer financial help. First, do you have available discretionary funds to tap into without jeopardizing your quality of life or retirement? Second, is it a need or a want for the young couple? Facing a sizable medical bill is necessary; having a new car is not. Third, has the couple asked for help, or do you believe they would accept the help if offered? Fourth, what would be the best way to provide financial support—a gift, matching grant, loan, or in-kind contribution? On the latter point, an in-kind donation may be a used car. The funding conditions should be clear, if not in writing. If it is an outright gift, it's essential not to have strings attached or hold the contribution over the couple's heads. Likewise, having an ulterior motive of what you want from the couple versus what they want will breed resentment and strain your relationship. At the same time, if you can contribute while exploring how they could participate and take responsibility for the financial help, that would be ideal. A matching grant or having the young adult couple do some work for the parent in exchange for a cash contribution can make sense. They may feel less indebted or dependent on such an arrangement. As a final check on your decision, ask yourself if your contribution will foster greater independence or dependence over the long run. The gift can create more dependency if they are likely to keep asking for continued subsidies. Parents with a lot of discretionary income who can give their young adult couple money need to be sure they are not doing this just because they can. Don't deprive your young adult couple of the opportunity to struggle. It will increase their resiliency in handling difficult circumstances, including financial demands. These conditions can be a helpful guide, but deciding when and how to help financially can be challenging.

Although I described how most parents continue to subsidize their young adult children after leaving home, doing so is not necessarily a sign that the young adult has failed to launch or you have yet to let go. Consider your financial capacity and circumstances that warrant parental financial help, and each parent must decide thoughtfully when such assistance is necessary or supports greater self-sufficiency and independence. Here are some common areas of subsidy parents may consider:

- Help with wedding costs
- Help with a down payment on a house
- Help with education, either of the parents or their children
- Help with daycare, in-kind, taking the children certain days a week, or providing childcare subsidies. A growing number of grandparents are providing some or all childcare services for young-adult couples.
- Help with unusual health insurance and excessive medical bills
- Contributing to a 529 educational plan for the grandchildren
- Funding medical or mental health assessments or services not covered by insurance. One example would be the young couple's costs of fertility treatment. Today's young couples are

marrying later and having more problems with infertility. The costs of pursuing other options, such as in vitro fertilization, can be daunting.
- Support for vocational testing or coaching relative to careers or jobs, which supports the young adult in becoming more independent.
- Help with some catastrophic events; this could be a medical emergency, car accident, a house fire, etc.
- Paying any out-of-pocket costs for the couple's mental and emotional well-being services. It may be used to address marital problems, depression, anxiety, or other mental health-related concerns. Such an offer removes one of the couple's excuses for not pursuing counseling. Many young couples take out high deductible insurance policies because they are healthy, don't think they will need medical services, and the insurance is cheap. Then, they learn about this high deductible they must pay when they seek counseling.

IN-LAWS ARE NOT OUTLAWS

Another challenging area for parents to be supportive and let go involves in-laws. There is an opportunity to practice including the new son or daughter-in-law while letting go of the need for control. The more you can engage and welcome these new in-laws with respect and appreciation, the more you will be able to let go. This goes back to the letting go principle and practice of expressing love and building a closer relationship in order to let go. In my survey of parents of married young adults (see appendix B), I found that one of the most significant challenges parents report is how to relate to the spouse of their young adult.

A young adult's spouse may be aloof, difficult to communicate with and control access to the parent's son, daughter, or grandchildren. The dilemma is supporting the marriage and their adult child while trying to engage the spouse positively. According to Madeleine Fugere, author and Professor at Eastern Connecticut State University, the reasons for difficulties between mothers-in-law and daughters-in-law may have evolutionary roots.[7] I have seen many more of the mother-in-law and daughter-in-law difficulties in my private practice. Figure further reports that mothers rate their relationships with sons-in-law more favorably than those with daughters-in-law. Over twenty years, Dr. Teri Apter, a writer, psychologist, and Fellow Emerita of Newnham College, found that seventy-five percent of couples reported having problems with their mothers-in-law.[8] Only 15 percent of mother-in-law and son-in-law relationships were problematic. She found that sixty percent of women admitted that their relationship with their female in-laws caused long-term unhappiness and stress. In either case, these strained relationships lead to conflict and frustration.

What are some underlying causes of the tension between mothers-in-law and daughters-in-law? The daughter or son-in-law becomes number one and replaces the parent. Facing this reality, it is critical for the parents to shift into a secondary position and support the marriage, not just their son or daughter. Being number two is a big "letting go" for mothers of sons. Sometimes, the son or daughter will confide in the parent about a problem with their spouse. One of the best things parents can say to a son or daughter who might disclose issues with their spouse is, "Have you discussed this with your spouse? If not, you need to, and if you can't work it out, get some professional help." Avoid colluding with your son or daughter or expressing criticism regarding their spouse. Such action puts your son or daughter in an untenable position of balancing loyalty to parents and spouse. This act is unsupportive of the marriage and will ultimately drive a wedge between you and your adult child. It ignores the fact that you can't be number one anymore. Accept this fact and be the best number two in supporting the marriage you can be.

A depressed client frustrated with her husband's relationship with her mother-in-law told me that her husband listened more to his mother than her. Sometimes, we must remind our young adults of the new number one in their lives. Another source of conflict is that mothers-in-law and daughters-in-laws have similar leadership roles in the household. In most cases, mothers-in-law may believe that they have, by experience and age, more expertise in such areas as decorating the house, cleaning, cooking, caring for children, and so on, if they have born these traditional homemaker responsibilities. Boomers grew up with Dr. Spock, but mothers today are heavily influenced by more recent writings on attachment, organic foods, and safety practices. One mother and daughter client of mine struggled over the value of the appearance of the grandchildren. The mother wanted her mother not to compliment the children on their looks or their appearance lest the children come to overvalue such outward characteristics more than their traits or strengths. The grandmother, a former teacher, struggled to hold back on the compliments that represented a habit she had with her children and in her job as a teacher. Each generation develops a new or different twist on childrearing practices.

> *My wife received an important and symbolic handoff on our wedding day. My mother was helping me with my cufflinks at the back of the church. While she completed this task, she said, in front of my soon-to-be wife, "This is the last time I will be doing something like this for you." From then on and throughout our marriage, my parents treated and supported us primarily as a couple. They stepped back, assumed a secondary role, and never took sides if issues arose between my wife and me. Their support for us as a couple has been a true gift. It is a model for a healthy transition for a mom who is shifting from number one in her son's life to number two.*

Various other differences can contribute to distance and strain in the relationship with a son- or daughter-in-law. They may include different values, religious orientations, childrearing practices, lifestyle decisions, management of money, and so on. In this short book, addressing all situations and challenges that might occur with in-laws isn't possible. We want to be able to hold—in love but also let go and support autonomy in our relationships with our married children. Here are a few principles that can be helpful:

Avoid "triangles," where you develop secrets with one of the young adults and leave the other out. Triangles can be especially damaging if you keep secrets from the young adult's spouse and if that spouse is the in-law. As much as possible, communicate directly with the in-laws. If your young adult and spouse seem unable to work out their problems, encourage them to seek professional help as a sign of their desire to strengthen and protect their marriage. In my situation, it is common for my wife to ask my daughters to request help from their spouses. When this chain of requests happens, the daughters will sometimes answer for their husbands and will not give their husbands a chance to respond. The son-in-law may wonder why I have not asked him directly for help.

The outcome of my observations has led me to begin asking my son-in-law for assistance directly.

Step back and take a secondary role, supporting your young adult's marriage. Encourage the couple to address issues they face between the two of them rather than bringing their trials to you. Respect the wishes, norms, and boundaries of the young adult couple. Take the time to get to know their preferences and respect them. If they want some notice before you visit, respect this request. They may choose different ways to celebrate special events and holidays as part of their new family traditions; we should honor those. Also, be clear and firm about your wishes, values, and norms, especially as they are at your home.

Be affirming of the couple and the daughter- or son-in-law. Find positive aspects about them that you can praise and recognize. Find common ground and ways to connect with your in-laws—shared interests, activities, events, practices, and so on. Seek to build a relationship with them through what you have in common. Take the lead and ask your son- or daughter-in-law for one or two suggestions of how you could be a better mother- or father-in-law. Then, follow through on as many of these suggestions as you can. Maybe they will reciprocate and ask for your feedback but don't expect it. You will generate more positive feelings toward them by acting more caringly and positively. They may also change to align with your desire for a reciprocal relationship. But please don't wait for them to transform their thoughts and actions towards you as a prerequisite for you to find and act on positive feelings toward them. Be the bigger person, reach out in love, and show kindness; your feelings will follow.

When problems arise, avoid blame and seek solutions. Suppose both sets of parents of the young adults have a tradition of celebrating Christmas Eve as a family. Both are resistant to discontinuing this family tradition. What solutions can you suggest that could respect these traditions while being careful not to give preference to one set of parents' wishes over the others? Ultimately, the young couple needs to make the call on how they will work out conflicting expectations. When problems persist with your young adult and spouse, please encourage them to seek professional help. Seek advice and counseling if you struggle to help your young adult and their spouse. Consider family counseling if problems persist with in-laws.

BE A PROACTIVE PARENT OF MARRIED YOUNG ADULT CHILDREN

We've been dealing with problems parents bring to my office and workshops. As a psychologist, it's easy to get pulled into these problems; it's my job. But the more effective focus should be preventing these problems and building a positive foundation with in-laws. Relate to your young adult couple as you would to other adult couples. Ask for their opinions and views. The more you treat them as adults, the more they will act that way.

Letting them pick up the tab when you dine out is a simple example. I suggest offering to pay the tip. Treat them as adults. Treat your son- or daughter-in-law as one of the family. Family rituals, celebrations, and recurring events that have been a part of the family history need to include the son- or daughter-in-law. Learn about your in-law's family rituals and celebrations. Welcome invitations to join their celebrations. It was very relaxing the first time my wife and I visited one of our daughters' homes for Thanksgiving. I thought this was great; let's do this more often. Make a point of developing a one-to-one connection with the daughter- or son-in-law. Discover together what you have in common. Find and share the activities you both enjoy and pursue those interests with them as they have time.

Respect their preferences in forms of communication as well as the content. Do they want to stay connected by text, phone, or face-to-face visits? When and how is it appropriate to contact them? Use their preferred form of communication to recognize their positive qualities and celebrate their achievements. My son will often not answer the phone when I make a call, but if I text him, he will text back quickly. It's a little weird, but it's okay if that's how he wants to connect. He may not be able to get into a long conversation at the time because of his involvement with his kids or because of his work, but he can give a quick text response. Sometimes, he texts that he can't talk now. That's helpful.

I can't address all your challenges with married young adults. As guidance, act in love, follow your principles, and support self-sufficiency and independence in your young adult couples. When I asked the parents of married young adults in a recent survey for ways to improve their relationships with their young adults, they had some helpful advice.

Please take a minute to review their suggestions, which I have listed in Appendix B-Survey Results.

DO YOU HAVE THE "RIGHT STUFF" TO LET GO?

In earlier chapters, I described the "right stuff" as character traits needed to succeed or do something well. In chapters one and two, I identified several qualities parents need to build healthy, connected relationships with their young adults while successfully launching them. These include compassion, patience, forgiveness, empathy, and gratitude. Let me add a few more relevant to this final letting-go stage.

We need to *embrace change*. Midlife is a time of change, whether you have adult children or not, but having adult children increases the need to change and learn new roles. It's a time to reinvest in your personal growth and the transformation of marriage without children. It's a time to let go and grow—to find new meanings, experiences, satisfaction, and value outside the children. Approach this time of change as an opportunity to grow as a person and in new family roles. We also need to practice *acceptance*. A daily review of the assumptions outlined in the Introduction and expanded upon in this chapter will be helpful to ensure the right mindset. Remember that we cannot continue to parent our children and must accept that the grandchildren are not ours. Such recognition requires acceptance and detachment—stepping back and letting go. Accepting and embracing a new description of "family" can be a bittersweet experience, but it is essential to our happiness at this last stage. Finally, successful midlife parents with the "right stuff" can *grieve* since letting go cannot occur without this. Grieving involves saying goodbye and letting go and is a normal response to the young adult's launch. There isn't a timetable for grieving the launch or for letting go. Grieving and saying goodbye are necessary for parents and young adults to move on with their respective lives. Reconstructing the relationship in new ways will help one overcome a sense of loss. We shouldn't try to suppress this grief; instead, embrace it as a sign of the importance of family relationships and the joy our children have brought us.

LET GO

When you are sorrowful, look again in your heart, and you shall see that, in truth, you are weeping for that which has been your delight.
—Kahlil Gibran, The Prophet

TIME TO SAY GOODBYE

One exercise I introduced in my workshops is asking parents to write, and in most cases send, a letter to their young adult. Since we use the phrase "launch" to describe what we are trying to do with our young adults, I ask the parents to imagine their young adult is leaving the country on a ship, and they may never see them again-literally launching. From day to day, we never know if we will continue to see our loved ones. Illness and accidents can quickly rob us of this assurance. What do you most want to say to your young adult as they prepare to sail away with the possibility of not seeing them again? If you strongly resist completing this exercise and believe there is nothing further your young adult needs to hear, that's fine. But please consider writing to discover and connect to special memories of your young adult and your hopes and dreams for them. Then, after completing this letter, ask yourself, "Is there something I have written that my young adult needs to hear, and am I willing to share with them verbally, if not in writing?" In either case, I'd suggest tucking the letter or a copy of it away as something you might share later, or they might find after you have passed. But why would you wait to share your heartfelt thoughts about them and your relationship? It would be a gift they would cherish. One colleague who read and contributed to this book shared the story of her mother's goodbye.

> *I found a letter two weeks after my mom died that she had written to my two brothers and me. Although I had seen this sealed letter in my mother's jewelry box earlier, I never opened it since I could see it was something she only wanted us to read in her passing. In that letter, she shared her feelings and values she wanted us to remember. It still brings tears to my eyes, but I am so thankful she wrote it!*

THE PARENT'S LAUNCH CODE

Here are some suggestions you might include in this letter.

1. What did you most enjoy about them as children and adolescents?
2. Share one or two special memories about your time with them growing up.
3. State regrets you might have as a parent for which you need to apologize.
4. Include actions or words you have said that you or they believe were harmful and for which you would like to ask their forgiveness.
5. Revisit those harmful actions or words for which they have apologized that you need to forgive.
6. Tell them what you wish you could do over.
7. What have you most appreciated about them as a person?
8. How have they been a blessing, helped you, or taught you valuable lessons?
9. What do you hope for them in the future?
10. What do you hope they will remember about you?
11. Write what you want them to know if you never see them again.
12. Also, include other areas you wish to address when saying goodbye.

I am including a sample letter. Only some of the questions above have been addressed, but that's okay. You can respond to one or more of the above questions or come up with some of your own memories or messages you wish to impart. The crucial aspect of the letter is not whether you have covered everything or how well you write the letter. The most important feature is that it comes from your heart.

Dear Son,
I am writing as if you are leaving the country, and I may never see you again. I know this is not happening, and I don't believe you have any plans as such, but I just wanted to share my reflections on your growing-up years and my hopes and dreams for you. We get swamped and don't take the time to share our deepest thoughts and desires, and I want you to know these.

LET GO

First, I wanted to mention some things I most enjoyed about your years growing up in our family. From the earliest of times, you were on the move. Even with a corrective device holding your two feet pointed the right way, you could fling yourself over the crib railing and escape. You were fearless in taking on a neighbor boy six inches taller than you, jumping on a two-wheel bicycle, and riding it for the first time without my push or help. Later, these athletic skills earned you opportunities to excel in high school sports, and your mother and I enjoyed watching every game you played. When I drive by the Little League fields and the high school, I fondly remember the sporting events you participated in at these sites.

Second, I wanted to say something about your character, of which I am most proud. You have always been goal-directed and achievement-oriented, which has taken you to the highest level in the medical profession. You always welcome a challenge with humility and some self-doubt, but in each case, you excel. Your heart and openness regarding your feelings and things that have been very difficult for you are equally important. This combination of a tough, ambitious, and competitive person who could be tender and vulnerable is unusual. I will always treasure this about you.

Third, I have tried to reflect on any regrets about you or our relationship, and I don't have many. You might have a few you could remind me of, and I would welcome these and an opportunity to apologize. Two incidents stand out. I remember holding your younger sister when you came up and continued bugging me about something you wanted, even after I said no. You were probably five years old. So, I did a leg sweep while sitting down and knocked your legs out from under you. It didn't hurt you, but I saw a stunned look on your face. I am not sure you will even remember it, but I was ashamed of what I did. Please forgive me. On another occasion, I got furious and verbally berated you. I remember coming out of the dry cleaners after picking up my clothes, and you were in the car and made some condescending remark that just set me off. I verbally let you have it. Again, afterward, I was very ashamed of this and knew I had overreacted. I don't remember apologizing to you, but please accept my apology now.

Fourth, I have pondered what I would do over in raising you, and I don't have an immediate answer. I know I was busy and could have given more time to you and could have done more things with you outside of attending sporting events. I have fond memories of your maiden freeway road trip to Hinckley after getting your license and of subsequent trips we took to Duluth. Little did I ever imagine you would end up living in Duluth. Those were great times just being together with you. As adults, we have had some additional ventures, like backpacking and sailing together, which are treasured memories.

Fifth, I have many hopes for you, some of which have already come true—being married and having children. I never envisioned you going into the medical field, but I am very proud of the effort and discipline you put into becoming a physician and your pride in your work. Along with the goal-directed and achievement side, there is a very conscientious side of wanting to do the best you can as a physician and provide your patients the best care they can get. My hopes for the future are that you will have a long and fulfilling marriage and family life and achieve all that you want in life. At the same time, I want to encourage you not to abandon your caring, sensitive, and vulnerable side. I also can't help but encourage you to continue to be a seeker of answers to life's more profound mysteries and questions.

Sixth, when I look back on my life, I hope you will remember me in some ways. I want you to remember me as always loving you deeply and unconditionally. Don't ever doubt my love for you. I want to be recognized as a person of integrity, true to his word, faithful to his marriage, and committed to the family. I want to be remembered not as an exceptional person but as a good and honorable person you are proud to call Dad.

Life is very short; good times become memories so quickly that we don't have time to savor them. This is all the more reason to take this time to treasure the relationship we have and how proud I am to call you, my son. Thanks for taking the time to read this, and don't feel obligated to respond in any way.

*With love and affection,
Dad*

MY FINAL REPORT CARD

Each day is one more day of saying goodbye. As each day passes, we must look in the mirror and ask ourselves how we did as a parent. A common theme in this book is the idea of doing your report card. If you have read and acted upon recommendations in this book, you are ready for your final self-exam. By this, I mean identifying how you have implemented the code- the six practices. Although asking for feedback and feedforward from your young adult is fair, only you can do your report card. Should their opinion matter? Absolutely. But at the end of the day, we can't control what others think, especially our young adult children. It's time for an honest reflection on our actions and an evaluation (grading) of our progress. We're all a work in progress, including our kids, so a grade less than an "A" only identifies an area of continued opportunity and growth.

I'll offer suggestions for the report card, but please list what **you** think is essential. Share your report card with your spouse, partner, or friend. Ask them to listen, ask questions, and challenge you if they think you may be grading yourself too hard or too easy. Once completed, focus on, and review these actions daily or weekly. At the end of the day or week, identify where you have done well and where you could improve and recommit to both areas. When you look in the mirror, the question is not, "Have I pleased my young adult or anyone else?" but, "Have I been the best parent I could be?"

THE PARENT'S LAUNCH CODE

My Final Report Card

Date:____/____/____

My Intended Actions	My Actual Action	My Grade	My Improvement Plan
Do I accept I can't control, fix, or be responsible for my young adult?			
Are my actions motivated by love and not fear, anxiety, etc.?			
Are my actions consistent with my principles: honesty, responsibility, etc.?			
Do my decisions and actions help my young adult become more independent?			
Do I show unconditional love?			
Do I invest in relating to and understanding my young adult?			
Do I practice apology and forgiveness?			
Am demonstrating backbone in love?			
Have I said goodbye?			

KEEPERS

As in earlier chapters, I try to pull out what I believe are essential "keepers," tips, or suggestions to keep in mind after reading this book. Please feel free to create your list of keepers because your takeaways may differ from mine. Here's my list of what I think is essential from this chapter. Please add yours.

1. Take the time to be sure you listen to, connect with, and understand your young adult and their spouse if married. Understanding is always the starting point.
2. Loving your daughter-in-law or son-in-law is a way of showing love for your child. Communicate unconditional love and extend this type of love to their spouse. Practice loving actions toward your son- or daughter-in-law; it will soften your heart and theirs.
3. Say goodbye, let go, and start to grow apart. If you are still emotionally entangled with your young adult due to anger, resentment, guilt, fear, or anxiety, revisit the need to apologize and forgive.
4. Approach the empty nest stage as a time of transformation and new opportunities—if married, a time to transform your marriage and relationship with your young adult. Embrace new experiences, friendships, and additions to the family.
5. Approach midlife as a time to reinvest in yourself, your health, and your well-being; reflect and turn inward to find new and deeper purposes for the second half of your life.
6. Expand the concept of family to include in-laws and grandchildren. Invest in these new relationships with a commitment to building positive and lasting bonds. If you're a grandparent, be the best one you can be.

THE PARENT'S LAUNCH CODE

7. Balance your needs for privacy, time alone, or marriage with clear communications of what you can give your young adult couple regarding time, presence, and help—financial and otherwise.
8. Reform your relationship with your young adult or young adult couple to be a good friend. Offer consultation or advice when asked, but always acknowledge that they can choose another path; if they do, you won't be angry with them.
9. _____
10. _____

EPILOGUE

A parent's job is there to be left.

—Anna Freud

We begin holding on and letting go from the moment we decide to have children. We hold them in the womb, and dads and moms feel the movement of the infant getting ready to arrive. If adopted, we joyfully anticipate the arrival of this new family member. Then they come, and the ritual of holding and letting go begins.

Actual letting go can't happen unless we first hold. The challenge is finding the music within that enables us to move close and hold on when needed and back away when required. Timing is everything, and finding this balance involves risk. There is a risk we might do the wrong thing and risk that our kids may stumble and suffer on their path to independence, but letting go leaves us with no choice.

The process isn't always smooth, but every child needs the holding message that they are loved no matter what. They need the " let go" message to become who they want to be and follow their dreams, even if those don't include us. This combination is the key launch code: *let go in love*. Remember: they are not our possessions, nor do we own their future. They are gifts we cannot keep. Our role as parents is to ensure they know they are loved and set them free.

I hope you find guidance and help in this book on how to do your best to love and let go. I hope you will provide the secure launch pad and the necessary benediction to free them so they can confidently fly off to their future happiness and success.

APPENDIX A

Chapter One

Unconditional Love Assessment

Answer the following questions, rating the extent to which you believe these characteristics are true about your parent. Use the following rating scale:

```
0    1    2    3    4    5    6    7    8    9    10
completely        somewhat true, and false      completely true
 not true
```

1. You give me your attention; you are emotionally available to me. _____
2. You tune in, listen, and understand me. _____
3. You tell and show them that you think I am important to you. I matter _____
4. You show acceptance of my feelings without ignoring or being judgmental. _____
5. You allow me to have different beliefs, values, and perspectives. _____
6. You show unconditional love for them regardless of my achievements or shortcomings. _____
7. You allow me to develop and have my own identity. _____

8. You allow and support my freedom and independence while staying connected to me._____
9. You allow me to make mistakes and fail while showing love and acceptance._____
10. You show a willingness to listen, consider, change your mind, and otherwise, be influenced by me while maintaining your values and beliefs_____

Chapter Two

How well do you know your young adult?

Put a checkmark next to any questions you believe you know how your young adult son or daughter would answer.

_____ 1. What do they like about themselves?
_____ 2. What do they dislike about themselves?
_____ 3. What was the most difficult challenge they faced in growing up?
_____ 4. What were their greatest achievements in growing up?
_____ 5. What were their greatest disappointments?
_____ 6. What do they most like about their life now?
_____ 7. What do they most dislike about their life now?
_____ 8. What are one or two of the most difficult challenges they believe they face at this time in their life?
_____ 9. What makes them happy?
_____ 10. What do they most appreciate about you as a parent?
_____ 11. What do they want to accomplish in the next five years?
_____ 12. What help, if any, do they want from you as the parent(s) to enable them to accomplish their goals in the next five years?
_____ 13. What strengths or skills do they believe they have to accomplish these tasks?
_____ 14. Where do they hope to be living and what do they hope to be doing five years from now?
_____ 15. How would they like to see the relationship change between them and you over the next five years?
_____ 16. What do think they would say is their aim or purpose in life?

APPENDIX A

Would you like to know your young adult's answers to these questions? Worth a breakfast or cup of coffee after you have completed your quiz and then ask them these questions but change the pronoun—they, them, and their to you, your, and so on.

How well do you listen?

Rate your parent's ability to listen to you on each of the following items, with 10 being the highest rating you can give your parent on listening and 0 being the lowest. The highest score possible for the whole assessment is 100.

Listening Self-Assessment

0	1	2	3	4	5	6	7	8	9	10
Not True at All										Completely True

My parent:

____ 1. Does not interrupt me when I am speaking.
____ 2. Does not think about what they will say next when listening to me.
____ 3. Does not finish my sentences.
____ 4. Maintains eye contact and won't allow interruptions such as phone calls, checking my cell phone, or other parties to interrupt the conversation.
____ 5. Routinely describe what they hear me say to ensure they understand.
____ 6. Ensures an important conversation is finished, and if not, they propose another time to come back to it.
____ 7. Does not try to fix or tell me what to do instead of listening.
____ 8. Pays attention to not only to the content of what I say but also to the emotions communicated through tone, words, or body language.
____ 9. Asks for clarification if they are unsure they understand what I am saying.
____ 10. Listens to understand and not judge.

Total Score:_____

How did you do? Circle some skills you may need to practice.

Chapter Three

Interview Questions to Surface Opportunities for a Parental Apology

1. What things would you like for me to have said as you were growing up?
2. What things, sayings, or other communications would you have wished I hadn't said?
3. What one or more things do you most remember about your experience with me that were disappointing? Follow-up question: Can you tell me how or why these disappointed you?
4. If we could go back to when you were a child, what one or two things would you like me to do differently?
5. How could I have been a better dad or mom to you when you were growing up?
6. What one or two things happened to you in our relationship that you still feel hurt or sad about?
7. What one or two things have I done or not done that have had a negative impact on your life today?
8. In the last two to three years, what have I done or said that have been most upsetting or frustrating to you?
9. What are some things I do or don't do today that are a source of frustration, hurt, or disappointment to you?
10. Has anything happened in our relationship over the years for which you would like to hear me say, "I'm sorry"?

APPENDIX A

Chapter Four

Engage Your Young Adult in A Dialogue on Forgiveness

To deepen your relationship with your young adult, discuss the application of forgiveness in your relationship with them. Some questions you might ask and discuss are below. It's important that the questions are the same for both of you. Go through and respond to the questions first so you can demonstrate self-disclosure. This will invite them to do the same. Then, they can go through the questions. Identify any actions either you or your emerging adult will take from going through these questions.

1. What decisions have I made or actions have I taken for which I would like to apologize? What are these?
2. Are there decisions I have made or actions I have taken for which I would like to forgive myself? What are these?
3. Are there decisions or actions I have made for which I would want your forgiveness? What are these?
4. Are there decisions or actions that the other (parent or child) has made that I would like to forgive?
5. Do I have anger or resentment toward others in the family or outside the family? What are these, and how will I move toward forgiveness?
6. What are one or two benefits of practicing forgiveness in our relationship be helpful?

Chapter Five

Interview Your Young Adult About Integrity Note: If you are one person interviewing a young adult, change "we" to "I."

1. In what ways were we either too strict or too lax during your childhood?
2. What values did we try to convey to you in your younger years? What about important truths, sayings, or principles to guide you in life?

3. What one or two ideas, principles, values, or lessons would you have liked for us to teach you in your younger years?
4. In what ways do we expect too much or too little of you now?
5. What would you have done differently if you were the parent? What would you do differently now if you are your parent?
6. What are your most important values, principles, and guidelines for living your life?
7. How do you define being independent of your parents?
8. As you move more toward independence, how would you like to stay connected or involved with us as your parents?
9. Where do you see yourself in five years? Where might you be living? Working? Married or with a girlfriend or boyfriend?
10. How do you want us to stay in touch or communicate with you when you are on your own?
11. In what ways are we too strict or too lenient in how we approach you at this time? What suggestions do you have as to how we might strike a better balance?
12. In what ways should we step back, let go, and allow you to make your own decisions?
13. In what ways do you want us to be more supportive or helpful to you?

Living at Home Agreement

Purpose of the agreement: To outline expectations of the living arrangements and responsibilities of both parents and (*young adult's name*) that will ensure we can have a positive experience in living together. This arrangement is temporary and provides an opportunity to transition to the young adult's living arrangements outside the home. The expectations and responsibilities as outlined below will be reviewed every two weeks by parents and (*young adult's name*), at which times adjustments in the terms can be considered.

Expectations: Some should be considered for the young adult.

- Rent-specific expectations: amount, due date, and so forth (parents may retain rent and make it available when young adults leave).

APPENDIX A

- Purchasing/chipping in on food, cooking (x nights week), laundry, and chores.
- Attendance at school and/or job.
- Quiet hours: Everybody needs to sleep, especially parents who are working and need to get up in the morning.
- Use of car, gas, upkeep.
- Insurance on vehicle.
- Cell phone.
- Guests and any overnight restrictions.
- Specific prohibitions if needed: no alcohol use if minor, no illegal drugs in the house or being used.
- No violence or threats of violence or damage to property.
- Respect by all members of the household: no swearing, name-calling, or personal attacks.

Expectations: some to consider for the parent.

- Show the investment the parents are making (optional).
- Provide a bedroom, bed, access to other areas of the house, TV, computer.
- Provide x meals a week and x amount of food for young adults to eat at other times.
- Will maintain the house: clean common areas, wash sheets and bedding.
- Respect the young adult's privacy and desire to be independent.
- Will provide consultation and coaching as requested by young adult.
- Will cover all costs related to the house: mortgage, insurance, utilities, Cable or other TV access, and Wi-Fi.

This agreement will be reviewed every two weeks and adjusted as agreed upon by all parties. If (*young adult's name*) does not adhere to the requirements of this agreement, a period of thirty days probation will be established. If (*young adult's name*) does not comply within this thirty-day period, (*young adult's name*) will be asked to find alternative living arrangements within the next thirty days.

Date of agreement: _____ _____ ____
Parties to the agreement:

_____

_____

Chapter Six

Protocol for Check-ins on Five-Year Plan

Once the young adult has created a five-year plan, the parents indicate what they will and will not do and their expectations. Establish meeting times, beginning with two weeks and move to a monthly check-in. The expectation is that this is a formal time to check in, and parents should avoid asking questions, criticizing, or nagging about the young adult's actions between the check-in periods. The tone should be positive, reinforcing small progress and collaborating on how parents can help young adults advance their plans.

Setting
Suggest meeting at the kitchen table or going out for coffee—make it adult or business-like.

Process
Pull out the young adult's five-year plan copy for parents and young adults.

Review plan as follows:

1. Ask the young adult how they have progressed on the plan (feedback on positives). Recognize and praise any progress.
2. Ask the young adult what one or two actions they can take before the next check-in to make progress on their plan (feedforward). Ask if the young adult is open to suggestions (feedforward), and if so, offer these but allow the young adult to use or not use these. Ask the young adult to note these on their plan.

APPENDIX A

3. Parents review their do's and don'ts for compliance on these and indicate one or two suggestions for improvement.
4. Parents ask what two or three actions the parents can take to support further progress by their young adult. Note these on your response sheet in writing and indicate one or more of these you are willing to carry out. Commit to these.
5. Note the young adult's proposed actions and parents' supportive actions to review in the next check-in.

Review the parents' expectations of the young adult if they are living at home.

1. Ask young adults how they have met these expectations. (feedback). Parents share positive observations.
2. Ask the young adult about one or two ways they could improve on expectations before the next check-in.
3. If things need to be improved, ask if there are negotiable expectations that the young adult would like to revise. Discuss and revise if the young adult is willing.
4. If there continues to be a lack of progress on expectations, propose that parents and young adults brainstorm—throw out three ideas for improving on expectations and ask young adults to commit to one or more of these actions.
5. Parents write these down for review at the next check-in.

Example of a Five-Year Plan: Twenty-one-year-old male on probation in college and moving home

How happy or satisfied with your life are you now? 0-10 = 0=completely unhappy. 10+completely happy

Current 2-3
In five years:

1. Where will you be living? Twin Cities or? Apartment or house? Best job/opportunities—an apartment

2. Alone, roommate, girlfriend?
   Alone not sure
3. What will you be doing to earn a living?
   My hobbies are playing video games and having short-term income opportunities, such as real estate or some business.
4. What will you be doing for fun?
   Outdoors, sports, watching sports, video games.
5. What are your skills, natural talents, or qualities that will help you succeed?
   Quick thinker, multiple languages, people skills, big picture, capacity to be goal oriented.
6. What roadblocks or difficulties might you have to face to get to your five-year plan?
   What has gotten him off course on goals—the pandemic, some bad decisions,
7. How will you overcome these?
   Get serious about academics; being at home will help and will cut out smoking weed.
8. What specifically can you do in the next six months to help you move toward your five-year plan?
   Move home, focus on classes, have a plan, and act on it versus procrastination.
9. What can you do in the next two weeks to begin moving to your five-year plan?
   Develop a plan to study at home and stop smoking pot.
10. What has been one of the most successful accomplishments you have had in your life?
    What skills did you use? Being present, attending classes, not falling behind, having goals, having a condensed schedule, and not having time to be distracted.
11. How could you apply these skills to support your five-year plan?
    Be more disciplined and have less distractions being at home.
12. What two or three ways can your parents be helpful in supporting your five-year plan?
    They are always there for me. They haven't done anything wrong. Don't blame themselves for his struggles—I am responsible. Wants to be more open.

13. In what different ways are your parents helpful now?
    Providing a home for senior year. They are always there for me. It's my issue.
14. Are there one or two ways your parents are not helpful in moving toward your five-year objective? Nothing comes to mind.
15. What one or two things do you want your parents to understand about you and your five-year plan?
    Current problems are not caused by them, and I am taking responsibility for fixing these problems. I need to walk the talk. Have not in the past.
16. What will your relationship with your parents be like in five years?
    It's good, but it could be better. I need to be more open—a good relationship.
17. How happy and satisfied with your life will you be when you attain your five-year plan? 0-10=. 6-7
18. What expectations should your parents have while living at home?
    Getting work done, helping around the house—making some money, Door Dash, coaching?? Eating healthy, getting exercise.

Parents' response to twenty-one-year-old male on probation with college and moving home

Son, you are our son, and we love you unconditionally. We will always love you no matter what the future brings. We want you to succeed in reaching your dreams and are willing to support you. However, our support for you is conditional and requires structure and guardrails.

We will do the following:

- Love and accept you for who you really are and support your personal life journey.
- Provide life skills guidance and support.

- Help you decide what you want out of life and assist you in planning to obtain it.
- Provide/pay for these items:
- Use of the car and car insurance
- Health and dental insurance
- Medical and dental expenses
- Counseling
- Cell phone service
- Cost of school or training to gain skills to support yourself with passing grades.
- Room and board at home

We will not do the following:

- Pay for personal items, entertainment, and so on.
- Treat you like a child instead of a young adult.
- Provide a "free ride" here at home if you are not actively progressing toward self-sufficiency and independence.

Expectations for living at home

- Attend school and/or have a job.
- Meet with your college advisor and have a plan for this fall and the overall degree.
- Be honest and open with us.
- Good self-care: eating, sleeping, exercising.
- Helping with chores and projects around the house when asked, cooking a meal or two.

The following rules are nonnegotiable and must be followed at all times.

- Do not engage in any dangerous or illegal activities.
- No drugs on the property.

APPENDIX B

Advice to couples in the empty-nest phase of the family life cycle, from a survey conducted in May 2018 with parents of young-adult couples. Many good suggestions. Highlights my belief in the wisdom of the community. In this case parents of married young adults.

Prepare for it by taking more time with each other in advance.	Establish a dating culture; pray together regarding the transition.
Explore new hobbies, careers, or passions.	Remember what brought you together and renew your relationship.
Be patient, relax, and don't be too hard on yourselves.	Don't act out of your neediness.
Prepare and plan for the empty nest.	Give your spouse space; don't try to meet all of your needs through your spouse.
Stay in touch with the children while enjoying the freedom.	Enjoy the possibilities and don't look back.
Let the children figure things out before jumping in.	Make a list of dreams and compare notes.
Spend quality time together.	Be open to innovation, creativity, play, detachment, and imperfection.
There's a lot of letting go.	Develop friends at a similar stage of life.

THE PARENT'S LAUNCH CODE

Everyone should look for joy in this phase of their lives; be grateful.	Find a balance with your spouse with each having interests outside the home.
Work things out; discuss difficulties and love one another.	Enjoy grandchildren; they are wonderful.
Act only as a consultant, not an adviser.	Be transparent and vulnerable.
Give them freedom to fail or succeed—to make their own mistakes.	Ask for their preferred method of contact.
Be a good listener; listen nonjudgmentally.	Let go of expectations.
Don't try to control them.	Wait to be invited; don't intrude.
Recognize their accomplishments.	Communicate without judgment.
Accept, connect with, and build up your spouse.	Show interest in them.
Hear what they didn't like about their childhood.	Ask for forgiveness for past failures.
Help them become financially independent.	Always be willing to help.
Initiate time and conversation with them.	Treat them with respect and expect they treat you likewise.
Be honest with yourself about your shortcomings.	Avoid criticism, especially of mistakes they make.
Be supportive and let them know you love them.	Don't take it personally when they spend time with other parents.
Accept their independence.	Be involved.
Keep communication lines open, always.	Treat them equally.
Be sure to support and include the spouse.	Respect their boundaries.
Never issue an ultimatum.	Don't let pride get in the way.
Honor their parenting style.	Recognize it is a privilege and not a right to have a say in their lives.

NOTES

Introduction
The Launch Code

1. Jeffrey Jensen Arnett, *Emerging Adults in America: Coming of Age in the 21st Century.* (Washington, DC: American Psychological Association. 2008).
2. Richard Fry, Jeffrey S. Passel, and D'Vera Cohn, "A Majority of Young Adults in the US Live with Their Parents for the First Time Since the Great Depression," Pew Research Center, September 4, 2020, accessed April 1, 2022, https://www.pewresearch.org/short-reads/2020/09/04/a-majority-of-young-adults-in-the-u-s-live-with-their-parents-for-the-first-time-since-the-great-depression/.
3. John Stoltzfus, a survey was conducted by the author of 123 parents of young adults in April and May of 2021.
4. Jeffrey J. Arnett and Joseph Schwab, Parents and Their Grown Kids: Harmony, Support, and (Occasional) Conflict, September 2013, Clark University.
5. Josh Coleman, *Rules of Estrangement: Why Adult Children Cut Ties and How to Heal the Conflict* (New York: Harmony Books, 2020).
6. Brené Brown, "The Power of Vulnerability," June 2010, accessed December 2022, https://www.ted.com/talks/brene_brown_the_power_of_vulnerability?language=en.

7. Personal conversation with Terry Paulson. For more information regarding Dr. Paulson, see http://www.terrypaulson.com.

Chapter One
Let Go with Love

1. Diane Klebold, *A Mother's Reckoning* (New York: Crown Publisher, 2016).
2. Brené Brown, *The Gifts of Imperfection* (Center City, MN: Hazelden, 2016).
3. Li, Pamela. "How Parental Love Helps a Child Succeed in Life. Parenting for the Brain, accessed January 2, 2022, https://www.parentingforbrain.com/parental-love.
4. Carl Whitaker, adviser, University of Wisconsin, Madison, in discussion with author, 1975.
5. Murray Bowen, written correspondence with author, April 14, 1976.
6. Lorna Benjamin, *Interpersonal Diagnosis and Treatment of Personality Disorders*, Second Edition (New York: Guilford Press, 1996).
7. Carl Whitaker, Carl, (adviser, University of Wisconsin, Madison) in discussion with author, 1975.
8. Sue Johnson, *Hold Me Tight: Seven Conversations for a Lifetime of Love (*New York: Little, Brown and Company, 2008).
9. Christine Metz Howard, "Relationships Benefit When Parents, Adult Children Connect through Multiple Channels," KU News, University of Kansas, October 24, 2014, accessed December 2022, https://news.ku.edu/relationships-benefit-when-parents-connect-adult-children-through-multiple-communication-channels-0.
10. Brené Brown, "The Power of Vulnerability, TED Talk, 2010, https://www.ted.com/talks/brene_brown_the_power_of_vulnerability.

NOTES

Chapter Two
Understand and Relate

1. Millennial descriptive data: These data come from various research reports from organizations like the Pew Research Center, the US Census Bureau, the Clark University Poll of Parents of Emerging Adults, the Council of Economic Advisors, the Goldman Sachs Millennial Study, McKinsey, Forbes, Gallop, and others. If you want to know the source of a specific research finding, please contact drjack@parentslettinggo.com.
2. Jeffrey Jensen Arnett, "Emerging Adulthood: A Theory of Development from the Late Teens Through the Twenties," *American Psychologist* 55 (May 2000): 469–480.
3. Richard Fry, Jeffrey S. Passel, and D'Vera Cohn, "A Majority of Young Adults in the US Live with Their Parents for the First Time Since the Great Depression," Pew Research Center, September 4, 2020, accessed April 1, 2022, https://www.pewresearch.org/short-reads/2020/09/04/a-majority-of-young-adults-in-the-u-s-live-with-their-parents-for-the-first-time-since-the-great-depression/.
4. Jeffrey Jensen Arnett and Joseph Schwab, The Clark University Poll of Parents of Emerging
5. Richard Reeves, *Of Boys and Men*, (Washington, DC: Brookings Institutional Press, 2022), 11.
6. Reeves, *Of Boys and Men*, 11.
7. Nicolas Eberstadt, *Men Without Work* (West Conshohocken, Pa: Templeton Press, 2022), 9-10.
8. Stella Chess and Audry Thomas, *Your Child Is a Person* (New York: Penguin Books, 1977).
9. Theodor Reik, *Listening with the Third Ear* (New York: Farrar, Straus, 1948).
10. Ray L. Birdwhistell, *Kinesics and Context: Essays on Body Motion Communication* (Philadelphia: University of Philadelphia Press, 1970).
11. Personal communication with Marshall on how he used feedback and feedforward to become a better dad, 2001.

Here a link to the description of feedback and feedforward by Marshall Goldsmith: <www.inc.com/marshall-goldsmith/power-of-feedforward.html>

Useful YouTube video of Marshall Goldsmith describing Feedforward: <https://www.youtube.com/watch?v=UqphNTu7mVI>

Chapter Three
Apologize

1. Roy J. Lewicki, Beth Polin, and Robert B. Lount Jr., "An Exploration of the Structure of Effective Apologies," Negotiation and Conflict Management Research, 9, no. 2 (May 2016): 177–96. DOI: 10.1111/ncmr.12073.
2. Kelly Dickenson, "Total Regret," *Psychology Today* (May/June 2014), accessed December 2022, https://www.psychologytoday.com/us/articles/201405/total-regret.
3. Harriet Lerner, *Why Won't You Apologize? Healing Big Betrayals and Everyday Hurts* (New York: Touchstone, 2017).
4. Brené Brown, *I Thought It Was Just Me* (New York: Gotham Books, 2007); *The Gifts of Imperfection* (Center City, MN: Hazelden, 2010).
5. See Joshua Coleman's website for specific help with the problem of estrangement, http://www.drjoshuacoleman.

Chapter Four
Forgive

1. Robert D. Enright, *Forgiveness Is a Choice: A Step-by-Step Process for Resolving Anger and Restoring Hope* (Washington, DC: American Psychological Association, 2001), 25.
2. Joan Borysenko, *Guilt Is the Teacher, Love Is the Lesson* (New York: Warner Books, 1991) 174.
3. Robin Casarjian, *Forgiveness: A Bold Choice for a Peaceful Heart* (New York: Bantam House, 1992), 23.
4. Ernest Kurtz and Katherine Ketcham, *The Spirituality of Imperfection: Storytelling and the Search for Meaning* (New York: Bantam, 2002, reissue), 222.

NOTES

5. X. Zheng and others, "The Unburdening Effects of Forgiveness: Effects on Slant Perception and Jumping Height," *Social Psychology and Personality Science*, 2014.
6. Carol Tavris, *Anger the Misunderstood Emotion* (New York: Touchstone, 1983).
7. Michael E. McCullough and others, "Interpersonal Forgiving in Close Relationships: II. Theoretical Elaboration and Measurement," *Journal of Personality and Social Psychology* 1998. vol. 75, no. 6, 1586–1603.
8. J. C. Karremans, P. A. Van Lange, and R. W. Holland, "Forgiveness and Its Association with Prosocial Thinking, Feeling, and Doing Beyond the Relationship with the Offender," *Personality and Social Psychology Bulletin*, October 2005.
9. Mayo Clinic staff, "Forgiveness: Letting Go of Grudges and Bitterness," Healthy Lifestyle, November 11, 2014, accessed December 2022, http://www.mayoclinic.org/healthy-lifestyle/adult-health/in-depth/forgiveness/art-20047692.
10. Dr. David Schramm, a professor at the University of Utah, accessed December 2022, https://www.drdaveschramm.com/dr-daves-blog/lessons-learned-from-empty-nesters.
11. Brené Brown, *I Thought It Was Just Me* (New York: Gotham Books, 2007); *The Gifts of Imperfection* (Center City, MN: Hazelden, 2010).
12. Robert D. Enright, *8 Keys to Forgiveness* (New York: Norton, 2015).
13. Fred Luskin, *Forgive for Good: A Proven Prescription for Happiness* (San Francisco: Harper Collins, 2002).
14. Everett Worthington, *Forgiving, and Reconciling: Bridges to Wholeness and Hope* (Downers Grove, Illinois: IVP Books, 2003).
15. Jack Stoltzfus, *Illuminations: Shedding Light on Depression* (Shoreview, MN: Advanced Self-Care Resources, 2001), 107.
16. Sue Klebold, *A Mother's Reckoning: Living in the Aftermath of Tragedy* (New York: Broadway Books, 2016), xxv.

Chapter Five
Show Backbone

1. Josephson, Michael, *Making Ethical Decisions*, Los Angeles: 2022.
2. Bill Millikin, *Tough Love* (Old Tappan, NJ: Fleming H. Revell Company, 1968).
3. Mark Murphy, *Hundred Percenters: Challenge Your Employees to Give It Their All, and They'll Give You Even More* (New York: McGraw Hill, 2009).
4. Christoper Peterson, Steven R. Maier, and Martin E. P. Seligman, *Learned Helplessness: A Theory for the Ages* (England: Oxford Press, reprint Edition, 1995).
5. Bryan Bruno, "What the Star*D Study Teaches Us Today," MidCityTMS, June 9, 2021, accessed June 2023, https://www.midcitytms.com/what-the-stard-study-teaches-us-today.
6. Joshua Coleman, *Rules of Estrangement: Why Adult Children Cut Ties and How to Heal the Conflict* (New York: Harmony Books, 2020).

Chapter Six
Love and Backbone in Action

1. Jeffrey Jensen Arnett and Joseph Schwab, "The Clark University Poll of Parents of Emerging Adults," Clark University, Worcester, Massachusetts, September 2013.
2. James O. Prochaska, John C. Norcross, and Carlo C. DiClemente, *Changing for Good* (New York: Quill-HarperCollins, 1994).

Chapter Seven
Let Go

1. John Stoltzfus, "Differentiations and Delinquent Youth" (PhD dissertation), Ann Arbor, Michigan: University Microfilms International Print Copy: 1982.
2. Jeanna Goudreau, "Nearly 60% of Parents Provide Financial Support to Adult Children," Forbes, May 20, 2011, updated January 11, 2021, accessed November 21, 2023,

NOTES

   https://www.forbes.com/sites/jennagoudreau/2011/05/20/parents-provide-financial-support-money-adult-children/?sh=1508cafe1987.
3. Jeffrey Jensen Arnett and Joseph Schwab, "The Clark University Poll of Parents of Emerging Adults," Clark University, Worcester, Massachusetts, September 2013.
4. Daniel Siegel, *Mindsight: The New Science of Personal Transformation* (New York: Bantam Books, 2011).
5. Jeffrey Jensen Arnett and Joseph Schwab, The Clark University Poll of Parents of Emerging Adults, Clark University, Worcester, Massachusetts, September 2013.
6. David Bredehoft, "Parents 'Just Want to be Friends' with Their Kids, accessed February 4, 2024, http://www.overindulgence.org/blog/parents-just-want-to-be.html.
7. Madeleine Fugere, "Why Getting Along with Mother-in-Law Is So Difficult, *Psychology Today*, October 28, 2016, https://www.psychologytoday.com/us/blog/dating-and-mating/201610/why-getting-along-mother-in-law-is-so-difficult.
8. Terri Apter, *What Do You Want from Me?* (New York and London: W.W. Norton and Company, 2009).

BIBLIOGRAPHY

The following books were those referenced in the introduction and chapters 1 through 7, as well as some others that would be helpful relative to the subjects of each chapter. For a brief description of many of these, see the annotated bibliography on the website parentslettinggo.com.

Introduction
The Launch Code

Arnett, Jeffrey Jensen, *Emerging Adulthood: The Winding Road from the Late Teens Through the Twenties*, Third Edition. New York: Oxford University Press, 2024.
Arnett, Jeffrey Jensen, and Elizabeth Fishel. *Getting to Thirty: A Parent's Guide to the 20-Something Years.* New York: Workman Publishing, 2014.
Arnett, Jeffrey J., and Joseph Schwab. *Parents and Their Grown Kids: Harmony, Support, and (Occasional) Conflict.* Clark University, 2013
Coburn, Karen Leven, and Madge Lawrence Treeger. *Letting Go: A Parent's Guide to Understanding College Years*, 1997.
Coleman, Josh. *Rules of Estrangement: Why Adult Children Cut Ties and How to Heal the Conflict.* New York: Harmony Books, 2020.
Devine, Michael and Lawrence V. Tucker. *Failure to Launch: Guiding Clinicians to Successfully Motivate the Long-Dependent Young Adult.* Lanham, MD: Rowman & Littlefield, April 1, 2015.
Konstan, Varda. *Parenting Your Emerging Adult: Launching Kids from 18-29.* Far Hills, New Jersey: New Horizon Press, 2013.

Levine, Madeline. *The Price of Privilege* Madeline. New York: Harper,.2006.
Lythcott-Haims, Julie. *How to Raise an Adult.* New York: Henry Holt and Company, 2015.
Sachs, Brad E. *Emptying The Nest.* 2010. New York: St. Martin's Press,2010.
Stoltzfus, Jack. *Can You Speak Millennial "ese"? How to Understand and Communicate with Your Young Adult.* Self-Published.: Shoreview, Mn. 2017

Chapter One
Let Go with Love

Benjamin, Lorna. *Interpersonal Diagnosis and Treatment of Personality Disorders*, Second Edition. New York: Guilford Press, 1996.
Brown, Brené. *The Gifts of Imperfection.* Center City, MN: Hazelden, 2016.
Campbell, Ross and Gary Chapman. *How To Really Love Your Adult Child.* Chicago, Illinois: Northfield Publishing, 2011.
Johnson, Sue. *Hold Me Tight: Seven Conversations for a Lifetime of Love.* New York: Little, Brown and Company, 2008.
Klebold, Diane. *A Mother's Reckoning.* New York: Crown Publisher, 2016.
Kohn, Alfie. *Unconditional Parenting.* New York: Atria Books, 2005.
Milliken, Bill. *Tough Love.* Chicago, IL: Fleming H. Revell, January 1, 1968.
Stoltzfus, John (Jack). "Differentiation and Delinquent Youth. Madison." Wisconsin: University of Wisconsin Press, 1980.
Stoltzfus, Jack. *Love to Let Go: Loving Our Kids into Adulthood.* Shoreview, Minnesota: Self-Published, 2017.
Twenge, Jean M. *Generations.* New York: Atria Books, 2023.

Chapter Two
Relate

Birdwhistell, Ray L. *Kinesics and Context: Essays on Body Motion Communication.* Philadelphia: University of Philadelphia Press, 1970.

BIBLIOGRAPHY

Chess, Stella and Audry Thomas. *Your Child Is a Person*. New York: Penguin Books, 1977

Eberstadt, Nicolas. *Men Without Work*. Conshohocken, Pa.: Templeton Press, 2022 edition

Hofer, Barbara, and Abigail Sullivan Moore. *The I Connected Parent: Staying Close to Your Kids in College (and Beyond) While Letting Them Grow Up*. New York: Free Press, 2010.

Henig, Robin Marantz. *Twenty-Something: Why Do Young Adults Seem Stuck?* New York: A Plume Book, 2012.

Hoolihan, Patricia. *Launching Your Teen into Adulthood*. Minneapolis, Minnesota: Search Institute Press, 2009.

Jensen, Frances E, and Amy Ellis Nutt. *The Teenage Brain*. New York: Harper, 2015.

Lancaster, Lynne C., and David Stillman. *The M-Factor*. New York: Harper-Collins Publishers, 2010.

Padilla-Walker, Laura M., and Larry J. Nelson. *Flourishing in Emerging Adulthood* New York: Oxford University Press, 2017.

Reeves, Richard. *Of Boys and Men*. Washington, D.C.: Brookings Institutional Press, 2022.

Reik, Theodor. *Listening with the Third Ear*. New York: Farrar, Straus, 1948.

Riera, Michael. *Staying Connected to Your Teenager*. Cambridge, Ma: Perseus Press, 2003.

Seigel, Daniel J. *Brainstorm: The Power and The Purpose of The Teenage Mind*. New York: Penguin, 2015.

Settersten, Richard and Barbara E. Ray. *Not Quite Adults: Why 20-Somethings Are Choosing a Slower Path to Adulthood and Why It's Good for Everyone*. New York: Bantam Books, 2010.

Stoltzfus, Jack. *Can You Speak Millennial"ese"?* Shoreview, Minnesota: Self-Published, 2017.

Walsh, David. *Why Do They Act That Way?* New York: Atria Books, 2014.

Chapter Three
Apologize

Brown, Brené. *Daring Greatly: How the Courage to Be Vulnerable Transforms the Way We Live, Love, Parent, and Lead.* New York: Penguin Putnam, 2012.

———. *I Thought It Was Just Me.* New York: Gotham Books, 2007.

———. *The Gifts of Imperfection.* Center City, MN: Hazelden, 2010.

Chapman, Gary, and Jennifer Thomas. *When Sorry Isn't Enough: Making Things Right With Those You Love.* Chicago: Northfield Publishing, 2013.

Engel, Beverly. The Power of Apology. New York: John Wiley and Sons, 2001.

Kador, John. *Effective Apology.* San Francisco: Berrett-Koehler Publishers, 2009.

Lazare, Aaron. On Apology. New York: Oxford University Press, 2004.

Learner, Harriet. *Why Won't You Apologize?* New York: Simon and Schuster, 2017.

Chapter Four
Forgive

Augsberger, David W. *Helping People Forgive.* Louisville, KY: Westminster John Knox Press, 1996.

Borysenko, Joan. *Guilt Is the Teacher, Love Is the Lesson.* New York: Warner Books, 1991.

Casarjian, Robin. *Forgiveness: A Bold Choice for a Peaceful Heart.* New York: Bantam, 1992.

Enright, Robert D. *8 Keys to Forgiveness.* New York: W.W. Norton and Company, 2015.

———. *Forgiveness Is a Choice: A Step-by-Step Process for Resolving Anger and Restoring Hope (APA Lifetools).* Washington, DC: American Psychological Association, 2001.

———. *The Forgiving Life: A Pathway to Overcoming Resentment and Creating a Legacy of Love (APA Lifetools).* Washington DC: American Psychological Association, 2001.

BIBLIOGRAPHY

Klebold, Sue. *A Mother's Reckoning: Living in the Aftermath of Tragedy.* New York: Broadway Books, 2016.

Kraybill, Donald B., Steven M. Holt, David L. Weaver-Zercher. *Amish Grace: How Forgiveness Transcended Tragedy.* Jossey-Bass, 2010.

Luskin, Fred. *Forgive for Good: A Proven Prescription for Happiness.* San Francisco: Harper Collins, 2002.

McCullough, Michael E., Steven J. Sandage, and Everett L. Worthington, Jr. *How to Put Your Past in the Past.* Downers Grove, IL: InterVarsity Press, 1997.

Simon, Sidney B., and Suzanne Simon. *Forgiveness: How to Make Peace with Your Past and Get on with Your Life.* New York: Grand Central Publishing, 1991.

Smedes, Lewis B. *Forgive and Forget: Healing the Hurts We Don't Deserve.* New York: Pocketbooks, 1984.

Stoltzfus, Jack. *Forgiveness: The Gift We Share with Our Young Adults and Ourselves.* Self-Published: Shoreview, Mn. 2017.

Stoltzfus, John. *Illuminations: Shedding Light on Depression.* Shoreview, Minnesota: Self-Published, 2003.

Tavris, Carol. *Anger the Misunderstood Emotion.* New York: Touchstone, 1983.

Tipping, Colin. *Radical Forgiveness.* Boulder, CO: Sounds True, 2009.

Worthington, E. L. Jr. *Moving Forward: Six Steps to Forgiving Yourself and Breaking Free from the Past.* New York: Waterbrook, 2013.

———. *Forgiving and Reconciling.* Downers Grove, IL: InterVarsity Press, 2003.

Chapter Five
Show Backbone

Bottke, Allison. *Setting Boundaries with Your Adult Children.* Eugene, Oregon: Harvest House Publishers; 2008.

Coleman, Joshua. *When Parents Hurt: Compassionate Strategies When You and Your Grown Child Don't Get Along.* New York: William Morrow, 2008.

Josephson, Michael S., Val J. Peter, and Tom Dowd. *Parenting to Build Character in Your Teen.* Boys Town, NE: Boys Town Press, 2001.

Katherine, Anne. *Boundaries: Where You End and I Begin.* Center City, Minnesota: Hazelden, 1991.
Levine, Madeline. *The Price of Privilege.* New York: Harper, 2006.
Milliken, Bill. *Tough Love.* Old Tappan, NJ: Fleming H. Revell Company, 1968.
Murphy, Mark. *Hundred Percenters: Challenge Your Employees to Give It Their All, and They'll Give You Even More.* New York: McGraw Hill, 2009.
Nemzoff, Ruth. *Don't Bite Your Tongue.* New York: Palgrave Macmillan, 2008.
Peters, Ruth. *Laying Down the Law: The 25 Laws of Parenting to Keep Your Kids on Track, Out of Trouble and (Pretty Much) Under Control.* Emmaus, Pennsylvania: Rodale Press, 2002.
Praeger, Dennis. *Happiness is a Serious Problem.* New York: Harper-Collins, 1998.
Prochaska, James O., John C. Norcross, and Carlo C. DiClemente. *Changing for Good.* New York: Harper Collins Paperback, 2006.
Sachs, Brad. *Family-Centered Treatment with Struggling Young Adults.* 2013. New York: Routledge, 2013.
Young, Joel L. and Christine Adamec. *When Your Adult Child Breaks Your Heart: Coping with Mental Illness, Substance Abuse, and the Problems That Tear Families Apart.* Guilford, CT: Lyons Press, 2013.

Resources on ~~Enabling~~ (Disabling)

Brown, Ann. *Anne Brown: Backbone Power: The Science of Saying No.* Amazon Digital Services, 2012.
Cloud, Henry, and John Townsend. *Boundaries: When to Say Yes, How to Say No to Take Control of Your Life.* Grand Rapids, MI: Zondervan, 1992.
Isay, Jane. *Walking on Eggshells: Navigating the Delicate Relationship Between Adult Children and Parents.* New York: Anchor Books, 2007.
Katherine, Anne. *Where to Draw the Line: How to Set Healthy Boundaries Every Day.* New York: Fireside, 2000.

BIBLIOGRAPHY

Levine, Madeline. *The Price of Privilege: How Parental Pressure and Material Advantage Are Creating a Generation of Disconnected and Unhappy Kids.* New York: Harper, 2006.

Miller, Angelyn. *The Enabler.* Tucson, Arizona: Wheatmark, 2008.

Nemzoff, Ruth. *Don't Bite Your Tongue: How to Foster Rewarding Relationships with Your Adult Children.* New York: Palgrave Macmillan, 2008.

Stockman, Larry V., and Cynthia S. Graves. *Grown-up Children Who Won't Grow Up.* Rocklin, CA: Prima Publishing, 1994.

Townsend. *Boundaries.* Grand Rapids, Michigan: Zondervan 1992.

Chapter Six
Backbone in Action

Adams, Jane. *When Our Grown Kids Disappoint Us.* New York: Free Press, 2004.

DeVine, Michael D. *Failure to Launch* New York: Jason Aronson, 2013.

Isay, Jane. *Walking on Eggshells.* New York: Anchor Books, 2007.

Metcalf, Linda. *Parenting Toward Solutions: How Parents Can Use Skills They Already Have to Raise Responsible Kids.* Upper Saddle River, New Jersey: Pearson, 1997.

Peterson, Christopher, Maier, Steven R., Seligman, Martin E. P. *Learned Helplessness: A Theory for the Ages.* England: Oxford Press, reprint Edition, 1995.

Chapter Seven
Let Go

Apter, Terri. *What Do You Want from Me?* New York and London: W.W. Norton and Company, 2009.

Carter, Betty, and Monica McGoldrick. *The Expanded Family Life Cycle: Individual, Family and Social Perspectives,* Third Edition. Boston, Mass: Pearson Education Company, 2005.

Casey, Karen. *Letting Go: Embracing Detachment.* San Francisco: Red Wheel/Weiser, 2010.

Coleman, Joshua. *When Parents Hurt.* New York: William Morrow, 2008.

Hawkins, Davis F. *Letting Go.* New York: Hey House, 2012.

Lesser, Elizabeth. *Broken Open: How Difficult Times Can Help Us Grow.* New York: Villard, 2005.
Seigel, Daniel. *Mindsight: The New Science of Personal Transformation.* New York: Bantam Books, 2011.
Stoltzfus, Jack. *Growing Apart.* Shoreview, Mn: Self-Published, 2018.

RESOURCES

AVAILABLE ON THE WEBSITE PARENTSLETTINGGO.COM

Resources
Quizzes or self-assessments
Interview Questions
Tip Sheets
Research—my survey of parents
Video Presentations
Young Adult Resources
Mental Health Resources
Drug and Alcohol Abuse Resources
Self-Help Groups and Resources

Under Blogs
There are over a hundred blogs that I have written that might address specific situations.

Go to the website or https://parentslettinggo.com/newsletter-sign-up/ and sign up to receive new blogs and announcements regarding webinars.

Printed in the USA
CPSIA information can be obtained
at www.ICGtesting.com
CBHW071936091224
18700CB00043B/822

9 781963 844641